Traditional CHRISTMAS *Two*

CREATIVE PUBLISHING international

MINNETONKA, MINNESOTA

CONTENTS

Christmas Traditions..5

Decorating the Tree..............................7

Tree Toppers 9
Ornaments 15
Garlands...70
Tree Trimming 76
Tree Skirts 78

Around the House.................................123

Decorations 124
Stockings 143
Mantels 148
Wreaths..150
Decorative Trees & Pine Balls 157

The Holiday Table 89

Floral Arrangements............................90
Coaster Sets 99
Table Linens...103

Appetizers, Snacks & Beverages............165

Appetizers 166
Snacks..178
Beverages 195

Copyright © 1997
Creative Publishing international, Inc.
5900 Green Oak Drive
Minnetonka, Minnesota 55343
1-800-328-3895
All rights reserved
Printed in U.S.A.

Traditional Christmas Two draws pages from the individual titles of the Home Decorating Institute®, the Recipes For Life® library, the Vegetarian Times® library, the Microwave Cooking Library®, and *Cookies!* Individual titles are also available from the publisher and in bookstores and fabric stores.

Library of Congress
Cataloging-in-Publication Data

Traditional Christmas two : cooking, crafts & gifts.
    p. cm.
  Includes index.
  ISBN 0-86573-899-8
  1. Christmas decorations. 2. Christmas cookery. I. Creative Publishing international.
TT900.C4T72 1997
745.594' 12 -- dc21   97-9479

Christmas Cookies.................................*203*

Basics...204
Cookies...207
Decorating with Frosting 242
Decorating with a Pastry Bag................244

Desserts & Sweets..................................*249*

Desserts 250
Sweets 260

Patterns *310*
Index...*316*

Gifts from the Kitchen..............................*281*

Pickles & Relishes................................282
Flavored Vinegars................................291
Jellies & Syrups....................................292
Softening Cream Cheese 300
For Fun...302
Dough Art 305

CREATIVE
PUBLISHING
international

President: Iain Macfarlane
Group Director, Book Development: Zoe Graul
Director, Creative Development: Lisa Rosenthal
Executive Managing Editor: Elaine Perry

Created by: The Editors of
Creative Publishing international, Inc.

Printed on American paper by:
R. R. Donnelley & Sons Co.
02 01 00 99 98/6 5 4 3 2

To: Carol
From: Mom

Christmas Traditions

Traditions enrich our lives, bond us with family and friends, and fill us with warm memories of times spent together. This is especially true at Christmas, when traditions are the heart of every gathering and celebration. Whether your traditions include making ornaments or baking cookies, stringing garlands or entertaining holiday guests, you will be delighted and inspired by the many projects and recipes in *Traditional Christmas Two*. Bursting with fresh ideas for Christmas crafting, decorating, and cooking, this book is sure to give you all kinds of ways to enhance your tried-and-true traditions, and even introduce you to a few new ones.

Traditional Christmas Two shows you how to spread Christmas cheer throughout your home with glorious mantel displays, original Christmas stockings, and even a holiday elf. Decorate wreaths with flair; make eye-catching wall trees and topiaries, or uniquely crafted tabletop trees. Create stunning floral arrangements to decorate the holiday table or buffet. Sew placemats, table runners, and toppers for elegant entertaining or everyday dining.

Trim your tree to suit your fancy, using ornaments, garlands, and tree toppers you make yourself. Select lace doily ornaments, trimmed fabric balls, and ribbon roses for a romantic Victorian tree. Or go for glitz, starting at the top with a bold wire-mesh bow and studding the tree with metallic folded stars, gold-leafed balls, and marbleized ornaments. For down-home country appeal, make ornaments from hand-cast paper or tea-dyed fabric and top the tree with a raffia-tied cinnamon-stick star. Sew a tree skirt that will be cherished for years, or try one of our quick and easy alternative skirt ideas.

The tastes and aromas from the Christmas kitchen build lasting memories. *Traditional Christmas Two* abounds with delicious recipes for entertaining your guests or simply treating the family. From appetizers and snacks to cookies and desserts, mouth-watering photographs entice you to try them all. Many of the recipes are microwavable, including specialty foods and crafts for inventive gift giving. Tantalize your tastebuds with savory Shrimp Wrap-ups or Antipasto Kabobs. Cater to your Christmas cravings with traditional favorites like Rosettes and Plum Pudding, or discover the exotic flavors of Poppy-Raspberry Kolachkes and Brandied Apricot Torte.

Christmas traditions, treasured and comfortably timeless, rekindle the holiday spirit every year. With vibrant photography and concise instructions, the ideas and recipes throughout these pages are sure to enliven the Christmas traditions in your home.

Decorating
The Tree

TREE TOPPERS

A tree topper adds the finishing touch to a Christmas tree. Select one that coordinates with the style or theme of the ornaments, such as a paper-twist angel to complement a tree with a homespun look. Make a wire-mesh bow to top a tree that is decorated with glittery or metallic objects, or make a cinnamon-stick star for a tree decorated with natural ornaments.

The angel shown opposite is crafted from paper twist, a tightly wrapped paper cording that, when untwisted, produces a crinkled paper strip. The angel is given dimension with the help of wire. The outline of the wings is shaped from paper twist with a wire inner core, and the garment and shawl have craft wire encased in the fold of the hems, allowing them to be shaped into drapes and folds. Embellish the angel as desired with a miniature artificial garland or tiny musical instrument.

For an elegant-looking tree topper, create a large wire-mesh bow from aluminum window screening. The window screening, available in shiny silver and dull charcoal gray, may be left unfinished or painted gold, brass, or copper. The bow may also be sprayed with aerosol glitter for added sparkle.

For a natural look, make a star from cinnamon sticks held together with hot glue and raffia. The star can be embellished with a raffia bow, miniature cones, and a few sprigs of greenery.

Angel *(opposite) is created from paper twist, sinamay ribbon, jute, and raffia, for a country look.*

Wire-mesh bow, *created from window screening, is sprayed with gold metallic paint for an elegant look.*

Cinnamon-stick star *is embellished with sprigs of greenery, red raffia, and miniature cones.*

9

MATERIALS

- Poster board.
- Packing tape.
- Three 1½" (3.8 cm) Styrofoam® balls.
- ½ yd. (0.5 m) paper twist, 4" to 4½" (10 to 11.5 cm) wide, in skintone or natural color, for head, neck, and hands.
- 1 yd. (0.95 m) paper twist, 4" to 4½" (10 to 11.5 cm) wide, for shawl.
- 2 yd. (1.85 m) paper twist, 7" to 7½" (18 to 19.3 cm) wide, for dress.

- 1 yd. (0.95 m) paper twist with wire inner core, for wings.
- Sinamay ribbon, at least 2" (5 cm) wide, for wings.
- Raffia.
- 3-ply jute.
- Dowel, ⅛" (3 mm) in diameter.
- 24-gauge craft wire.
- Thick craft glue.
- Hot glue gun and glue sticks.
- Wire cutter or utility scissors.
- Miniature garland or other desired embellishments.

CUTTING DIRECTIONS

From skintone or natural paper twist, cut one 4" (10 cm) piece for the head, one 10" (25 cm) piece for the underbodice, and three ¾" (2 cm) pieces for the neck and hands.

From the paper twist for the dress, cut two 4½" (11.5 cm) pieces for the sleeves, six 8½" (21.8 cm) pieces for the skirt, and one 7" (18 cm) piece for the dress bodice.

From the paper twist with a wire inner core, cut one 12" (30.5 cm) length for the arms and one 24" (61 cm) length for the wings.

1 Cut a semicircle with 8" (20.5 cm) radius from poster board. Trim 6" (15 cm) pie-shaped wedge from one end; discard. Form cone with base 15" (38 cm) in diameter; secure with packing tape. Press the Styrofoam balls between fingers to compress to 1¼" (3.2 cm) in diameter.

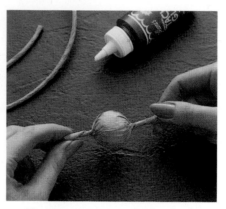

2 Untwist paper twist for head; glue width of paper around Styrofoam ball, using craft glue. Apply craft glue to ball at top and bottom, and tightly retwist paper; apply additional glue as necessary so paper stays twisted. Allow glue to dry.

3 Trim one end of the twisted paper close to foam ball; this will be top of head. Poke remaining twisted end into top of cone; trim top of cone, if necessary. Remove head, and set aside.

4 Poke a hole through each side of the cone, 1" (2.5 cm) from top; for the arms, insert the paper twist with the wire inner core through the holes. Push each wire arm through the center of Styrofoam ball; for shoulders, slide balls up to the cone. Shape balls to fit snugly against cone by pressing with fingers; secure to cone with hot glue, applying the glue to the cone.

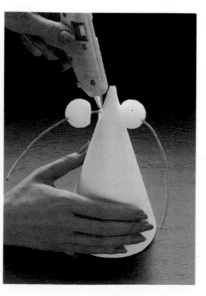

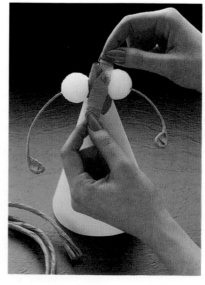

5 Bend each wire arm 1" (2.5 cm) from end; bend to form triangle shape for hands. Untwist a paper strip for hand; mist it with water. Wrap paper around the hand; secure with craft glue. Repeat for the other hand.. Untwist and mist the paper strip for neck. Wrap paper around top of cone; secure with craft glue.

6 Untwist underbodice piece; cut a small slit in center. Position slit in paper over top of cone; smooth paper around shoulders and cone. Secure with craft glue. Glue head in place.

7 Untwist skirt pieces. Join the skirt pieces together by overlapping long edges ¼" (6 mm); secure with glue to form tube. Fold ½" (1.3 cm) hem on one edge; insert wire into fold, overlapping ends of wire about 1" (2.5 cm). Secure hem with craft glue, encasing wire.

8 Place cone on a soup or vegetable can. Slide skirt over cone, with the hem about 2" (5 cm) below the lower edge of the cone. Hand-gather upper edge to fit smoothly around the waist; secure with wire. Shape wired hem into graceful folds.

9 Untwist sleeve piece. Overlap the edges ¼" (6 mm) to form a tube; secure with craft glue. Fold the hem, encasing the wire as in step 7. Slide sleeve over arm, placing hem at wrist. Glue sleeve at shoulder, sides, and underarm, concealing underbodice at underarm. Shape wired hem. Repeat for other sleeve.

10 Untwist dress bodice piece; cut in half lengthwise. Fold strips in half lengthwise. Drape one strip over each shoulder, placing folded edges at neck; cross the ends at front and back; glue in place. Wrap wire around waist; trim excess.

11 Cut several lengths of raffia, about 25" (63.5 cm) long; mist with water. Tie raffia around waist, concealing the wire; trim ends. Cut thicker raffia lengths, and separate into two or three strands.

12 Bend the paper twist with wire inner core for wings as shown; allow the ends to extend 1" (2.5 cm) beyond center. Wrap ends around center; secure with glue.

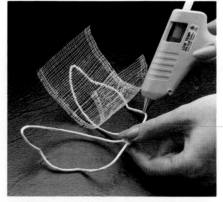

13 Bend edges and curve of wings as shown. Glue sinamay ribbon to back of wings, using hot glue. Allow glue to dry; trim away excess ribbon.

14 Position wings on back of angel at center, so wings curve away from back; secure, using hot glue.

(Continued)

15 Cut jute, and separate to make three single-ply 30" (76 cm) lengths. Wrap each ply tightly and evenly around dowel, securing the ends. Saturate jute with water. Place the dowel in 200°F (95°C) oven for 2 hours or until dry.

16 Remove jute from the dowel. Cut and glue individual lengths of coiled jute to head for hair, working in sections; for the bangs, glue short pieces across the front of the head.

17 Untwist the shawl piece. Fold ½" (1.3 cm) hem on one long edge. Insert wire into fold; glue hem in place, encasing wire. Repeat on opposite side.

18 Drape shawl around the shoulders. Shape the wired hems to make a graceful drape; adjust the shawl in back to conceal the lower portion of the wings. Fold ends of shawl to underside of the skirt. Glue shawl in place in several areas, using hot glue.

19 Shape the wire arms to hold desired accessories. Secure any other embellishments to angel as desired, using hot glue.

HOW TO MAKE A WIRE-MESH BOW TREE TOPPER

MATERIALS

- Aluminum window screening.
- 24-gauge or 26-gauge craft wire.
- Utility scissors.
- Aerosol acrylic paint in metallic finish, optional.
- Aerosol glitter, optional.

CUTTING DIRECTIONS

Cut the following rectangles from window screening, cutting along the mesh weave: one 8" × 38" (20.5 × 96.5 cm) piece for the loops, one 8" × 28" (20.5 × 71 cm) piece for the streamers, and one 2½" × 7" (6.5 × 18 cm) rectangle for the center strip.

1 Paint both sides of each rectangle, if desired; allow to dry. Fold up ½" (1.3 cm) on long edges, using a straightedge as a guide. Fold up ½" (1.3 cm) along short edges of streamers and one short edge of center strip.

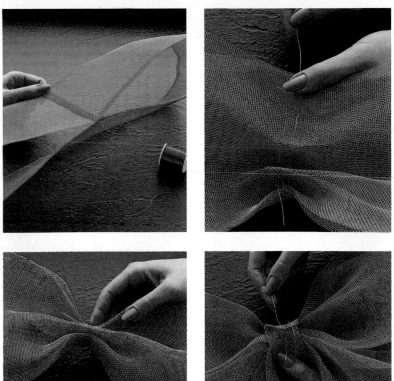

2 Cut 16" (40.5 cm) length of wire. Form a loop from rectangle for loops, overlapping the short ends about ¾" (2 cm) at center. Insert wire at one overlapped edge; twist wire to secure, leaving 2" (5 cm) tail.

3 Stitch through the center of overlapped mesh with long end of wire, taking 1" to 1½" (2.5 to 3.8 cm) stitches. Pull up wire firmly to gather mesh; wrap wire around center, and twist the ends together; trim the excess.

4 Hand-pleat width of streamer at the center; place below the gathered loop. Wrap length of wire around the center of loop and streamers; twist ends together. Paint wire to match bow, if necessary.

5 Wrap center strip around the bow, concealing the wire. Stitch ends together with length of wire. Apply aerosol glitter, if desired. Secure a length of wire to the back of center strip for securing bow to tree.

HOW TO MAKE A CINNAMON-STICK STAR TREE TOPPER

MATERIALS

- Five 12" (30.5 cm) cinnamon sticks.
- Hot glue gun and glue sticks.
- Raffia.
- Embellishments, such as cones and sprigs of greenery.

1 Arrange two cinnamon sticks in an "X"; position a third stick across the top, placing one end below upper stick of "X" as shown.

2 Place remaining two sticks on top in an inverted "V." Adjust spacing of cinnamon sticks as necessary, to form star. Secure sticks at ends, using hot glue.

3 Tie raffia securely around ends at intersection of cinnamon sticks. Tie several lengths of raffia into bow; glue to top of star. Secure embellishments with glue.

TEA-DYED ORNAMENTS

Add an old-fashioned, homespun look to a Christmas tree with a variety of stitch-and-turn ornaments, such as stockings, stars, trees, and snowmen. Embellish the ornaments to make each one unique.

For an aged appearance, make the ornaments from cotton quilting fabrics, and tea dye the fabrics before cutting the ornaments. Tea dying works well on light-colored fabrics. The color change will vary with the type of tea used. Orange tea, for example, gives a yellowed look to fabrics, while cranberry tea produces a reddish appearance. The amount of color change will depend on the concentration of tea used and the length of time the fabric is soaked.

MATERIALS

- Scraps of cotton quilting fabrics, such as muslin, calico, and ticking.
- Polyester fiberfill.
- Embellishments, such as buttons, cinnamon sticks, artificial or preserved greenery, and artificial berries.
- 9" (23 cm) length of cording for hanger of each snowman, star, and tree ornament.
- Large-eyed needle.
- Small twigs and round toothpick, for snowman ornament.
- Orange acrylic paint and black acrylic paint or fine-point permanent-ink marker, for details of snowman ornament.
- Drapery weight or marble, for stocking ornament.
- Hot glue gun and glue sticks.

CUTTING DIRECTIONS

Transfer the ornament pattern pieces (page 314) onto paper. For a star or stocking ornament, cut two pieces from fabric, right sides together. For a snowman or tree ornament, cut two pieces from fabric, placing the dotted line of the pattern on the fold of the fabric. For the snowman, also cut one hat piece, placing the dotted line of the pattern on the fold of the fabric.

HOW TO TEA DYE FABRIC

1 Prewash the fabric to remove any finishes. Brew strong tea, about four tea bags per 1 qt. (1 L) of water; leave tea bags in water. Soak fabric in tea until desired color is achieved; areas with air pockets will not dye as dark, and areas of fabric touching tea bags will be darker.

2 Remove fabric from the tea, and squeeze out excess; do not rinse fabric. Place the fabric on paper towel; allow to dry. Press fabric to heat-set color; use scrap of fabric to protect ironing surface from any excess tea.

HOW TO MAKE A STOCKING ORNAMENT

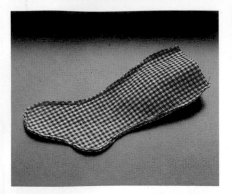

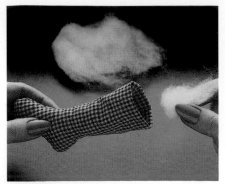

1 Place stocking pieces right sides together. Stitch ⅛" (3 mm) seam around stocking, using short stitch length: leave top open.

2 Turn stocking right side out; press. Fold fabric to inside along dotted line; press. Placing drapery weight or marble into toe of stocking, loosely stuff stocking with polyester fiberfill.

3 Tear ½" × 6" (1.3 × 15 cm) strip of fabric for hanger; fold strip in half. Place folded strip at top of stocking; secure by stitching a button to strip, ⅜" (1 cm) from the ends, through all layers. Secure embellishments inside stocking, using hot glue.

HOW TO MAKE A STAR ORNAMENT

1 Cut a ¾" (2 cm) slit through center of one star piece. Place the pieces right sides together; stitch ⅛" (3 mm) seam around star, using a short stitch length. Trim off the points, and clip the inner corners.

2 Turn star right side out through the slit; stuff star firmly with polyester fiberfill. Hand-stitch opening closed, and take two or three stitches through center of star; pull stitches to indent center. Secure thread.

3 Glue embellishments to star over stitched opening in center. Thread cord for hanger through the needle; take a stitch through star at desired location. Knot ends of cord together.

HOW TO MAKE A TREE ORNAMENT

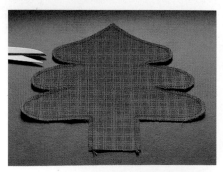

1 Place pieces for the tree right sides together. Stitch ⅛" (3 mm) seam around the tree, using a short stitch length; leave opening on lower edge of trunk. Clip corners and curves.

2 Turn tree right side out. Stuff tree with polyester fiberfill, stuffing branches first.

3 Turn raw edges to inside on lower edge of trunk; slipstitch closed. Stitch or glue buttons to the ends of the branches. Secure the hanger as in step 3, above.

HOW TO MAKE A SNOWMAN ORNAMENT

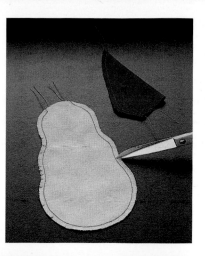

1 Place snowman pieces right sides together. Stitch ⅛" (3 mm) seam around the snowman, using short stitch length; leave a 1" (2.5 cm) opening at top. Clip seam allowances as necessary. Fold hat in half, right sides together, matching raw edges; stitch ⅛" (3 mm) seam on the edge opposite fold.

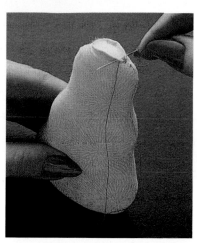

2 Turn snowman right side out; stuff firmly with polyester fiberfill. Turn raw edges to inside on upper edge; slipstitch opening closed.

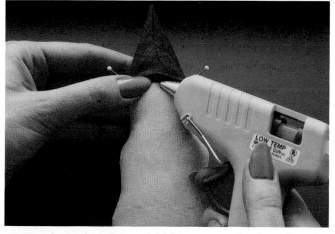

3 Turn hat right side out; fold fabric to inside along dotted line. Position hat on snowman with seam at center back; secure with hot glue. Fold the peak of the hat over to one side; secure with a dot of hot glue.

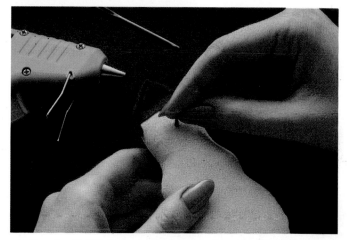

4 Break off ½" (1.3 cm) from round toothpick for nose; paint nose orange. Using a large-eyed needle, poke hole in fabric at desired location for nose. Apply a dot of hot glue to blunt end of nose; insert in hole.

5 Make dots for eyes and mouth, using acrylic paint or a fine-point permanent-ink marker. Tear ½" × 8" (1.3 × 20.5 cm) fabric strip for scarf; tie scarf around neck of snowman.

6 Poke holes in fabric on each side of snowman at the desired location for twig arms; apply glue to end of each twig and insert into the holes. Secure any embellishments with hot glue. Secure cord for hanger as in step 3 for star, opposite.

COOKIE-CUTTER ORNAMENTS

Cookie cutters provide a variety of shapes to be used as patterns for tree ornaments. To make patterns, simply trace around the cookie cutters and add ¼" (6 mm) seam allowances. Stitch the ornaments wrong sides together and leave the seams exposed for a homespun look.

Make the ornaments from cotton or cotton-blend fabrics. Add decorative details to the ornaments with fabric paints in fine-tip tubes. Hand-paint your own designs or follow the imprints of plastic or metal cookie cutters as a guide for painting the details.

For best results in painting, prewash the fabrics to remove sizing. Practice painting on a scrap of fabric before painting on the ornaments to perfect the painting techniques. To keep the paint flow even, tap the tip of the bottle gently on the table to eliminate air bubbles. Wipe the tip of the bottle often while painting, to prevent paint buildup. If the tip becomes clogged, squeeze the tube to force paint through the tip onto a sheet of paper or a paper towel. If necessary, remove the cap and unclog the tip with a toothpick or needle.

HOW TO MAKE A COOKIE-CUTTER ORNAMENT

CUTTING DIRECTIONS

Make the patterns as below, step 1. For each ornament, cut two pieces from fabric, wrong sides together.

MATERIALS

- Scraps of cotton fabric in desired colors.
- Polyester fiberfill.
- 9" (23 cm) length of ribbon or cording, for hanger.
- Fabric paints in fine-tip tubes, for decorating ornaments.

1 Transfer cookie-cutter design to paper by tracing around cookie cutter with a pencil; add ¼" (6 mm) seam allowances.

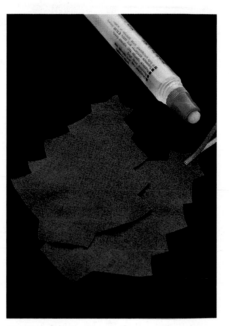

2 Cut fabric pieces for ornaments as in cutting directions. Fold ribbon in half to make hanger; glue-baste to top of ornament as shown.

3 Place the fabric pieces wrong sides together; pin. Stitch ¼" (6 mm) from raw edges, using short stitch length; leave 1" (2.5 cm) opening for stuffing.

4 Stuff the ornament with polyester fiberfill; use the eraser end of a pencil to push the stuffing into smaller areas.

5 Stitch the opening closed, using a zipper foot. Trim seam allowance to ⅛" (3 mm), taking care not to trim off hanger.

6 Add painted details to ornaments as desired, using fabric paints.

SPICE
ORNAMENTS

Spice ornaments are fragrant and colorful additions to the holiday tree. They are made by covering Styrofoam® balls with powdered or crushed dried spices. To create a variety of looks, the simple ornaments can be embellished with ribbons and preserved or artificial leaves or berries. For durability, the spice-covered ornaments are sprayed with an aerosol clear acrylic sealer.

MATERIALS

- Powdered or crushed dried spices, such as nutmeg, cinnamon, oregano, mace, paprika, parsley, poppy seed, crushed red pepper, allspice, mustard seed, chili powder, or dried orange peel.
- Aerosol acrylic paints in colors that blend with spices.
- Styrofoam balls.
- 20-gauge craft wire.
- 9" (23 cm) length of ribbon or cording, for hanger.
- Thick craft glue; hot glue gun and glue sticks.
- Aerosol clear acrylic sealer.
- Embellishments as desired.

Spice ornaments, *arranged in a bowl, are made with paprika, crushed red pepper, mace, allspice, mustard seed, cinnamon, and chili powder.*

HOW TO MAKE A SPICE ORNAMENT

1 Roll Styrofoam ball lightly against table to compress the Styrofoam slightly.

2 Spray Styrofoam ball with aerosol acrylic paint; allow to dry.

3 Apply craft glue to the Styrofoam ball; roll in spice to cover. Allow to dry. Apply aerosol acrylic sealer.

4 Knot the ends of the ribbon or cording together. Bend 4" (10 cm) length of wire in half. Attach ribbon or cording to the ornament with wire as shown; secure with dot of hot glue.

5 Secure any additional embellishments to the ornament as desired, using hot glue.

METAL
ORNAMENTS

Metal ornaments made from either copper or tin add a whimsical look to a tree. The metals are available at craft stores in sheets of various sizes. Copper is the thinner of the two and cuts easily with household utility scissors; tin can be cut best with a jeweler's snips, available at jewelry-making supply stores. Both metals are suitable for flat ornaments; however, tin can also be used to make spiral ornaments. To create chained ornaments, two or more ornaments can be wired together.

Metal ornaments can be embellished, if desired, with craft wire or a punched design. Simple shapes for the ornaments and the punched designs can be found on gift-wrapping paper, greeting cards, and cookie cutters.

You may enlarge or reduce simple designs on a photocopy machine, if desired.

For a country or rustic look, copper can easily be given a weathered or aged appearance through a process called oxidizing. Heat oxidizing is done by placing the copper ornament over a flame until the color changes. The copper ornament is moved randomly over the flame to produce uneven coloring. A gas stove works well for oxidizing copper, because it produces a clean flame. Hold the copper with tongs while heating, because the metal becomes very hot. For additional texture, sand the surface of the copper before it is heated, using medium-grit sandpaper.

MATERIALS

- Copper or tin sheet.
- Awl and rubber mallet, or tin-punching tool.
- Utility scissors or jeweler's snips.
- Scrap of wood.
- Tracing paper and transfer paper.
- Masking tape.

- 22-gauge to 28-gauge brass or copper craft wire.
- Fine steel wool.
- 100-grit sandpaper.
- Tongs with handles that do not conduct heat, for oxidizing copper.
- Aerosol clear acrylic sealer.

HOW TO MAKE A COPPER OR TIN FLAT ORNAMENT

1 Cover the work surface with a newspaper. Transfer the desired design for the ornament onto tracing paper. Transfer design to metal sheet, using transfer paper.

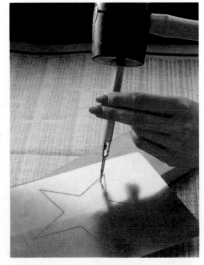

2 Place ornament design over scrap of wood. Punch hole for hanger about 1/8" (3 mm) inside edge of design, using an awl and mallet. Embellish interior of ornament with a punched design, if desired (page 25).

3 Cut out ornament, using scissors or jeweler's snips. Trim the tips off any sharp points.

4 Sand edges of ornament lightly, using sandpaper to smooth any sharp edges of metal; avoid sanding surface of ornament if smooth finish is desired.

5 Rub the ornament with fine steel wool to remove any fingerprints. Oxidize copper, if desired (opposite). Spray with aerosol clear acrylic sealer.

6 Embellish the ornament, if desired, by wrapping it with wire; for additional textural interest, layer two ornaments, then wrap with wire. Twist ends of wire together on back side; trim off excess.

7 Cut 7" (18 cm) length of wire, for hanger. Twist end of wire around awl, to make a coil, as in step 1, opposite. Insert opposite end of wire through the hole from the front of ornament; bend end to make hook for hanging.

HOW TO MAKE A TIN SPIRAL ORNAMENT

1 Cut ¼" × 6" (6 mm × 15 cm) strip of tin; trim ends at an angle. Trim off any sharp points, using jeweler's snips. Sand edges lightly with sandpaper. Punch a hole for hanger about ⅛" (3 mm) from one end of the strip, using an awl and mallet.

2 Wrap tin strip around pencil to make spiral; remove ornament from the pencil. Spray with aerosol clear acrylic sealer. Add hanger as in step 7, above.

HOW TO CONNECT METAL ORNAMENTS WITH WIRE

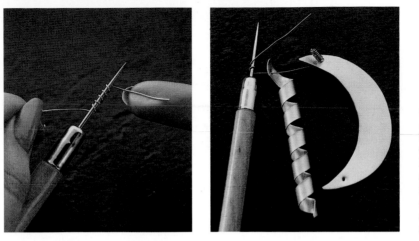

1 Cut 6" (15 cm) length of wire. Twist end of wire around awl to make a coil, using about 2¼" (6 cm) of wire. Press coil together between fingers to compress slightly.

2 Insert opposite end of the wire through hole in one ornament from front. Insert wire through second ornament from back. Repeat coiling process to secure the wire to second ornament.

HOW TO PUNCH A DESIGN IN A METAL ORNAMENT

1 Transfer the design for punching to tissue paper as on page 23, step 1. Tape the design for punching to metal sheet inside lines for ornament.

2 Punch holes around the edges of design at ⅛" (3 mm) intervals, using awl and mallet. Remove tissue pattern.

HOW TO OXIDIZE COPPER

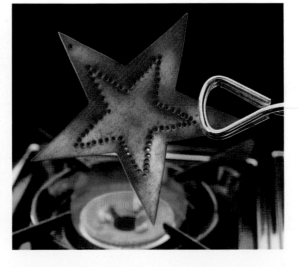

1 Texturize copper sheet, if desired, by sanding lightly with sandpaper.

2 Hold the copper ornament over flame with tongs; move it through flame randomly to produce color change. Remove the ornament from heat occasionally to check for desired color; holding the copper in flame too long can cause the copper to lose all its natural color.

FOLDED STAR
ORNAMENTS

Using simple folding techniques, turn strips of paper or ribbon into delicate and dimensional folded star ornaments, sometimes called German stars. Each star ornament is made from only four strips of paper or ribbon. The width of the paper strips or ribbon determines the size of the ornament. Use the chart at right to help determine the width and length of the strips needed to make a folded star ornament of the desired size.

For folded star ornaments from paper, select papers of medium weight, such as parchment papers and gift-wrapping papers. Many art supply stores have large sheets of decorative papers with unique textures. To make gift-wrapping paper decorative on both sides, you can fuse two sheets together, using lightweight paper-backed fusible web. Test-fuse small pieces of paper to be sure the paper does not become too stiff to crease easily.

For folded star ornaments made from ribbon, select ribbons that are attractive on both sides and that hold a crease well, such as some craft and metallic ribbons; avoid satin or taffeta ribbons.

CUTTING DIRECTIONS

For each folded star ornament from paper, cut four strips of paper, using the chart below as a guide for determining the width and length of the strips.

For a folded star ornament from ribbon, cut four lengths of ribbon, using the chart below as a guide for determining the length of the strips; the length depends on the width of the ribbon used.

MATERIALS

• Paper or ribbon, amount depending on size of star desired.

• Lightweight paper-backed fusible web, for use with papers that are decorative on one side only.

• Thick craft glue; decorative thread or cording, for hanger.

SIZE CHART FOR FOLDED STAR ORNAMENTS

APPROXIMATE SIZE	WIDTH OF STRIP	LENGTH OF STRIP	RIBBON YARDAGE REQUIRED
2" (5 cm)	½" (1.3 cm)	15" (38 cm)	1¾ yd. (1.6 m)
3" to 3½" (7.5 to 9 cm)	⅝" to ¾" (1.5 to 2 cm)	18" (46 cm)	2 yd. (1.85 m)
4½" (11.5 cm)	1" (2.5 cm)	27" (68.5 cm)	3 yd. (2.75 m)
6½" to 7" (16.3 to 18 cm)	1⅜" to 1½" (3.5 to 3.8 cm)	36" (91.5 cm)	4 yd. (3.7 m)
9" (23 cm)	2" (5 cm)	46" (117 cm)	5⅛ yd. (4.7 m)

HOW TO FUSE PAPER

1 Fuse adhesive side of paper-backed fusible web to the wrong side of decorative paper, using dry iron set at medium temperature; press for 1 to 3 seconds. Remove paper backing; set aside to use as press cloth.

2 Place second sheet of paper over the first piece, with wrong sides together. Using paper backing as a press cloth, fuse layers together for 1 to 3 seconds.

HOW TO MAKE A FOLDED STAR ORNAMENT

1 Fold each of the four strips in half; trim ends to points. Place two folded strips vertically, with the tips of the left strip pointing up and tips of right strip pointing down.

2 Place the left vertical strip between layers of a third strip, positioning it near fold of third strip. Place ends of third strip between the layers of the right vertical strip.

3 Weave the fourth strip below third strip by placing ends of right vertical strip between layers of fourth strip. Place ends of fourth strip between layers of left vertical strip. Pull ends tightly.

4 Fold top layer of left vertical strip down; crease. Rotate woven square one-quarter turn clockwise.

5 Repeat step 4 to fold the next two top layers down; insert fourth strip between layers of the lower left square as shown. Crease and rotate one-quarter turn clockwise.

6 Fold upper right strip over itself at 45° angle as shown; crease.

7 Fold same strip over itself at 45° angle as shown; crease.

8 Fold same strip to left, aligning folded edges; insert end of strip between layers of upper right square to make one star point. Rotate woven square one-quarter turn clockwise.

9 Repeat steps 6 to 8 to make four star points.

10 Turn star over. Repeat steps 6 to 8 to make four more star points, for a total of eight star points.

11 Lift horizontal strip at upper right corner to the left, out of the way. Fold up vertical strip at lower right; crease.

12 Fold same strip over itself at 45° angle as shown; crease. Grasp end of strip; keep this side of the strip facing up as you complete step 13.

13 Turn the strip counterclockwise; insert end of strip between layers of upper left square. Strip will come out through star point; open point of star with finger or tip of scissors, if necessary. Pull tight to make star point that projects upward.

14 Rotate star one-quarter turn clockwise and repeat steps 11 to 13 to make four projecting star points.

16 Thread needle; insert needle through star between two outer points. Knot ends of thread for hanger.

15 Turn star over. Repeat steps 11 to 14 to make four additional projecting star points. Trim ends of strips even with edge of outer star points. Secure by applying dot of glue to both sides of ends, if necessary.

TRIMMED FABRIC ORNAMENTS

Create elegant ornaments by covering Styrofoam® balls with rich fabrics and trims. Four wedge-shaped fabric pieces are used to cover the Styrofoam ball. Use one fabric, or select up to four different coordinating fabrics, to cover the ball. The fabric pieces are glued to the ball, and the raw edges are concealed with flat trim, such as ribbon or braid. Cording, pearls, sequins, or beads can also be used to embellish the ornament. The hanger of the ornament is made from a decorative cord and an ornamental cap.

MATERIALS

- 3" (7.5 cm) Styrofoam ball.
- Fabric scraps.
- Cording and flat trims, such as ribbon or braid.
- Decorative beads, pearls, sequins, and bead pins, optional.
- 9" (23 cm) length of cording and ornamental cap, for hanger.
- Thick craft glue; hot glue gun and glue sticks.

HOW TO MAKE A TRIMMED FABRIC ORNAMENT

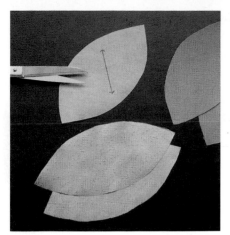

1 Transfer the pattern (page 314) to paper, and cut four pieces from fabric scraps.

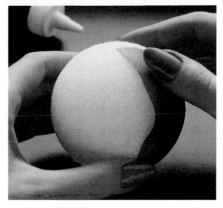

2 Apply craft glue near the edges on the wrong side of one fabric piece. Position the fabric piece on Styrofoam ball; smooth edges around the ball, easing fullness along sides.

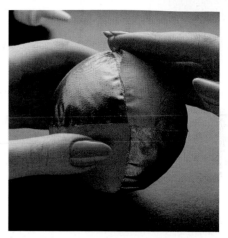

3 Apply remaining fabric pieces to ball; match points and align raw edges to cover ball completely.

4 Glue trim over the raw edges of the fabric pieces, butting raw edges of trim at top of ornament.

5 Poke hole in Styrofoam ball at top of ornament. Insert end of one or two pieces of cording into hole; secure with craft glue. Apply glue to fabric as shown; wrap the cording tightly around the ball in one continuous spiral, until desired effect is achieved. Poke end of cording into Styrofoam; secure with glue.

6 Embellish with additional cording, if desired. Attach decorative beads, pearls, and sequins, if desired, using bead pins; secure with dot of craft glue.

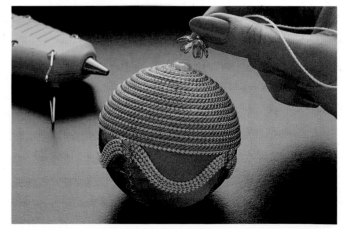

7 Insert cord in decorative cap; knot ends. Shape cap to fit top of ornament; secure with hot glue. Add bead or decorative cap to bottom, if desired.

GOLD-LEAF ORNAMENTS

urn papier-mâché craft ornaments into elegant gold-leaf ornaments, using imitation gold leaf.

Imitation leaf, also available in silver and copper, can be found at craft and art supply stores. Several sheets are packaged together, with tissue paper between the layers. When working with the sheets of gold leaf, handle the tissue paper, not the gold leaf, whenever possible. The gold leaf is very fragile and may tarnish.

MATERIALS

- Papier-mâché ball.
- Aerosol acrylic paint, optional.
- Imitation gold, silver, or copper leaf.
- Gold-leaf adhesive; paintbrush.
- Soft-bristle brush.
- Ribbon, for bow.
- Thick craft glue; aerosol clear acrylic sealer.

HOW TO MAKE A GOLD-LEAF ORNAMENT

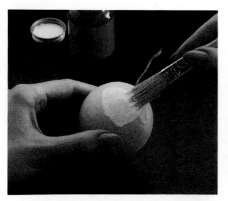

1 Apply aerosol paint to the papier-mâché ball, if desired; allow paint to dry. Apply gold-leaf adhesive to the ornament in small area, feathering out edges; allow the adhesive to dry until clear.

2 Cut the gold leaf and tissue paper slightly larger than adhesive area. Press the gold leaf over the adhesive, handling the tissue only. Remove the tissue paper.

3 Remove excess gold leaf with a soft-bristle brush. Apply gold leaf to additional areas of ball as desired. Apply aerosol clear acrylic sealer. Tie ribbon in bow around base of hanger; secure with dot of craft glue.

MARBLEIZED ORNAMENTS

Elegant marbleized ornaments are easy to make, using clear glass ornaments and craft acrylic paints. For best results, use paints that are of pouring consistency; paints may be thinned with water, if necessary. The marbleized effect is created by pouring two or three colors of paint into a glass ornament and swirling the paint colors together. Allow the paints to dry slightly after each color is applied, to avoid a muddy appearance.

MATERIALS

- Clear glass ornament, with removable top.
- Craft acrylic paints in desired colors.
- 9" (23 cm) length of cording or ribbon, for hanger.
- Ribbon, for bow.
- Disposable cups; hot glue gun and glue sticks.

HOW TO MAKE A MARBLEIZED ORNAMENT

1 Remove cap from ornament. Pour first color of paint into disposable cup; thin with water, if necessary. Pour small amount of paint into ornament; rotate to swirl paint. Place ornament, upside down, on the cup; allow any excess paint to flow out.

2 Repeat step 1 for each remaining color of paint. Place the ornament, upside down, on a cup, and allow the excess paint to flow out. Turn ornament right side up; allow to dry. Paint colors will continue to mix together during the drying process. Use additional coats of paint as necessary for opaque appearance.

3 Replace cap on ornament. Insert cording or ribbon through wire loop in cap; knot ends. Make a bow from ribbon; secure to top of ornament, using hot glue.

STRING BALL ORNAMENTS

Oversized string balls filled with nothing but air seem to magically keep their shape. An ornament is created by wrapping a balloon with string and decorative cords or narrow ribbons, then applying a liquid fabric stiffener and allowing it to dry. When the balloon is popped and removed, the stiffened string ball can be decorated with ribbons and other embellishments. Hang the ornaments on the Christmas tree, or arrange them around an evergreen garland on a buffet or mantel.

MATERIALS

- Round latex balloons, in desired sizes.
- Liquid fabric stiffener.
- Foam applicator.
- Wrapping materials, such as string, metallic cord, narrow braid, and narrow ribbon.
- Clothespins, dowel 3/8" (1 cm) or smaller in diameter, and deep cardboard box, for suspending wet balloon.
- Metallic cord, for hanger; large-eyed needle.
- Ribbon, for bows.
- Embellishments, such as glitter, sequins, and confetti, optional.

HOW TO MAKE A STRING BALL ORNAMENT

1 Inflate balloon to desired size; knot end. Grasp balloon by the knot; apply thin layer of liquid fabric stiffener to entire surface of balloon, using foam applicator.

2 Wrap end of string loosely around base of knot. Wrap string around balloon and back to knot.

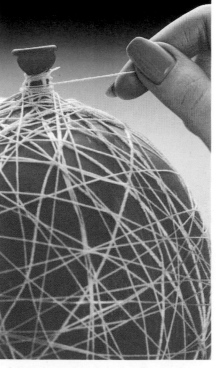

3 Continue to wrap string around the balloon, changing directions gradually; sparsely cover entire surface of balloon. Wrap string loosely around knot; cut string. Apply another layer of fabric stiffener to string.

4 Repeat steps 2 and 3 for each additional layer of wrapping material. Continue to add layers of string until surface of balloon is evenly covered to desired density.

5 Apply generous coat of liquid fabric stiffener over the entire wrapped balloon. Sprinkle with glitter, if desired.

6 Suspend balloon from dowel, using clothespin; prop dowel across opening of deep cardboard box, allowing balloon to drip into box. Allow to dry completely.

7 Pop balloon; loosen any areas of balloon that may stick, using eraser end of pencil. Pull deflated balloon out of the ball through hole left by balloon knot at top. Remove any remaining residue between strings with eraser end of pencil or a pin.

9 Insert ribbons into same holes as cord; tie into bows. Embellish ornament as desired.

8 Attach cord at top of ball, using large-eyed needle; insert needle into hole left by balloon knot, and exit through any space, about ½" (1.3 cm) away. Knot ends of cord to form loop for hanging.

SCHERENSCHNITTE ORNAMENTS & GARLANDS

Simple folding and cutting techniques turn ordinary paper into beautiful ornaments. The German craft of scherenschnitte (shear-en-shnit-tah), or scissors' cuttings, produces an intricate paper filigree that can be displayed as a single, flat ornament or a garland of repeated motifs. Single ornaments, glued to card stock, also make unique gift tags or Christmas cards. Two identical scherenschnitte pieces can be made and sewn together down the center for a three-dimensional ornament. Several patterns for each style are given on page 312. Ornaments can be antiqued, if desired, or painted with watercolor paints. For added sparkle, glitter may be applied to the ornament.

Choose art papers that have a sharp edge when cut. Parchment papers are particularly suitable for scherenschnitte, due to their strength and ability to accept stain or watercolors. Scissors with short, sharp, pointed blades are necessary for intricate work. Tiny detail cutting on the interior of the design is easier to do with a mat knife and cutting surface.

Three-dimensional ornament is created by stitching two identical symmetrical designs together through the center. You can also make single ornaments or a garland as shown opposite.

HOW TO MAKE A SINGLE SCHERENSCHNITTE ORNAMENT

MATERIALS

- Tracing paper.
- Art paper.
- Graphite paper, for transferring design; removable tape; scrap of corrugated cardboard.
- Scissors with short, sharp, pointed blades.
- Mat knife and cutting surface.
- Needle; thread, for hanger.
- Instant coffee and cotton-tipped swab, for antiquing, optional.
- Watercolor paints and glitter, optional.

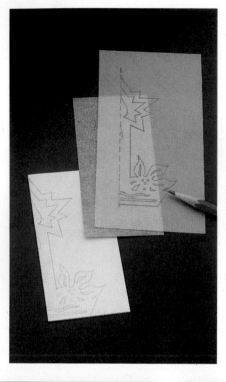

1 Cut a piece of art paper larger than the pattern dimensions (page 312); for a symmetrical design, fold paper in half, right sides together. Trace pattern onto tracing paper. Transfer the design from tracing paper to wrong side of folded art paper, using graphite paper; align the dotted line on design to fold of art paper.

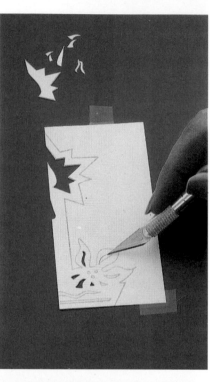

2 Tape folded art paper to cutting surface, placing the tape in area outside design. Cut out interior shapes, using mat knife; begin with shapes nearest fold, and work toward cut edges of paper. Make any small holes by punching through paper with a needle.

3 Remove art paper from cutting surface, and cut outer edge of design with scissors. Open cut design.

4 Press flat with a warm iron. Antique or embellish as desired, using one of the three methods on page 17. Attach thread hanger at center of the ornament, ¼" (6 mm) from the upper edge, using a hand needle; knot the thread ends.

HOW TO MAKE A THREE-DIMENSIONAL SCHERENSCHNITTE ORNAMENT

1 Follow steps 1 to 4, opposite, for two identical designs, omitting thread hanger. Place the cut designs on top of each other, aligning edges; secure to scrap of corrugated cardboard, using removable tape. Punch holes with pushpin every ¼" (6 mm) along the center fold, through both layers.

2 Thread a needle with 18" (46 cm) length of thread in same color as ornament. Sew in and out of holes from top to bottom of ornament.

3 Turn ornament over, and stitch back up to top hole. Tie the ends of thread together at desired length for hanger. Arrange the ornament sections at right angles to each other.

1 Cut strip of art paper 11" (28 cm) long and 2¾" (7 cm) wide. Fold in half, wrong sides together, to make 5½" × 4¼" (14 × 10.8 cm) strip. Fold short ends to center fold, right sides together, so the strip is accordion-folded, with wrong side facing out.

2 Trace design for garland (page 312) onto tracing paper. Transfer design from tracing paper to wrong side of folded art paper, using graphite paper; align dotted lines on design to double folded edges of paper.

3 Cut out the design, following steps 2 and 3 for single ornament on page 40. Open out garland. Embellish, if desired, using one of the three methods opposite.

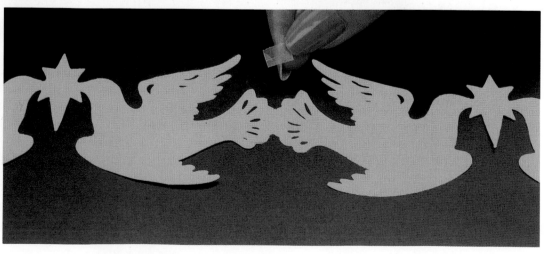

4 Repeat steps 1 to 3 as necessary to make as many garland lengths as desired. Press the garland pieces flat with a warm iron. Join garland lengths with small pieces of tape on wrong side.

HOW TO EMBELLISH SCHERENSCHNITTE ORNAMENTS

Watercolored ornaments. Paint scherenschnitte ornament with watercolor paint and soft brush. Allow to dry; press with warm iron. Repeat on back side.

Glittered ornaments. Apply glue over areas to be glittered, using glue pen. Sprinkle with glitter; shake off the excess. Repeat on back side.

Antiqued ornaments. Mix 1½ teaspoons (7 mL) instant coffee with ½ cup (125 mL) hot water. Apply coffee to outer edge of ornament and around large openings with cotton swab. Allow to dry; press. Repeat on back side.

PAPIER-MÂCHÉ
ORNAMENTS

Create easy-to-make papier-mâché ornaments from ready-made forms, available at craft shops. Simply embellish the forms with a variety of paints, beads, or glitter for a shimmering holiday display.

TIPS FOR EMBELLISHING
PAPIER-MÂCHÉ ORNAMENTS

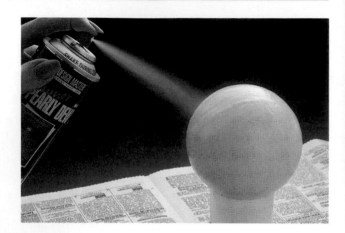

Paint the ornaments with aerosol acrylic paint; use pearlescent paint for a lustrous finish.

Apply glitter glue to painted ornaments to create a shimmering raised design.

Embellish the ornaments with beads; secure with craft glue.

HAND-CAST PAPER ORNAMENTS

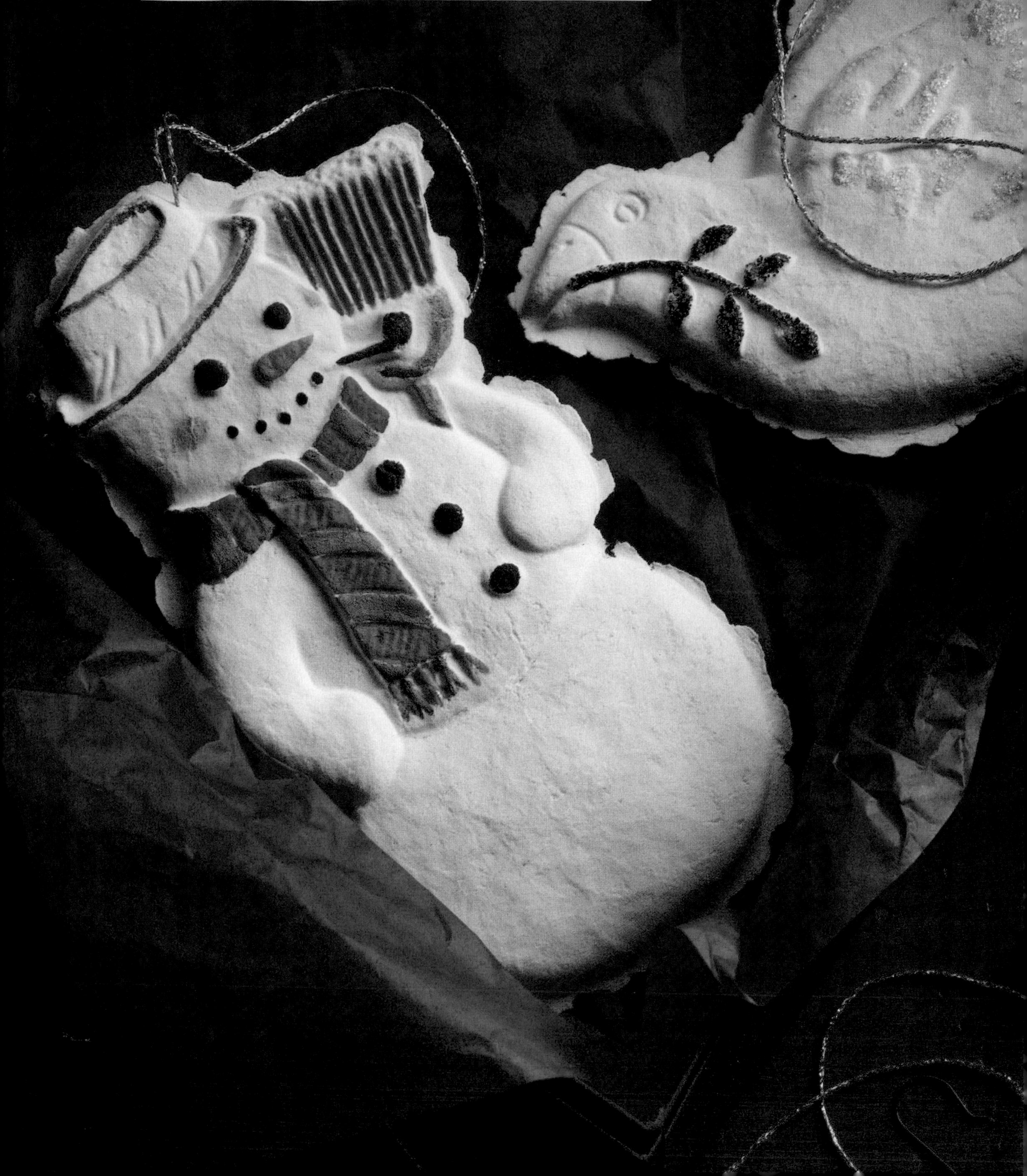

Though they may appear to be very delicate, these hand-cast paper ornaments are durable enough to become lasting keepsakes. Cotton linter is soaked in water and processed to a pulp, using a household blender. Paper-casting powder is added to the pulp for strength. Water is then strained from the mixture, and the pulp is pressed into a ceramic mold and allowed to dry.

After the ornament is removed from the mold, it may be painted, using water-color paints, or shaded, using chalk pastels. Tiny sprigs of dried floral material and narrow ribbons may be added for a Victorian look. For sparkle, fine glitter may be applied.

Supplies for making hand-cast paper ornaments are available at craft or art supply stores. They may be purchased separately or in kit form. One sheet of cotton linter measuring 8" × 7" (20.5 × 18 cm) will produce enough pulp for three hand-cast paper ornaments. The decorative ceramic molds have many other uses, making them a worthwhile purchase. Preparation of the mold before casting may vary with each brand; read manufacturer's instructions before beginning the project.

Leftover pulp can be saved for later use. Squeeze out excess water, and spread the pulp out in small clumps to dry. It is not necessary to add more paper-casting powder when resoaking and processing leftover pulp.

MATERIALS

- Cotton linter.
- Paper-casting powder, such as paper clay or paper additive.
- Household blender.
- Strainer.
- Ceramic casting mold.
- Sponge.
- Kitchen towel.
- Narrow ribbon or cord, for hanger; darning needle, for inserting hanger.
- Watercolor paints or chalk pastels, optional.
- Embellishments, such as dried floral materials, narrow ribbons, and glitter, optional.
- Craft glue, or hot glue gun and glue sticks, optional.

HOW TO MAKE A HAND-CAST PAPER ORNAMENT

1 Tear 8" × 7" (20.5 × 18 cm) sheet of cotton linter into 1" (2.5 cm) pieces. Put in the blender with 1 quart (1 L) water; allow to soak for several minutes.

2 Blend the water and linter for 30 seconds on low speed. Add 1 teaspoon (5 mL) of paper-casting powder to mixture; blend on high speed for one minute.

3 Pour about one-third of mixture into strainer, draining off water. Put wet pulp into mold.

4 Spread pulp evenly around mold and out onto flat outer edges; pulp on flat edges will form deckled edge around border of ornament.

5 Press damp sponge over pulp, compressing it into the mold and drawing off excess water; wring out sponge. Repeat two or three times until excess water is removed.

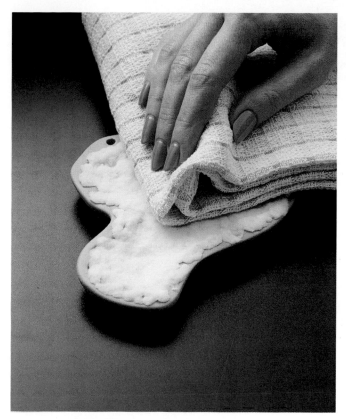

6 Press a folded kitchen towel over the compressed pulp, absorbing any remaining water and further compressing pulp.

7 Allow compressed pulp to dry completely in the mold. To speed drying, place the mold in an oven heated to 150°F (65°C) for about three hours.

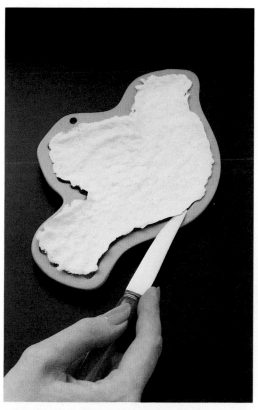

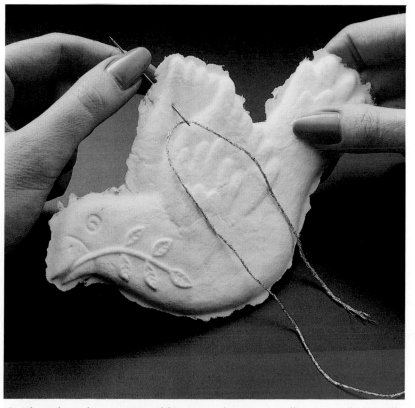

8 Loosen deckled edge of border around hand-cast paper ornament, using blade of knife; gently remove ornament from mold.

9 Thread cord or narrow ribbon into darning needle. Insert the needle through top of ornament at inner edge of border; knot ends of cord. Embellish ornament as desired (page 50).

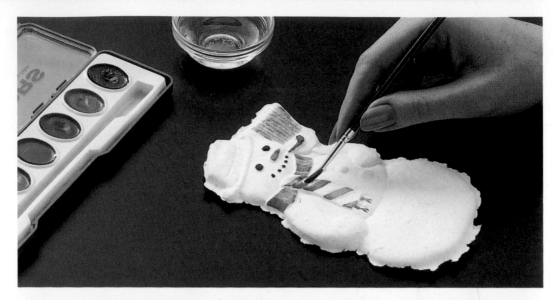

Painted ornaments.
Paint hand-cast paper ornaments, using diluted watercolors and small brush. Allow a painted area to dry before painting the adjacent area.

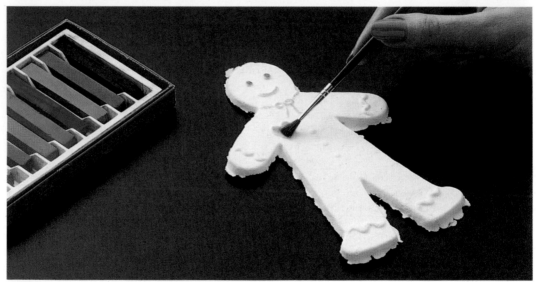

Color-shaded ornaments. Shade hand-cast paper ornaments, using chalk pastels or cosmetic powders. Apply with small brush or small foam applicator.

Glittered ornaments.
Outline or fill in small areas, using glitter glue in fine-tip tubes. Or, for large areas, apply glue over areas, using glue pen or glue stick. Sprinkle with glitter; shake off excess.

LACE DOILY ORNAMENTS

Lace doily ornaments, shaped as wreaths, semicircles, and baskets, give a Victorian look to a Christmas tree.

By using the ornaments, instead of bows, on packages, they become an extra keepsake gift.

Make the ornaments easily from Battenberg lace or cutwork doilies. Add ribbon hangers, and embellish the ornaments with trimmings such as dried or silk flowers or pearl strands.

MATERIALS (for lace doily wreath or semicircle ornament)

- Two 6" (15 cm) Battenberg or cutwork doilies, for lace wreath, or one for lace semicircle.
- Polyester fiberfill.
- 9" (23 cm) length of ribbon or braid trim, for hanger.
- Embellishments, such as dried or silk floral materials, pearl strands, and ribbon.
- Hot glue gun and glue sticks, optional.

MATERIALS (for lace doily basket ornament)

- One 8" (20.5 cm) Battenberg or cutwork doily: one doily makes two ornaments.
- 9" (23 cm) length of ribbon or braid trim, for hanger.
- Embellishments, such as dried or silk floral materials, optional.
- Hot glue gun and glue sticks, optional.

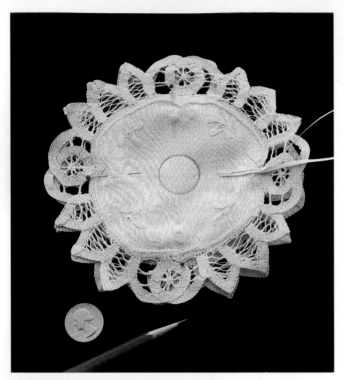

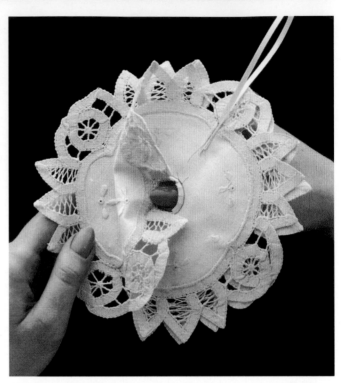

1 Baste ends of ribbon to wrong side of doily, about 1¼" (3.2 cm) from center. Mark 1" (2.5 cm) circle in center of one doily on wrong side. Pin the doilies right sides together.

2 Stitch around circle on marked line, using short stitch length. Trim away the fabric on the inside of circle ⅛" (3 mm) from stitching; turn right side out through center.

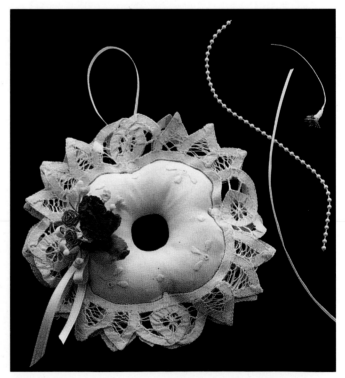

3 Stitch around the doilies, along the inner edge of lace trim, or 1" (2.5 cm) from the previous stitching; leave 2" (5 cm) opening.

4 Stuff the wreath with polyester fiberfill; stitch the opening closed by machine, using zipper foot. Secure embellishments with hot glue or by hand-stitching them in place.

HOW TO SEW A LACE DOILY SEMICIRCLE ORNAMENT

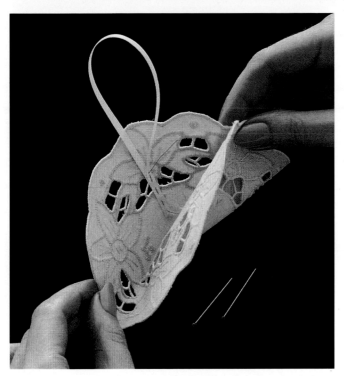

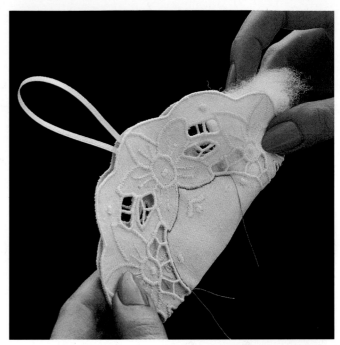

1 Baste ends of ribbon to wrong side of doily, about ¾" (2 cm) from center of doily. Fold doily in half.

2 Stitch around the semicircle, along inner edge of lace, or 1" (2.5 cm) from outer edge, using a short stitch length; leave 1" (2.5 cm) opening. Complete as in step 4, opposite.

HOW TO SEW A LACE DOILY BASKET ORNAMENT

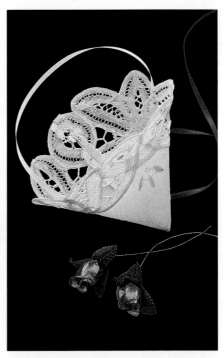

1 Cut doily in half. Fold one doily piece in half again, right sides together; mark point on raw edge at fold. Mark point on outer curved edge ½" (1.3 cm) from cut edge; draw line connecting points.

2 Cut on the marked line. Stitch ¼" (6 mm) from the raw edge, using short stitch length. Turn right side out; press.

3 Stitch ribbon to each side of the basket; seam is at the center back. Secure any embellishments with hot glue or by hand-stitching in place.

FELT ORNAMENTS

These finely detailed ornaments are fun and easy to make, using craft felt or synthetic suede. Choose from a traditional dove or reindeer, or a whimsical cat and mouse. The body of each ornament is stitched before it is cut, making for quick assembly. Polyester stuffing gives added dimension.

HOW TO MAKE A MOUSE ORNAMENT

MATERIALS

- Felt.
- Polyester fiberfill.
- Thick craft glue.
- Black fine-point permanent-ink marker.
- Scrap of fabric for shawl.
- Gray embroidery floss.

- Scrap of yellow cellulose sponge, about 3/8" (1 cm) thick, for cheese.
- 9" (23 cm) length of ribbon, 1/8" (3 mm) wide, for bow on cheese.
- 8" (20.5 cm) length of fine brass wire, for glasses.

CUTTING DIRECTIONS

From felt, cut two ears and four arms, using patterns on page 310. Also cut one 5" (12.5 cm) strip of felt a scant 1/4" (6 mm) wide, for tail. From fabric, cut one shawl, using pattern on page 310. Transfer mouse body pattern on page 310 onto heavy paper or cardboard; body is cut on page 56, step 3.

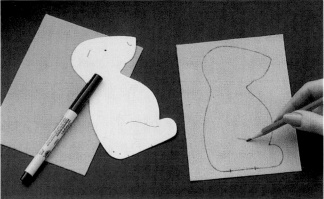

1 Place pattern for body on felt; using fine-point marker, trace around pattern. Lightly mark stitching line for leg definition, using pencil or chalk. Pin-mark tail placement. Place marked felt on second layer of felt.

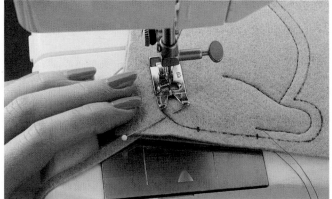

2 Stitch around body ¼" (6 mm) inside marked line and on markings for leg definition, inserting tail as indicated on pattern; leave opening for stuffing at lower edge of body.

(Continued)

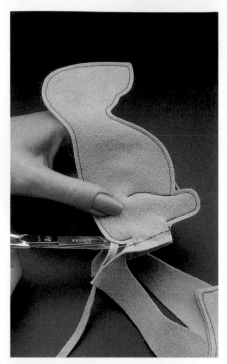

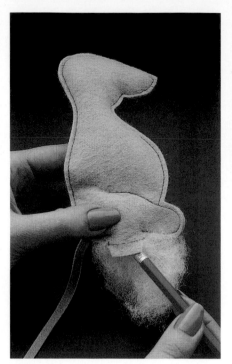

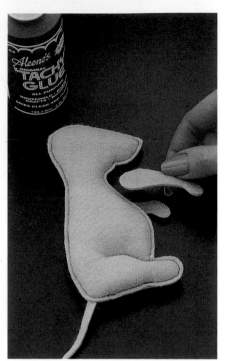

3 Trim felt ⅛" (3 mm) from the stitching, taking care not to trim off tail; do not trim at opening for stuffing.

4 Stuff body with polyester fiberfill. Stitch the opening closed, using zipper foot; trim felt ⅛" (3 mm) from stitching.

5 Glue two arm pieces together, matching edges; repeat for remaining arm. Allow glue to dry. Glue one arm to each side of body, as indicated on pattern. Allow glue to dry.

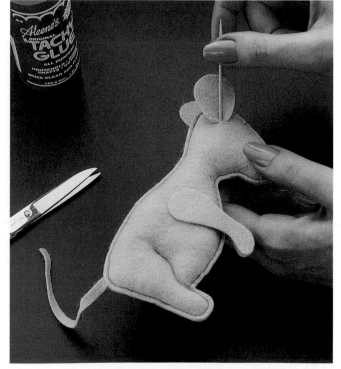

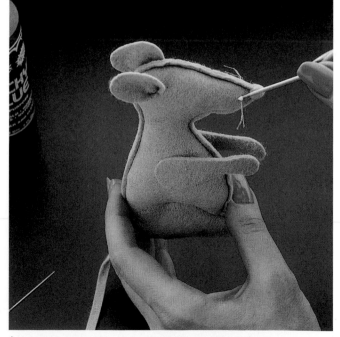

6 Cut slit for ear, about ¼" (6 mm) long, as indicated on pattern. Insert lower edge of ear into opening, using a toothpick. Secure the ear with small dot of glue. Repeat for remaining ear.

7 Cut two ¼" (6 mm) circles from pink felt; glue to each side of the snout as shown. Thread needle with three strands of gray embroidery floss, and insert through nose for whiskers; trim to ¾" (2 cm) on each side of nose. Using toothpick, place small dot of glue at the base of whiskers to secure.

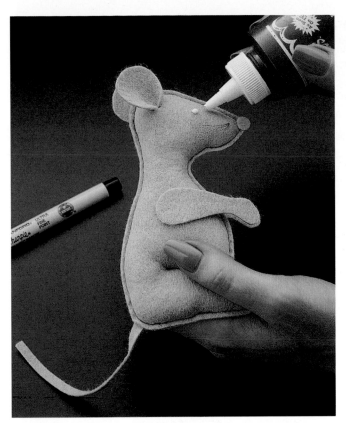

8 Apply small dot of fabric glue to felt at eye marks, as indicated on pattern. When glue is dry, mark each eye, using black permanent-ink marker.

9 Form glasses by wrapping wire around a pen to make the first lens opening; twist wire to secure. Repeat to make the second lens, spacing circles about ½" (1.3 cm) apart. Place glasses on nose; secure by wrapping ends of wire around ears. Trim excess wire.

10 Cut wedge about 1" (2.5 cm) long from sponge, for cheese. Tie ribbon bow around cheese. Make gift tag from scrap of colored paper; secure to ribbon bow, using thread. Glue cheese to front paws.

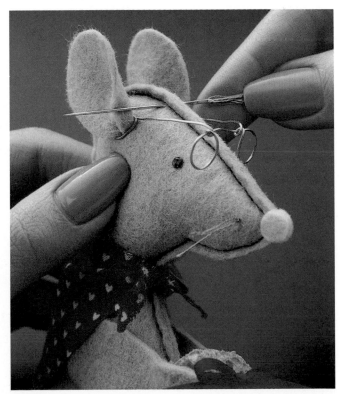

11 Tie shawl around neck of the mouse. Secure loop of embroidery floss through top of the ornament, for hanger.

HOW TO MAKE A CAT ORNAMENT

MATERIALS

- Felt.
- Polyester fiberfill.
- Thick craft glue.
- Black fine-point permanent-ink marker.
- Miniature novelty mouse.
- 9" (23 cm) length of ribbon, 1/8" (3 mm) wide, for bow at neck.
- Brown embroidery floss, for whiskers.
- Pipe cleaner.

CUTTING DIRECTIONS

Cut two ears and one muzzle, using patterns on page 310. Cut two 1 1/4" × 5" (3.2 × 12.5 cm) rectangles, for tail. Transfer body and hindquarters patterns on page 310 onto heavy paper or cardboard; these pieces are cut below.

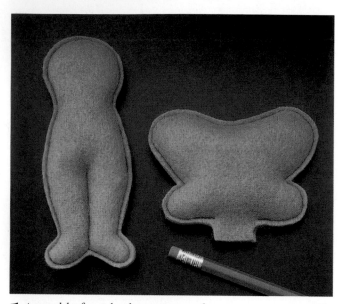

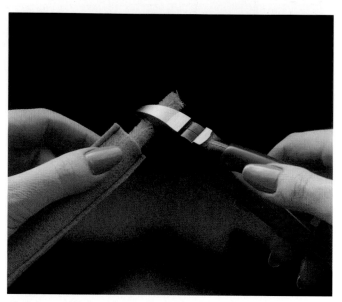

1 Assemble front body section as for mouse on pages 55 and 56, steps 1 to 4, omitting reference to tail; in step 2, leave opening just below neck, for stuffing. Repeat to make hindquarters section, leaving opening at lower edge, for stuffing and tail placement; do not stitch hindquarters section closed.

2 Layer tail pieces. Stitch around tail, using 1/4" (6 mm) seam allowance and rounding corners at one end; leave opposite end open. Trim felt 1/8" (3 mm) from stitching. Insert pipe cleaner into tail; trim pipe cleaner 1/2" (1.3 cm) from edge of felt.

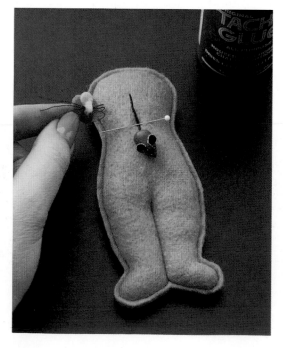

3 Insert the tail into hindquarters section; complete stitching. Trim the excess felt, taking care not to cut tail.

4 Cut one scant 1/4" (6 mm) circle each from pink and red felt; glue to wrong side of muzzle piece as shown. Glue three 2" (5 cm) strands of brown embroidery floss to wrong side of muzzle, for whiskers. Glue muzzle unit to face, as indicated on pattern, tucking tail of novelty mouse under the muzzle.

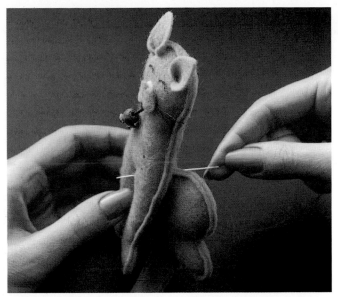

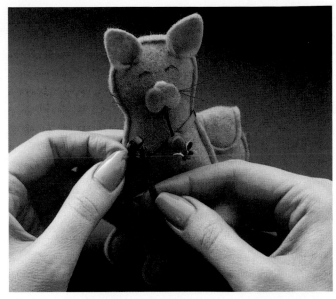

5 Attach the ears as on page 56, step 6. Mark the eyes as on page 57, step 8. Hand-stitch or glue the body to the hindquarters.

6 Shape the tail into desired position. Tie ribbon around the neck. Secure loop of embroidery floss through top of ornament, for hanger.

HOW TO MAKE A REINDEER ORNAMENT

MATERIALS

- Felt.
- Polyester fiberfill; pipe cleaner.
- Thick craft glue; embroidery floss.
- Black fine-point permanent-ink marker.
- Golf tee, for horn; craft acrylic glitter paint.

CUTTING DIRECTIONS

From felt, cut two ears, two antlers, and one tail, using patterns on page 311. Cut one ½" × 8" (1.3 × 20.5 cm) rectangle for the scarf. Transfer body and leg patterns on page 311 onto heavy paper or cardboard; these pieces are cut below.

1 Glue antler pieces together, matching edges. Fold tail in half lengthwise; pin. Assemble reindeer leg section as for the mouse body on pages 55 and 56, steps 1 to 3, omitting reference to tail. Insert pipe cleaner into leg; trim pipe cleaner ¼" (1.3 cm) from edge of felt.

2 Repeat step 1 on page 55 to prepare reindeer body section for stitching; pin-mark placement for antlers, tail, and extended leg. Stitch around body, inserting the antlers, tail, and leg at markings; leave opening at upper edge of back for stuffing.

(Continued)

3 Trim felt ⅛" (3 mm) from stitching, taking care not to cut antlers, tail, or front leg. Stuff body with polyester fiberfill. Stitch opening closed, using zipper foot.

4 Attach ears as on page 56, step 6. Mark eyes as on page 57, step 8.

5 Apply glitter paint to golf tee; allow to dry. Glue golf tee to leg as shown, for horn.

6 Cut slits at ends of scarf piece to make fringe, using scissors. Tie scarf around neck of reindeer. Secure loop of embroidery floss through top of ornament, for hanger.

HOW TO MAKE A DOVE ORNAMENT

MATERIALS

- Felt.
- Polyester fiberfill.
- Thick craft glue; embroidery floss.
- Black fine-point permanent-ink marker.
- Small artificial leaves.

CUTTING DIRECTIONS

Transfer body and wing patterns on page 311 onto heavy paper or cardboard; these pieces are cut below.

1 Assemble body section as for mouse on pages 55 and 56, steps 1 to 4, omitting reference to tail. Repeat to make two wings, omitting stuffing.

2 Glue a wing to each side of the body, staggering the placement slightly so both the wings are visible from each side.

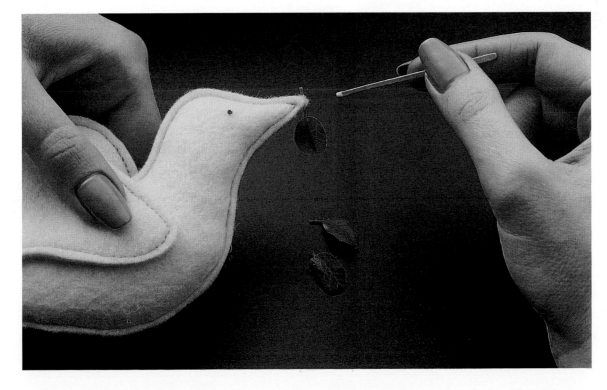

3 Mark eyes as on page 57, step 8. Glue artificial leaves to beak. Secure a loop of embroidery floss through the top of ornament, for the hanger.

RIBBON ROSES

Ribbon roses add an elegant touch to the Christmas tree. They are constructed using either standard ribbon for a traditional rose or wired ribbon for a cabbage-style rose, and are secured to wire stems. The stems are wrapped with floral tape, with artificial leaves inserted for a finishing touch.

Make roses of different sizes, using ribbon in different widths. The length of the ribbon needed for each rose varies with the width of the ribbon and the desired finished size. A rose made with 5⁄8" (1.5 cm) ribbon may require ½ yd. (0.5 m) of ribbon, while a rose made with 2¼" (6 cm) ribbon may require 1½ yd. (1.4 m) of ribbon. For impact, cluster several roses of different colors and sizes, forming a ribbon rose bouquet. Simply twist the wire stems of the roses around the tree branches to secure them to the tree.

MATERIALS

- Medium-gauge stem wire.
- Fine-gauge paddle floral wire, for traditional ribbon roses.
- Ribbon in desired width, for traditional rose, or wired ribbon in desired width, for cabbage-style rose; width of ribbon and desired finished size of rose determine length needed.
- Artificial rose leaves.
- Floral tape.

HOW TO MAKE A TRADITIONAL RIBBON ROSE

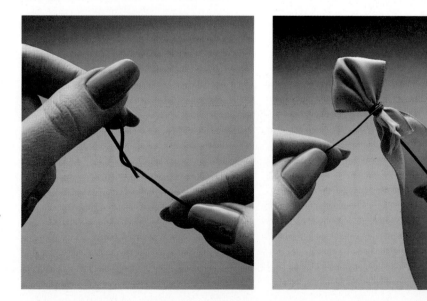

1 Bend a 1" (2.5 cm) loop in the end of stem wire; twist to secure.

2 Fold ribbon end over loop; wrap with paddle floral wire to secure.

(Continued)

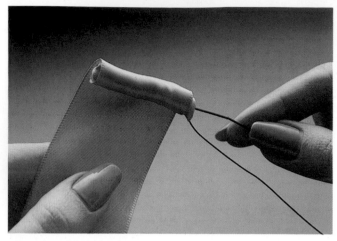

3 Hold ribbon taut in left hand and stem wire in right hand; roll stem wire toward left hand, wrapping ribbon tightly around the fold three times, forming rose center. Wrap paddle wire tightly around base to secure.

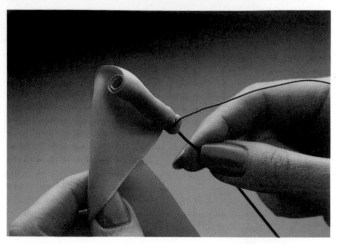

4 Fold ribbon back diagonally as shown, close to rose. Roll rose center over fold, keeping upper edge of rose center just below upper edge of fold; lower edges of ribbon will not be aligned.

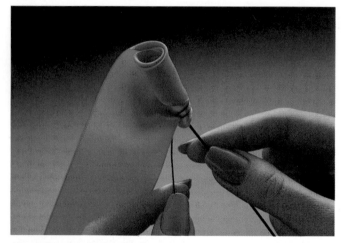

5 Roll to end of fold, forming petal. Wrap paddle wire tightly around base.

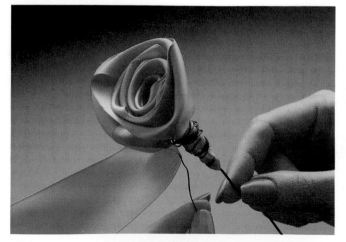

6 Repeat steps 4 and 5 for desired number of petals. Fold ribbon back diagonally, and secure with paddle wire at base; cut ribbon and paddle wire.

7 Wrap end of floral tape around base of rose, stretching tape slightly for best adhesion. Wrap entire base of rose, concealing wire. Continue wrapping floral tape onto stem wire. Place stem of artificial rose leaf next to stem wire; wrap stem wire and leaf stem together with floral tape. Continue wrapping until entire stem wire is covered with floral tape.

HOW TO MAKE A CABBAGE-STYLE ROSE

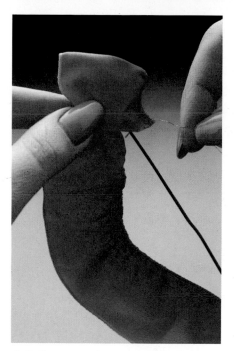

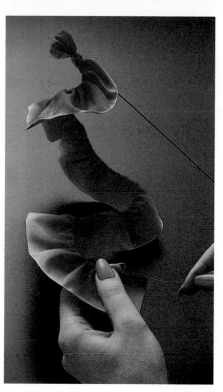

1 Follow step 1 on page 63. Cut a 1 to 1½-yd. (0.95 to 1.4 m) length of wired ribbon. Pull out about 2" (5 cm) of wire on one edge of one end of ribbon. Fold ribbon end over loop; secure with pulled wire, forming rose center.

2 Gather up one edge of remaining length of ribbon tightly by sliding ribbon along ribbon wire toward the rose center.

3 Wrap the gathered edge around the base of the rose, wrapping each layer slightly higher than the previous layer.

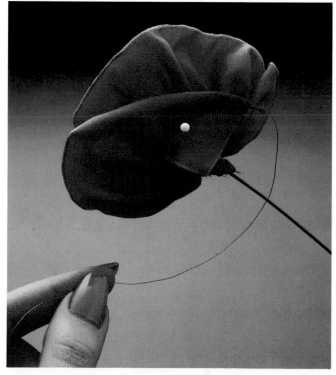

4 Fold the ribbon end down and catch under last layer. Wrap ribbon wire tightly around base several times to secure. Cut off excess ribbon wire.

5 Follow step 7, opposite, covering gathered edge of ribbon and wire.

MORE
IDEAS FOR
ORNAMENTS

Nature elements are used to embellish a miniature basket and wreath, creating clever ornaments. Miniature basket ornament is filled with sprigs of greenery and artificial berries. Miniature wreath is embellished with a small craft bird, sprigs of greenery, and artificial berries.

Ribbon, lace, and small cones (right) turn a plain ornament into an elegant tree decoration. Secure the embellishments using dots of clear-drying glue.

Torn fabric strips are tied around a cinnamon stick to make a Christmas tree ornament (below) Whole allspice and anise are used for embellishment. Secure raffia hanger with hot glue.

Large cones, painted like Santas, (below) make quick and inexpensive ornaments. Secure strings for the hangers, using a drop of hot glue. Form the face, beard, and hairline, using artificial snow paste; then paint the ornament, using acrylic paints. Trim the top of the completed ornament with snow paste.

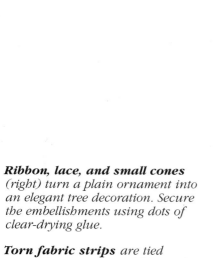

QUICK & EASY ORNAMENTS

Wheat bundles (left), hung upside down, are attractive accents on trees with natural or country decorating styles. The wheat stems are secured in bundles with a rubber band, which is concealed with a fabric bow. Secure the ornaments to the tree using floral wire.

Wire garland, shaped into spirals, adds glitz to a Christmas tree. Wrap a 26" (66 cm) length of wire garland around a pen or pencil. Remove the wire, then gradually untwist the coil from one end to make the ornament. At the widest end, bend the wire to form a hanger.

Glitter adds sparkle to plain ornaments. Mark designs on the ornaments using a glue-stick pen, then sprinkle with extra-fine glitter.

Dried fruit slices *make aromatic ornaments. Orange slices, glued together, are decorated with sprigs of greenery, berries, and ribbon hangers. The apple slices have jute hangers and are embellished with anise and cinnamon sticks. Dried fruit slices are available at craft stores, or make your own as on pages 70 and 72.*

Torn fabric strips *are wrapped and glued around Styrofoam® balls to make country-style ornaments. Secure raffia bows and hangers with hot glue.*

Ribbons and berries *embellish the tops of purchased glass ornaments. Ribbons also replace the traditional wire hangers.*

Glitter glue *in fine-tip tubes is applied to a glass ball ornament, creating a unique dimensional design.*

GARLANDS

Tree garlands can be made in a variety of styles. Shown top to bottom, choose from a rope garland, wrapped ball-and-spool garland, a dried-fruit-slice garland, or a wired-ribbon garland.

For ease in assembling, make the garlands in lengths of about 72" (183 cm). The wired-ribbon garland can be made any length. Most garlands are constructed with loops at the ends for securing the garlands to the branches.

Decorate a tree with a country or natural look, using a rope garland embellished with berry or floral clusters. The clusters may be purchased ready-made, or you can make your own.

To make a wrapped ball-and-spool garland with a country look, wrap torn fabric strips around Styrofoam® balls and wooden spools, then string them together with a piece of jute or twine. Buttons can be added to the garland for more color. Adding buttons decreases the number of wrapped balls and spools needed.

For a dried-fruit-slice garland, combine dried apple and orange slices with cinnamon sticks and fresh cranberries. String the items together with a piece of raffia for a natural look. You can dry your own fruit slices by placing them in a low-temperature oven for several hours. The drying time will vary, depending on the moisture content of the fruit. Remove the fruit slices from the oven when they feel like leather. If the slices are dried too long, they will be brittle and break; if the drying time is too short, they will be soft and spoil. The fresh cranberries will dry naturally on the garland after it is made.

A wired-ribbon garland can be made inexpensively from fabric strips, beading wire, and paper-backed fusible web. Decorate a tree with one continuous garland or several shorter ones. Arrange the garland by weaving the ribbon between and into the branches to create depth.

HOW TO MAKE A ROPE GARLAND

MATERIALS

- 1⅓ yd. (1.27 m) two-ply or three-ply manila or sisal rope, ¼" or ⅜" (6 mm or 1 cm) in diameter.
- Sheet moss.
- Eight berry or floral clusters with wire stems, either purchased or made as on page 152.
- Wire cutter.
- Hot glue gun and glue sticks; thick craft glue.

1 Make 3" (7.5 cm) loops at ends of rope by inserting each end between plies; secure with hot glue.

2 Make eight berry or floral clusters, if necessary (page 152). Insert the wire stems of clusters between the plies of rope at 8" (20.5 cm) intervals, and secure them with hot glue; trim any excess wire, using wire cutter.

3 Conceal wire ends of clusters with pieces of sheet moss; secure with craft glue.

HOW TO MAKE A WRAPPED BALL-AND-SPOOL GARLAND

MATERIALS

- Scraps of cotton fabrics.
- Twenty-four ⅞" (2.2 cm) Styrofoam® balls.
- Twenty-four wooden craft spools.
- Assorted buttons, optional.
- Lightweight jute or twine.
- Large-eyed needle.
- Thick craft glue.

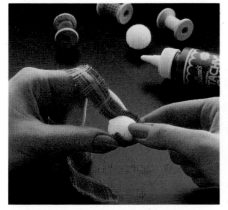

1 Tear twenty-four ¾" × 2¼" (2 × 6 cm) fabric strips on crosswise grain. Wrap around wooden spools; secure with glue. Tear twenty-four ½" × 13" (1.3 × 33 cm) fabric strips. Wrap randomly around Styrofoam balls; secure with glue.

2 Cut an 84" (213.5 cm) length of jute or twine. Form 3" (7.5 cm) loop at one end, and secure with knot; thread a large-eyed needle on opposite end.

3 String wrapped balls and spools onto jute or twine, alternating with buttons, if desired. Form loop at end; secure with knot.

HOW TO MAKE A DRIED-FRUIT-SLICE GARLAND

MATERIALS

- Firm apples and oranges.
- Fresh cranberries.
- Cinnamon sticks.

- 2 cups (500 mL) lemon juice.
- 1 tablespoon (15 mL) salt.

- Parchment paper.
- Raffia.
- 24-gauge floral wire.

- Wire cutter.
- Aerosol clear acrylic sealer.
- Paper towels.

1 Mix lemon and salt together; set aside. Cut fruit into scant ¼" (6 mm) slices, cutting crosswise as shown. Soak apple slices in lemon solution for 1 minute. Pat slices with paper towels to absorb excess moisture.

2 Place apple and orange slices on cookie sheet lined with parchment paper. Bake in 150°F (65°C) oven for 8 to 12 hours, until slices are dry, but still pliable; turn slices over and open oven door periodically while drying.

3 Apply aerosol clear acrylic sealer to cooled fruit slices. Break cinnamon sticks into 2" (5 cm) lengths. Select length of sturdy raffia; form loop at one end, and secure with knot.

4 Create needle for stringing fruit by folding a 6" (15 cm) length of floral wire in half around the unknotted end of raffia. Twist wire together at ends; trim excess, using wire cutter. Crimp the wire at fold, using pliers.

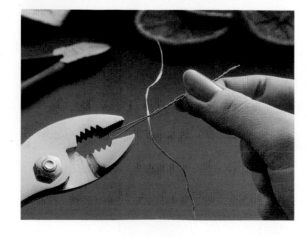

5 String the fruit slices, cranberries, and cinnamon sticks onto raffia; pierce fruit slices about ⅜" (1 cm) from the edges and gently ease along the raffia. Tie lengths of raffia together as necessary to make the garland about 72" (183 cm) long. Form a loop at end; secure with knot.

HOW TO MAKE A WIRED-RIBBON GARLAND

MATERIALS

- Fabric.
- One or more rolls of paper-backed fusible web, 3/8" (1 cm) wide.
- 26-gauge beading wire or craft wire.

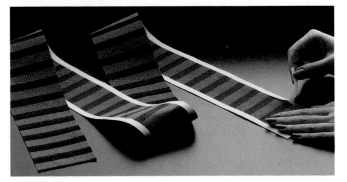

1 Cut fabric strips to desired width of ribbon plus 3/4" (2 cm). Piece strips as necessary, as on page 80, step 7. Apply strip of fusible web to wrong side of fabric along both long edges, following the manufacturer's directions. Remove paper backing.

2 Cut wire slightly longer than the length of fabric. Place the wire along inner edge of one fused strip. Fold and press fused edge to wrong side of fabric, encasing wire. Repeat for opposite side. Trim wire at ends.

MORE IDEAS FOR GARLANDS

Spice garland *is made by stringing spice ornaments (page 20) and cranberries to create a richly textured garland.*

Metal garland *is made by joining metal ornaments (page 23) with brass wire.*

Dough-cutout garland, *full of country charm, is strung together with raffia. To create the look and scent of ginger-bread cookies, simply add 1 tablespoon (15 mL) each of cinnamon, allspice, and cloves to the recipe on page 307.*

QUICK & EASY GARLANDS

Candy canes and mint candies are tied together with red ribbon for a colorful garland.

Large bells embellished with cones and sprigs of greenery are tied together with raffia.

Holiday garlands are traditionally used to decorate the Christmas tree. Make your own garlands by securing items such as candies, cookie cutters, or floral materials together with ribbon, raffia, or fabric strips.

Mini cookie cutters in Christmas shapes are strung on lengths of jute. Beads are interspersed between the cookie cutters to add color to the garland.

Pretzels, tied to torn strips of fabric, make a country-style garland.

Collectible metal toys and cookie cutters *are used as ornaments to create a country-style tree. Popcorn garland and fabric bows are used for contrast, and raffia streamers add to the country look.*

A variety of ornaments can be mixed successfully on a tree. Create a unified look by emphasizing a particular color or style, repeating it in several areas of the tree. For interest, add a few elements of surprise, such as an artificial bird's nest, oversize decorations, dried or silk flowers, or raffia streamers.

Wired-ribbon bow *is used as a tree topper. Streamers of ribbon cascade down the tree and are tucked into the branches. Gold and bronze foliage and berry picks are tucked into the branches to complete the elegant look.*

Dried floral materials, *such as baby's breath, German statice, roses, and pepper berries, are tucked into the tree, creating a garland effect. Several craft bird's nests and birds add to the natural look. Dried flowers, tied with a bow, are used as a tree topper.*

Artificial fruit garland *gives a natural look to this tree. Aromatic dried-fruit-slice ornaments (pages 68 and 69) and honeysuckle vine are used to decorate the tree.*

Oversize decorations, *such as snowmen, can be used for impact on a tree. Place the oversize decorations on the tree first, securing them with floral wire, if necessary. Candy canes and frosted twigs are used to fill in bare areas.*

TREE SKIRTS

A tree skirt offers the finishing touch to a Christmas tree. This simple lined tree skirt, finished with bias binding, has a layer of polyester fleece or batting for added body. It can be embellished in a variety of ways, using fused appliqués.

Make the patterns for appliqué designs by enlarging simple motifs found on Christmas cards or gift-wrapping paper. Use machine quilting or hand stitching around the outer edges of the appliqués to give them more definition.

MATERIALS

- 1¼ yd. (1.15 m) fabric, for tree skirt.
- 1¼ yd. (1.15 m) lining fabric.
- 45" (115 cm) square polyester fleece or low-loft quilt batting.
- ¾ yd. (0.7 m) fabric, for binding.
- Scraps of fabric, for fused appliqués.
- Paper-backed fusible web.

CUTTING DIRECTIONS

Cut the fabric, lining, and fleece or batting as in steps 1 to 3, below. Cut bias fabric strips, 2½" (6.5 cm) wide, for the binding.

HOW TO SEW A TREE SKIRT

1 Fold fabric for tree skirt in half lengthwise, then crosswise. Using a straightedge and a pencil, mark an arc on the fabric, measuring 21" to 22" (53.5 to 56 cm) from folded center of fabric. Cut on the marked line through all layers.

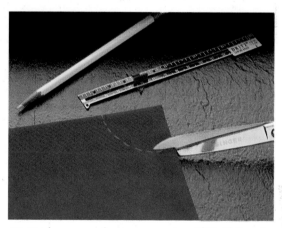

2 Mark a second arc, measuring 1¾" (4.5 cm) from the folded center of the fabric. Cut on the marked line.

3 Cut along one folded edge; this will be the center back. Cut lining and fleece or batting, using fabric for tree skirt as a pattern.

4 Apply the paper-backed fusible web to the wrong side of fabric scraps, following the manufacturer's directions. Transfer design motifs onto paper side of the fusible web; turn pattern over if the design is asymmetrical.

(Continued)

5 Cut design motifs from paper-backed fabric; remove paper backing. Fuse motifs to the tree skirt as desired.

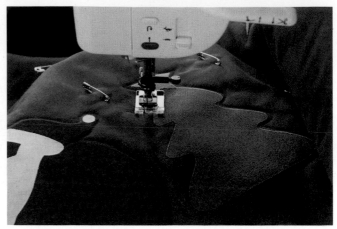

6 Layer the lining, fleece, and fabric for tree skirt, right sides out. Baste the layers together, using safety pins or hand stitching. Quilt design motifs by stitching around the outer edges of designs.

7 Piece binding strips to form 5½-yd. (5.05 m) length; join the strips together as shown; trim ¼" (6 mm) from stitching. Press seams open; trim off points.

8 Press the binding strip in half lengthwise, wrong sides together; fold back ½" (1.3 cm) on one short end. Pin binding to tree skirt, matching raw edges and starting at center back.

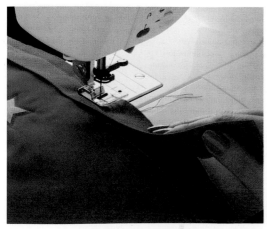

9 Stitch a scant ⅜" (1 cm) from raw edges, overlapping ends of binding ½" (1.3 cm); trim close to stitching.

10 Wrap binding strip snugly around edge of tree skirt, covering the stitching line on the wrong side; pin. Stitch in the ditch on right side of tree skirt, catching the binding on the wrong side.

MORE IDEAS FOR TREE SKIRTS

Gingerbread-men appliqués embellish this tree skirt. The outer edge is defined with contrasting bias binding and jumbo rickrack. The rickrack is applied to the underside of the tree skirt after the binding is applied. The gingerbread men are embellished with fabric paints in fine-tip tubes.

Star-and-moon theme is created using appliqués from lamé fabric. To prevent the delicate fabric from fraying, the raw edges of the appliqués were sealed, using fabric paints in fine-tip tubes.

Bullion fringe adds an elegant edging to a brocade tree skirt. Applied to the underside of the tree skirt, the fringe is secured in place by edgestitching along the inside edge of the binding from the right side.

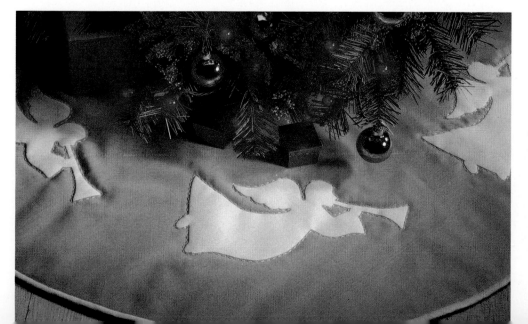

Sheer organza overlay, placed over the fused angel appliqués, creates a shadow embroidery effect. The tree skirt is quilted around the outer edges of the appliqués, using two strands of embroidery thread and a hand running stitch.

Decorate the base of a Christmas tree with a layered tree skirt embellished with ribbon bows. When arranged around the tree, it resembles an eight-pointed star. The skirt can be made for either an elegant or casual look, depending on the choice of fabrics and ribbon.

Easy to make, the tree skirt is simply two lined squares of fabric, stitched together around center openings. Back

openings in the layers allow for easy placement around the tree. Safety pins, used in place of permanent stitching, gather the fabric along each side, saving time and allowing the tree skirt to be stored flat.

Choose a lightweight lining fabric to prevent adding bulk to the skirt. For an inexpensive lining that is also a good choice for sheer fabrics, use nylon net.

Layered tree skirt is made from printed and plaid complementary holiday fabrics. Solid-colored fabrics are used for the lining. The tree skirt is embellished with wired ribbon bows.

MATERIALS

- 1¼ yd. (1.15 m) each, of two coordinating fabrics.
- 1¼ yd. (1.15 m) each, of two lining fabrics.
- Eight large safety pins.
- Wired ribbon.

HOW TO MAKE A LAYERED TREE SKIRT

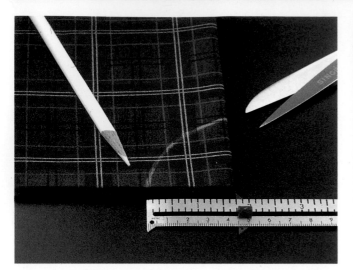

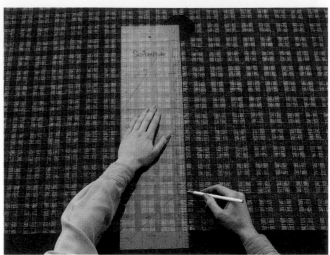

1 Cut outer fabric into a square, trimming selvages. Fold fabric in half lengthwise, then crosswise. Mark an arc, measuring 1¾" (4.5 cm) from folded center of fabric. Cut on marked line.

2 Pin-mark one folded edge at raw edges for the center back opening; open fabric and mark cutting line from raw edge to center opening, on wrong side of fabric.

3 Place face fabric on lining, right sides together; pin the layers together. Stitch ¼" (6 mm) seam around tree skirt, stitching around all edges and on each side of center back line; leave 6" (15 cm) opening for turning. For sheer fabrics, stitch a second row scant ⅛" (3 mm) from first stitching.

4 Cut on marked line; trim lining even with edges of outer fabric. Clip seam allowances around center circle; trim corners diagonally. Turn right side out; press. Slipstitch opening closed.

5 Repeat steps 1 to 4 for the remaining tree skirt layer. Align skirts, right sides up, matching center back openings. Shift the upper skirt so corners of the lower skirt are centered at sides of upper skirt. Mark opening of lower skirt on upper skirt. Pin layers together around the center from marked point to opening in the upper skirt.

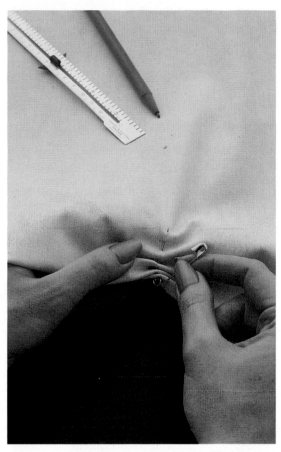

6 Topstitch ¼" (6 mm) from the raw edges around center, from opening to marked point, securing the two tree skirt layers together.

7 Gather and bunch fabric at the center of one long edge by inserting point of safety pin in and out of fabric for about 6" (15 cm) on lining side of the tree skirt as shown; close the pin. Repeat at center of each side for each tree skirt layer; do not pin back opening sides.

8 Place skirt around base of tree. Overlap back opening at outer edge; gather and bunch fabric for underlayer with safety pin. Repeat for remaining center back opening of upper layer of skirt.

9 Make four ribbon bows. Position a bow at each side of the upper layer, concealing safety pin; secure with pin.

MORE IDEAS FOR TREE SKIRTS

Polar fleece tree skirt *(above) is a quick and cozy project. Simply cut a polar fleece circle to the desired size; cut out a center circle for the trunk, and cut an opening slit, if desired. Fringe the skirt, keeping the blade of the scissors perpendicular to the fabric edge. Blanket-stitch fleece appliqués around the skirt for rustic appeal.*

Lace tablecloth, *draped around the base of a tree, complements a Victorian-style tree.*

Excelsior, highlighted with gold spray paint, is arranged around the base of a Christmas tree for a unique accent.

The Holiday Table

FRESH FLORAL ARRANGEMENTS

Decorate for the holidays with fresh flowers by making a centerpiece or a buffet arrangement. A centerpiece used on a dining table is usually short in height so it does not interfere with conversation. A buffet arrangement is designed to be placed against a wall and can be taller, for more impact.

To make a holiday arrangement, use long-lasting flowers such as those on page 92 and add sprigs of greenery, such as Scotch pine, spruce, or juniper. For a more festive look, embellish the arrangement with canella berries, decorative pods, pepper berries, pinecones, feathers, or seeded eucalyptus.

A fresh holiday arrangement can be displayed in any container that holds water. For baskets, terra-cotta pots, or metal pots, use a plastic waterproof container as a liner.

Fresh flowers can be held in the arrangement by either of two methods, depending on the container selected. For glass containers, the flowers are held in place by making a grid over the mouth of the container with clear waterproof tape. For nonglass containers, the flowers are held in place by inserting them into floral foam designed for fresh flowers.

TIPS FOR FRESH FLOWERS

Cut off 1" (2.5 cm) from stems, at an angle, before arranging; for roses, cut stems at an angle while submerging them in water.

Remove any leaves that will be covered by water in the finished arrangement; leaves left in the water will shorten the life of the flowers.

Add cut-flower food to the water.

Add fresh water to the floral arrangement as necessary.

Keep flowers out of direct sunlight and drafts.

MATERIALS

- Flowers in three sizes.
- Sprigs of two or more varieties of greenery.
- Tall linear floral material, such as gilded devil's claw heliconia, curly willow, or branches, for the buffet arrangement.
- Gilded pods, berries, or twigs, for the centerpiece.
- Floral foam, designed for fresh flowers, for use with nonglass containers.
- Clear waterproof floral tape.
- Sharp knife.

Centerpiece (above) *combines chrysanthemums, roses, ornithogalum, leatherleaf, seeded eucalyptus, lotus pods, and cedar. Buffet arrangement* (opposite) *uses mums, lilies, leptosporum, roses, gilded devil's claw heliconia, leatherleaf, and seeded eucalyptus to create a dramatic display.*

Chrysanthemums

Ornithogalum

Lily

Carnations

Orchid

Yarrow

Heather

Roses

Alstroemeria

Stock

Leptosporum

Flowers shown above can be used to make long-lasting holiday arrangements.

HOW TO PREPARE THE CONTAINER

1 **Nonglass containers.** Soak the floral foam in water for at least 20 minutes.

2 Cut foam, using a knife, so it fits the container and extends about 1" (2.5 cm) above rim. Round off the upper edges of foam, if necessary, to prevent foam from showing in the finished arrangement. Secure with clear waterproof tape. Add water.

Glass containers. Make a grid over the mouth of container, using clear waterproof floral tape.

HOW TO MAKE A FRESH FLORAL BUFFET ARRANGEMENT

1 Prepare glass or nonglass container (above). Insert first variety of greenery into container, placing taller stems into center near back and shorter stems at sides and front.

2 Insert remaining varieties of greenery. Insert tall linear materials into container, spacing them evenly.

3 Insert largest flowers into the arrangement, one variety at a time, spacing them evenly throughout to keep arrangement balanced on three sides.

4 Insert second largest flowers into arrangement, spacing evenly. Insert the smaller flowers into the arrangement to fill any bare areas. Mist arrangement lightly with water.

HOW TO MAKE A FRESH FLORAL CENTERPIECE

1 Prepare the glass or nonglass container (opposite). Cut sprigs of greenery to lengths of 5" to 8" (12.5 to 20.5 cm); trim away any stems near the ends of sprigs.

2 Insert sprigs of greenery into the container, placing longer sprigs around the outside and shorter sprigs near the center.

3 Insert the largest flowers into the container, placing one stem in the center and several stems on each side to establish the height and width of the arrangement. Insert remaining large flowers, spacing evenly.

4 Insert the second largest flowers into the arrangement, one variety at a time, spacing evenly, so the arrangement appears balanced from all sides.

5 Insert additional sprigs of greenery as necessary to fill in any bare areas. Insert gilded pods, twigs, or berries, if desired, for further embellishment. Mist arrangement lightly with water.

Country arrangement *is created by filling small brown bags with popcorn, nuts, and dried fruits. The bags are tied with torn strips of fabric and placed in a rustic basket.*

Elegant decorating accent is created from a dried grapevine wreath, an artificial vine of grape leaves, dried artichokes, and gilded cones. Refer to pages 150 to 153 for information on embellishing wreaths.

Natural setting *is created with a pine garland used as the base of the arrangement. Pillar candles placed in glasses and smaller votive candles are embellished with cinnamon sticks and raffia. Spice ornaments and dried flowers are scattered throughout, for additional interest.*

95

HOLIDAY FLORAL ARRANGEMENTS

Use this unique floral arrangement to add color to your holiday table. Make the arrangement from the floral materials shown, or select floral materials to coordinate with your decorating scheme.

To help create the elegant natural look of the arrangement, the preserved leaves are highlighted with gold paint. Try this simple highlighting technique on other floral materials to achieve interesting effects. The gold highlights complement the gilded terra-cotta pots that are used for the base of the arrangement.

MATERIALS

- Two terra-cotta pots, about 5" (12.5 cm) in diameter.
- Gold aerosol paint, plus optional second color.
- Floral foam, for silk arranging.
- Artificial pine boughs.
- Latex grape clusters and apples; dried pomegranates.
- 3 yd. (2.75 m) stiff decorative cording.
- Artificial or preserved leaves on branches; twigs.
- Hot glue gun and glue sticks.

HOW TO MAKE A HOLIDAY FLORAL ARRANGEMENT

1 Place a sheet of plastic on a tabletop. Spray a generous pool of aerosol paint onto the plastic; drag the preserved leaves through the paint to gild them. Allow to dry. Repeat with additional paint colors, if desired.

2 Place one pot on its side, next to the other; secure pots together, using hot glue. When dry, apply gold aerosol paint to the containers.

(Continued)

97

3 Cut floral foam, using knife, so it fits container snugly and is even with edge of container; secure with hot glue. Repeat for remaining container.

4 Insert pine boughs and leaf branches into foam, so they rise from 5" to 8" (12.5 to 20.5 cm) above foam. Cut pine branches into small pieces to fill area around edges of containers. Insert a few twigs into vertical pot.

5 Insert apples and grape clusters, allowing some of the grapes to cascade slightly over sides of containers. Secure pomegranates into arrangement as desired with hot glue.

6 Apply tape to decorative braid at 8" to 12" (20.5 to 30.5 cm) intervals; cut braid through center of tape. Form loops from lengths of braid; wrap ends together with tape. Insert loops of decorative braid into arrangement, securing braid to foam with hot glue.

HOLIDAY COASTER SETS

As a gift for the hostess, make a set of holiday coasters and package them in a decorative box. Purchase a small cardboard box and lid in a holiday-motif shape, such as a star, heart, or tree. Make the padded coasters in the same shape as the box, using cotton quilting fabric and needlepunched cotton batting. Paint the box, and adorn the lid with an additional coaster, giving a clue to the contents of the box.

MATERIALS

- Cardboard box in holiday-motif shape, such as a star, heart, or tree, measuring about 2" (5 cm) high and 4" to 5" (10 to 12.5 cm) in diameter.
- ½ yd. (0.5 m) cotton quilting fabric in Christmas print.
- ½ yd. (0.5 m) needlepunched cotton batting.
- Pinking shears.
- Embellishments, such as tiny buttons or ribbons, optional.
- Acrylic paint and paintbrush.
- Craft glue.

1 Prewash fabric and batting, following the manufacturer's instructions. Fold fabric in half, wrong sides together, matching selvages. Trace the box bottom on right side of fabric eight times, for eight coasters; allow ½" (1.3 cm) between coasters. Trace the box lid once for larger coaster.

2 Insert batting between the layers of fabric. Secure fabric and batting layers together, using two or three pins in each traced coaster.

3 Cut coasters apart through all layers, leaving irregular margins around each coaster. Stitch layers together, using small stitches, and stitching ¼" (6 mm) inside traced lines.

4 Cut out coasters just inside traced lines, using pinking shears. Embellish the coasters with small buttons or other embellishments, if desired.

5 Paint all surfaces of cardboard box and lid, using acrylic paint and paintbrush. Allow to dry.

6 Insert the eight small coasters into box. Embellish large coaster for lid with bow or other embellishment, if desired. Secure large coaster to lid, using craft glue.

HOLIDAY PLACEMATS & TABLE RUNNERS

Create a variety of looks for the holiday table using simple stitched-and-turned placemats and table runners. Choose to make placemats and a matching rectangular table runner, or sew a table runner that has pointed ends. Embellish the placemats and table runner with coordinating braid, ribbon, or other flat trims.

The instructions that follow are for placemats with a finished size of 13" × 18" (33 × 46 cm). The length of the table runner is determined by the length of the table and the desired drop length, or overhang, at the ends of the table.

MATERIALS (for four placemats)

- 1⅝ yd. (1.5 m) fabric, for the placemat top and backing pieces.
- 1⅝ yd. (1.5 m) fusible interfacing.
- Braid or other flat trim.

MATERIALS (for table runner)

- Fabric, for table runner top and backing pieces; yardage varies, depending on length of runner.
- Fusible or sew-in interfacing; yardage varies, depending on length of runner.
- Braid or other flat trim.

CUTTING DIRECTIONS

For each placemat, cut two 13½" × 18½" (34.3 × 47.3 cm) rectangles from fabric, for the placemat top and backing. Cut one 13½" × 18½" (34.3 × 47.3 cm) rectangle from fusible interfacing.

For a table runner, cut two rectangles from fabric for the table runner top and backing, and cut one rectangle from fusible interfacing. The width of the rectangles is 18½" (47.3 cm); the length is equal to the length of the table plus two times the desired drop length, plus ½" (1.3 cm) for the seam allowances.

HOW TO SEW A BASIC PLACEMAT OR TABLE RUNNER

1 Apply interfacing to the wrong side of placemat or table runner top; if using fusible interfacing, follow manufacturer's directions.

2 Pin top to backing, right sides together. Stitch around placemat or table runner, ¼" (6 mm) from raw edges; leave 4" (10 cm) opening for turning. Trim corners.

3 Turn the placemat or table runner right side out; press. Slipstitch the opening closed. If desired, embellish with braid trim (page 104).

HOW TO SEW A TABLE RUNNER WITH POINTED ENDS

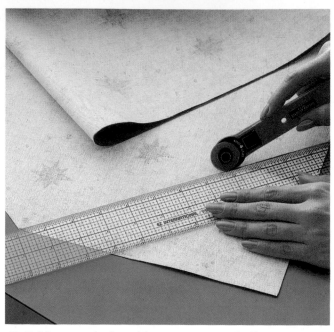

1 Mark the center of one short end on rectangle for table runner top. From same short end, measure distance on each long edge equal to the desired drop length plus ¼" (6 mm) for seam allowance; mark. Draw lines from marking on short end to markings on long edges.

2 Fold rectangle for table runner top in half crosswise; align the raw edges. Cut on marked lines through both layers. Cut backing and interfacing to match table runner top. Complete table runner as on page 103, steps 1 to 3.

HOW TO EMBELLISH A PLACEMAT OR TABLE RUNNER WITH BRAID TRIM

1 Pin braid trim to the placemat or table runner at desired distance from edge; miter the braid trim at corners by folding it at an angle. Fold end of braid diagonally at final corner; trim excess.

2 Edgestitch along inner and outer edges of braid trim; hand-stitch mitered corners in place.

MORE IDEAS FOR PLACEMATS & TABLE RUNNERS

Braid trim (left) is used to make a mitered border around a placemat.

Purchased appliqués add a festive touch to a plain placemat. The appliqués are fused to the placemat tops before the backing is applied.

Assorted trims (above) are stitched to the placemat top before the backing is applied.

Layered trims are positioned 1" (2.5 cm) from the outer edges of a pointed table runner (right). A tassel is stitched to each point.

PACKAGE
PLACEMATS

Dress up a holiday table with pieced placemats that have the three-dimensional look of wrapped packages. The dimensional illusion is achieved by using fabrics in light, medium, and dark colors. A simple bow, created from a pleated fabric square and a fabric loop, completes the package.

The placemat is made from either lightweight cotton or cotton blends, using quick cutting and piecing techniques for easy construction. The instructions that follow are for a set of four placemats that measure about 13" × 17" (33 × 43 cm). Stitch the placemats using 1/4" (6 mm) seam allowances.

MATERIALS (for four placemats)

- 1/4 yd. (0.25 m) light-colored fabric, for package top.
- 1/2 yd. (0.5 m) medium-colored fabric, for package front.
- 1/4 yd. (0.25 m) dark-colored fabric, for package side.
- 5/8 yd. (0.6 m) fabric, for ribbon and bow.
- 7/8 yd. (0.8 m) fabric, for backing.
- Low-loft quilt batting.
- Quilter's ruler with an edge at 45° angle.

CUTTING DIRECTIONS

Cut the following strips on the crosswise grain, cutting across the full width of the fabric: two 6½" (16.3 cm) strips from the fabric for the package front; two 2" (5 cm) strips from the fabric for the package side; and four 2" (5 cm) strips from the fabric for the package top. From the fabric for the ribbon and bow, cut: four 1½" (3.8 cm) strips and one 1¼" (3.2 cm) strip, for the ribbon; eight 6½" (16.3 cm) squares, for the bows; and one 2½" × 15" (6.5 × 38 cm) strip, for the loop of the bow. Cut four 13½" × 17½" (34.3 × 44.3 cm) rectangles each from the backing fabric and batting.

HOW TO SEW A SET OF PACKAGE PLACEMATS

1 Stitch package front strips to each side of one 1½" (3.8 cm) ribbon strip, to make pieced strip for package fronts. Press the seam allowances toward ribbon strip. From pieced strip, cut four 9½" × 13½" (24.3 × 34.3 cm) rectangles.

2 Stitch package side strips to each side of one 1½" (3.8 cm) ribbon strip, to make pieced strip for package sides. Press the seam allowances toward ribbon strip. Cut off one end of pieced strip at 45° angle, as shown.

(Continued)

107

3 Measure and mark strip at 9¾" (25 cm) intervals. Cut four parallelograms for package sides, as shown.

4 Stitch package top strips to each side of one 1½" (3.8 cm) ribbon strip, to make the pieced strip for the package tops. Repeat to make two pieced strips. Press seam allowances toward ribbon strips. Cut off one end of each pieced strip at a 45° angle, as shown; the angle is cut in the opposite direction from the angle of package side strips.

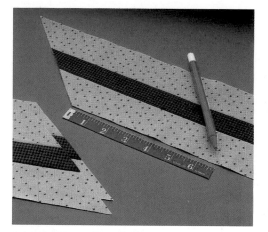

5 Measure and mark the package top strips at 6¾" (17 cm) intervals. Cut into eight parallelograms for package tops.

6 Stitch the 1¼" (3.2 cm) ribbon strip to one angled end of one of the parallelograms for package top; allow excess fabric from ribbon strip at each end. Press seam allowances toward ribbon strip; trim strip even with edges of the parallelogram. Stitch second parallelogram for package top to the opposite side of ribbon strip; press the seam allowances toward the ribbon strip. Repeat to make four package tops.

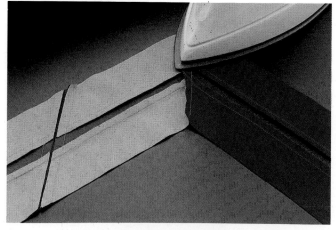

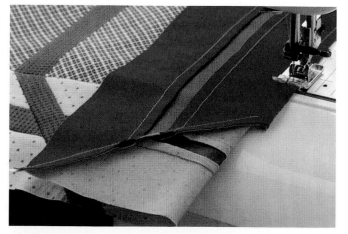

7 Align one package top to one package side along the angled edges, with right sides together and raw edges even. Stitch from sharply pointed end to ¼" (6 mm) from inside corner; backstitch to secure stitching. Press the seam allowances toward package top.

8 Align pieced strips for side and top to package front, matching ribbon strips of top and front. Stitch from outer edges exactly to the seam intersection. Press seam allowances toward top and side.

9 Place the backing and placemat top right sides together. Place fabrics on batting, with pieced design on top; pin or baste layers together.

10 Stitch around the placemat top, ¼" (6 mm) from raw edges; leave 4" (10 cm) opening for turning. Trim the excess backing and batting; trim corners.

11 Turn the placemat right side out; press. Slipstitch opening closed. Quilt placemat by stitching on seamlines, using monofilament nylon thread in needle and thread that matches backing fabric in the bobbin. (Contrasting thread was used to show detail.)

12 Fold strip for loop of bow in half lengthwise, right sides together. Stitch ¼" (6 mm) seam; turn tube right side out. Press, with the seam centered on one side. Cut tube into four 3" (7.5 cm) strips.

13 Press raw edges ¼" (6 mm) to inside at one end of each tube; tuck opposite end inside the tube to make a loop. Stitch ends together. Pin loop, as shown, over intersecting ribbons on package top. Slipstitch in place.

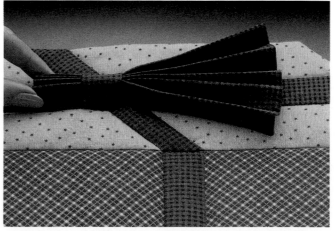

14 Place two fabric pieces for bow right sides together, matching raw edges. Stitch ¼" (6 mm) from raw edges, leaving 2" (5 cm) opening for turning. Trim the corners; press the seams open.

15 Turn bow piece right side out; press. Slipstitch the opening closed. Hand-pleat fabric, and insert into loop for bow.

HOLIDAY PLACEMATS & NAPKINS

For a festive place setting at the table, make a set of quilted placemats that portray a winter landscape. A round napkin, folded to represent an evergreen tree, completes the setting.

The placements and napkins are made from 100 percent cotton fabric, using techniques for quick construction. Narrow piping or cording trims the edges of the lined napkin, making the napkins easy to turn and press. Simple stitch-and-turn construction eliminates binding on the placemats. The trees on the placemat are secured with machine-blindstitched appliqué.

The finished placemats measure about 12" × 18" (30.5 × 46 cm).

MATERIALS (for six placemats and napkins)

- ⅔ yd. (0.63 m) fabric, for sky section.
- ¾ yd. (0.7 m) fabric, for lower ground section of placement.
- ½ yd. (0.5 m) fabric, for upper ground section.
- 1⅛ yd. (1.05 m) fabric, for backing.
- 1½ yd. (1.4 m) each of two coordinating fabrics, for napkins and appliquéd trees on placemat.
- 9½ yd. (8.7 m) cording or piping, for trim on napkin.
- Cardboard, spray starch, and monofilament nylon thread, for blindstitched appliqués.
- Low-loft quilt batting.

CUTTING DIRECTIONS

Cut the fabric for the napkins as on page 112, step l.

Make the pattern for the placemat and cut the fabric for the sky and ground pieces as on pages 113 and 114, steps 1 to 4. For each placemat, cut one 12½" × 18½" (31.8 × 47.3 cm) rectangle from backing fabric, and one 14" × 20" (35.5 × 51 cm) rectangle from batting.

Transfer tree templates for appliqués (pages 312 and 313) onto cardboard; cut. Using templates, cut one of each tree for each placemat, adding ¼" (6 mm) seam allowances when cutting.

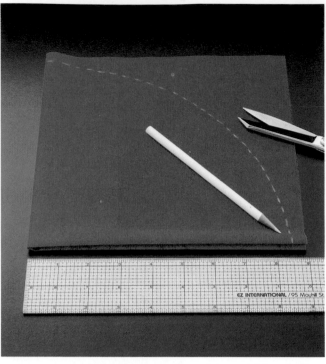

1 Cut one 18" (46 cm) square from fabric; fold in half lengthwise, then crosswise. Using a straightedge and pencil, mark an arc on the fabric, measuring 8½" (21.8 cm) from the folded center of fabric. Cut on the marked line through all layers. Using circle as pattern, cut six circles from each of the two napkin fabrics.

2 Pin trim to right side of one napkin piece, with raw edges even; curve ends of trim into seam allowance as shown, so ends overlap and trim tapers to raw edge. Machine-baste trim in place, using a zipper foot.

3 Place the napkin and lining right sides together, matching raw edges; pin. Stitch around the napkin, stitching just inside the previous stitches, crowding stitches against the trim; leave a 2" (5 cm) opening. Trim the seam allowance, using pinking shears.

4 Turn the napkin right side out; press. Edgestitch around napkin, using zipper foot and stitching opening closed.

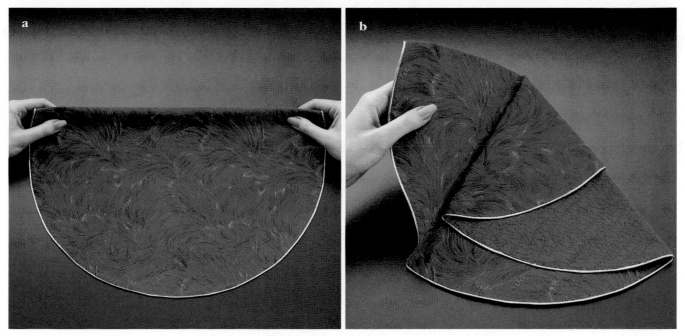

5 Fold under upper one-third of napkin **(a).** Fold right side over, then left side over, folding napkin into thirds **(b).**

HOW TO MAKE A LANDSCAPE PLACEMAT

1 Cut piece of paper 12" × 18" (30.5 × 46 cm). On left side of paper, make a mark 2½" and 9" (6.5 and 23 cm) from lower edge as shown. On right side of paper, mark 7½" (19.3 cm) from lower edge as shown.

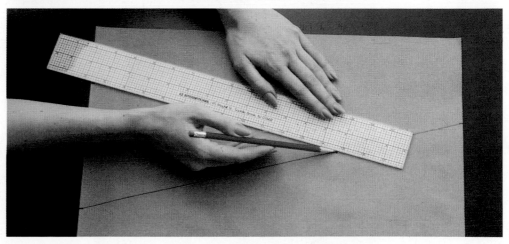

2 Draw a diagonal line connecting lower left mark to right mark as shown. Mark point on diagonal line 12" (30.5 cm) from left edge of the paper; draw a line connecting this point to the remaining mark on the left side.

(Continued)

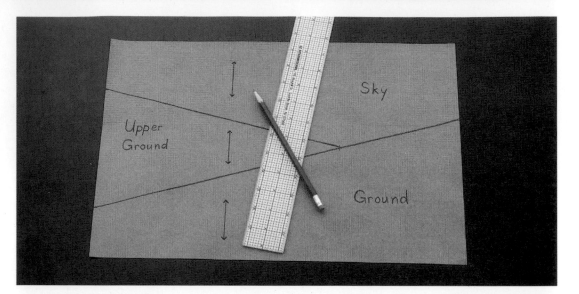

3 Label pattern sections for ground and sky, as shown; mark the grainline on each section.

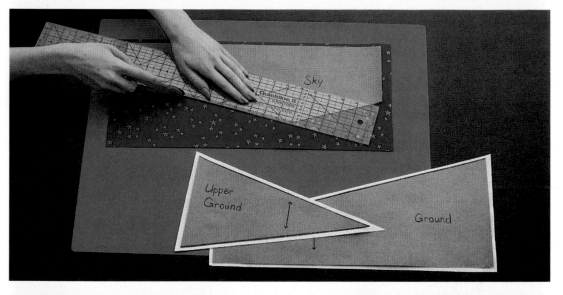

4 Cut pattern on marked lines. For each placemat, cut one of each piece from fabric, adding ¼" (6 mm) seam allowances to each side of pattern.

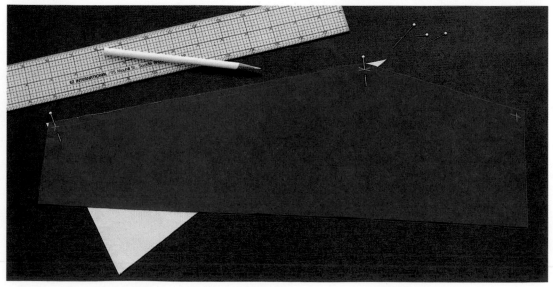

5 Mark each section on the wrong side of the fabric where ¼" (6 mm) seams will intersect. Align the upper ground piece and the sky piece, right sides together, matching markings for seam intersections. Stitch ¼" (6 mm) seam. Finger-press seam allowances toward upper edge of the placemat.

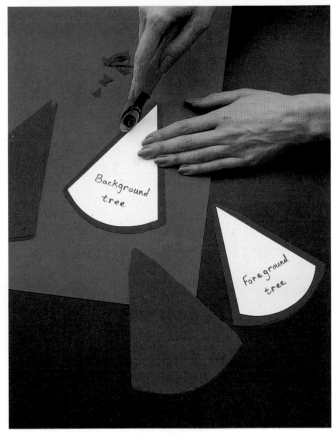

6 Align pieced unit and remaining ground piece, right sides together, matching markings for the seam intersections. Stitch ¼" (6 mm) seam. Press seam allowances toward upper edge of placemat.

7 Cut tree appliqués from fabric (page 111). Center tree templates on wrong side of fabric pieces. Trim points.

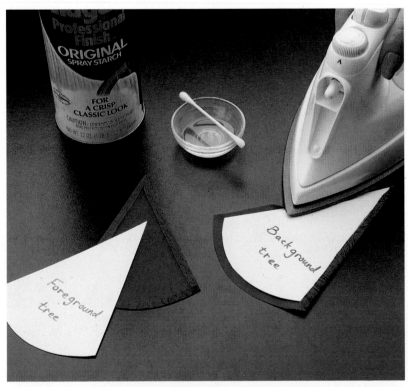

8 Spray starch into small bowl; dab starch on a section of the seam allowance. Using tip of dry iron, press seam allowance over edge of template. Continue around appliqués. Remove templates; press pieces, right side up.

9 Arrange trees on right side of pieced placemat top. Glue-baste background tree in place. Mark placement of foreground tree, using chalk; set aside.

(Continued)

115

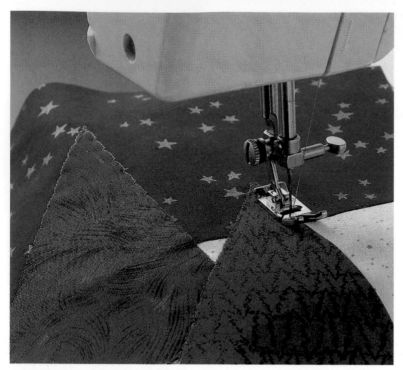

10 Blindstitch around the outer edge of background tree, using monofilament nylon thread in the needle; stitch as close to the edge as possible, just catching the appliqué with the widest swing of blindstitch. Glue-baste the foreground tree in place; blindstitch. (Contrasting thread was used to show detail.)

11 Place backing and placemat top right sides together. Place fabrics on batting, with backing piece on top; pin or baste the layers together.

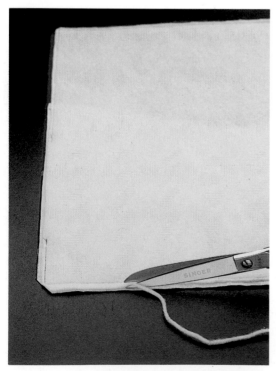

12 Stitch around placemat top, ¼" (6 mm) from the raw edges; leave 4" (10 cm) opening for turning. Trim batting to ⅛" (3 mm); trim corners.

13 Turn placemat right side out; press. Slipstitch opening closed. Quilt placemat by stitching around appliqués and on seamlines, using matching thread. Topstitch ¼" (6 mm) around outside edges. (Contrasting thread was used to show detail.)

MORE IDEAS FOR THE TABLE

Motifs *cut from printed fabric are fused to a solid background to make an interesting table covering. Simply fuse motifs to background fabric, using fusible web; then conceal cut edges of fabric, using acrylic craft paints in fine-tip tubes.*

Ribbon, *wrapped package-style around a table, creates a holiday atmosphere. Secure the ribbon in place on the underside of the table, using masking tape.*

PIECED STAR
TABLE TOPPERS

This eight-pointed reversible star adds a decorative touch to tables. Use it as a table topper over a skirted round table. Or drape it over a dining table, sofa table, or end table.

The star is made by stitching eight diamonds together. The outer half of each diamond is cut longer than the inner half, creating extended points that can be draped over the edges of a table. The finished star measures about 50" (127 cm) in diameter. Tassels can be added to the points of the stars for additional embellishment.

The star and the lining can be sewn from a single fabric. Or use two or more fabrics for variety. If more than one fabric is used, become familiar with the piecing technique in order to plan the placement of the pieces before you

begin to stitch. The lining is constructed using the same method as for the star, making the table topper reversible.

MATERIALS

- 3 yd. (2.75 m) fabric, for star and lining from one fabric, or ¾ yd. (0.7 m) each of four fabrics, for star and lining from four fabrics.
- Eight tassels, optional.

CUTTING DIRECTIONS

Make the pattern as on page 120. Cut eight diamonds from the fabric or fabrics for the star. Also cut eight diamonds from the fabric for the lining.

Pieced star table toppers can be made in a variety of styles. Above, the star topper with a country look is made from four different cotton fabrics. Opposite, an elegant star topper is made from a single fabric and embellished with tassels at each of the points.

HOW TO MAKE A PIECED STAR TABLE TOPPER PATTERN

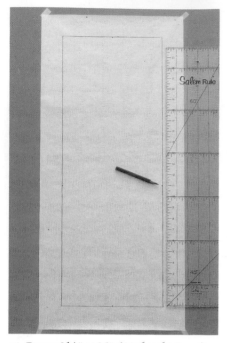 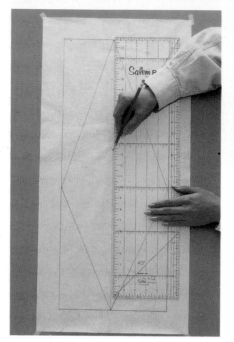 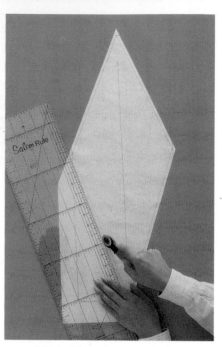

1 Draw 9¼" × 25" (23.6 × 63.5 cm) rectangle on paper. Mark a dot at the center of each short side. Mark a dot along each long side, 11" (28 cm) from one end.

2 Draw lines connecting the dots as shown. Mark grainline parallel to long sides of rectangle.

3 Add ¼" (6 mm) seam allowances to the diamond pattern, outside the marked lines. Cut out pattern.

HOW TO SEW A PIECED STAR TABLE TOPPER

1 Align two of the diamonds, right sides together and raw edges even. Stitch ¼" (6 mm) seam on one short side, stitching toward narrow point. Repeat for remaining pieces to make four 2-diamond units.

2 Stitch two of the 2-diamond units, right sides together, along one short side; finger-press seam allowances in opposite directions as shown. Repeat for the remaining two units.

3 Place the two 4-diamond units right sides together. Pin, matching inner points of diamonds at center. Fold seam allowances of each unit in opposite directions; stitch seam from outer edges toward center.

4 Release the stitching within the seam allowances at center of star, so seam allowances will lie flat. Press from wrong side, working from center out.

5 Repeat steps 1 to 4 for lining. Pin the star and the lining, right sides together, matching the raw edges and seams; the seam allowances will face in opposite directions. Stitch around star, stitching from inside corners to points; leave 6" (15 cm) opening on one side, for turning.

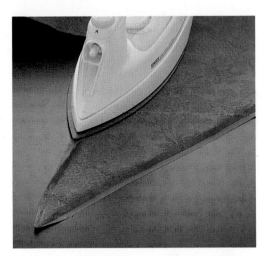

6 Clip inside corners, and trim points. Press the seam allowances open around the outer edges.

7 Turn star right side out; press. Slipstitch opening closed. Stitch a tassel to each point, if desired.

Around The
House

WOODEN BASKETS

Handcrafted wooden baskets are ideal for gift giving and can be used as decorative accents throughout the holiday season. Make the baskets using either a snowman or a Christmas tree design. An aged look, achieved by sanding the edges and applying stain, gives the baskets a rustic charm. They are inexpensive to make and require only basic woodworking skills and tools.

When cutting with a jigsaw, it is helpful to clamp the wood in place, protecting it with wood scraps or felt pads, if necessary. This also allows you to hold the saw firmly with both hands, to reduce vibration, and move the saw smoothly while cutting. Cut inside corners by sawing into the corner from both directions; cut curves slowly to avoid bending the blade.

MATERIALS

- 12 ft. (3.7 m) of ¼" × ¾" (6 mm × 2 cm) pine screen molding.
- 1 × 8 pine board.
- Wooden dowel, ½" (1.3 cm) diameter, 11¼" (28.7 cm) long.
- Jigsaw.
- Drill; ¹⁄₁₆" and ½" drill bits.
- Sanding block; medium-grit and fine-grit sandpaper.
- Acrylic paints; artist's brushes.
- Stain in medium color, such as medium walnut.
- 17 × ¾" (2 cm) brads.
- Wood glue; tracing paper; graphite paper.
- Scrap of wool fabric, for snowman scarf, optional.

HOW TO MAKE A WOODEN BASKET

1 Fold sheet of tracing paper in half lengthwise. Trace the partial pattern (page 313) for tree or snowman onto tracing paper, placing fold of tracing paper on dotted line of pattern. Cut out pattern. Open the full-size pattern. Transfer the pattern to 1 × 8 pine board twice, using graphite paper; align the arrow on pattern with grain of wood. Transfer mark for handle.

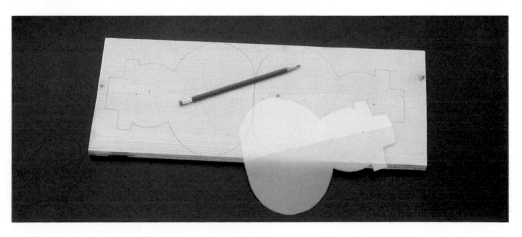

(Continued)

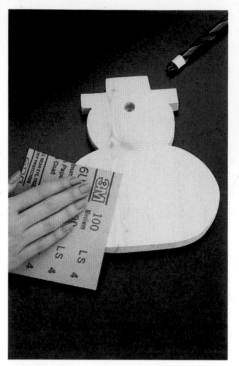

2 Cut along marked lines, using jigsaw.

3 Drill hole at mark for handle to ⅜" (1 cm) depth, using ½" drill bit; use masking tape on drill bit as guide for the depth. Sand basket ends smooth, using medium-grit sandpaper.

4 Mark and cut twelve slats from screen molding, in 12" (30.5 cm) lengths. Sand ends. Predrill nail holes ⅜" (1 cm) from each end of each slat, using ¹⁄₁₆" drill bit.

5 Paint outer surface of basket ends as desired, using acrylic paints and foam applicator. Allow to dry.

6 Sand edges of the basket ends lightly, using fine-grit sandpaper, to remove some paint and give an aged appearance.

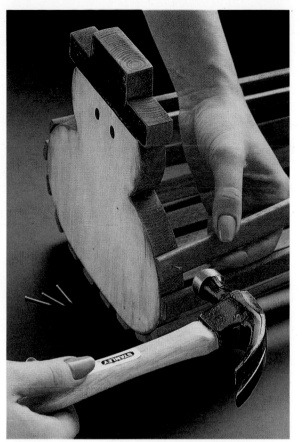

7 Apply stain to all pieces, using soft cloth; allow to dry.

8 Mark placement for slats on the basket ends, using pattern as guide. Secure slats to one basket end, using $17 \times \frac{3}{4}$" (2 cm) brads; align the end of slat to outer edge of basket end, with the rounded edges of the slat facing outward.

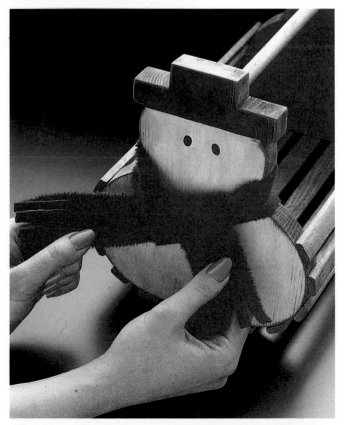

9 Apply small amount of wood glue in the holes for handle. Insert dowel ends into holes.

10 Secure slats to remaining basket end. For snowman basket, cut two $1\frac{1}{2}$" × 22" (3.8 × 56 cm) fabric strips; clip ends to make fringe, and tie around necks, for scarves.

FRINGED
FABRIC TREE

Make a grouping of fabric trees in various sizes to display on a mantel. The trees are made from fringed strips of cotton fabric that are wrapped around a Styrofoam® cone. The fringe is given a frayed appearance by wetting it, then machine drying it with towels. Decorate the trees with purchased decorations or miniature dough cutout ornaments (page 307).

MATERIALS

- Styrofoam cone with height of 6" (15 cm), 9" (23 cm), or 12" (30.5 cm), depending on desired tree size.
- ½ yd. (0.5 m) fabric for small tree or ¾ yd. (0.7 m) for medium or large tree.
- Thick craft glue.
- 4" (10 cm) lengths of wire, for securing embellishments.
- Embellishments, such as miniature decorations and raffia, if desired.

HOW TO MAKE A FRINGED FABRIC TREE

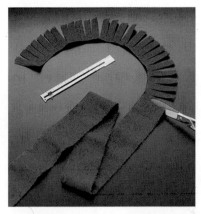

1 Tear fabric strips, 4¼" (10.8 cm) wide, on crosswise grain; reserve sufficient fabric for covering cone. Fold fabric strip in half lengthwise, wrong sides together; edgestitch close to fold. Repeat for remaining strips.

2 Make the fringe by clipping the strips at ½" (1.3 cm) intervals, along the edges opposite the fold; clip to, but not through, stitching. Wet clipped strips, and squeeze out any excess water; machine dry with towels to create frayed edges.

3 Trim Styrofoam cone to a point. Roll trimmed end gently on table to make smooth.

4 Wrap fabric around the Styrofoam cone; trim off excess. Secure fabric to cone, using craft glue.

5 Apply glue to upper edge of the fringe, gluing about 4" (10 cm) at a time. Wrap fringe around the cone, starting 1" (2.5 cm) from lower edge of tree; continue to glue and wrap fringe to end of strip.

6 Continue to glue and wrap additional fringed fabric strips around cone until entire cone is covered; overlap ends of strips slightly. Trim off excess at top.

7 Embellish tree as desired, securing ornaments to tree with bent lengths of wire.

SANTA'S ELVES

Pose an elf or two on a table or mantel to add a whimsical touch to your holiday decorating. The body of the elf is stuffed with polyester fiberfill and is weighted down with a small bag of sand. Small quantities of sand are available, packaged as paint additives, at many paint stores.

MATERIALS

- Fabric scraps.
- 3" (7.5 cm) square of paper-backed fusible web.
- Assorted two-hole or four-hole buttons.
- Two small shank buttons, for eyes.
- Polyester fiberfill.
- Sand; plastic bag, such as a sandwich bag.
- Jute and ¼" (6 mm) dowel, for hair.
- Hot glue gun and glue sticks.
- Heavy-duty thread, such as carpet thread.
- Pink cosmetic blush.
- Embellishments as desired.

CUTTING DIRECTIONS

Make the full-size patterns for the upper body, lower body, and hat as in steps 1 to 3, opposite. Cut two lower body pieces and two upper body pieces from scraps of fabric for the body. Using the pattern for the upper body, also cut two hat pieces from scraps of fabric for the hat.

Trace the pattern pieces for the boot and ear (page 310) onto paper. Cut four boots and four ears from scraps of fabric.

For the pants legs, cut two 5½" × 6" (14 × 15 cm) rectangles from scraps of fabric that match the lower body. For the sleeves, cut two 4½" × 5½" (11.5 × 14 cm) rectangles from scraps of fabric that match the upper body.

1 Draw a 9½" (24.3 cm) vertical line on center of tracing paper. Draw a perpendicular line at lower end, 3¼" (8.2 cm) long. Mark a point 3½" (9 cm) above lower edge and 2½" (6.5 cm) from vertical line. Mark a second point 6½" (16.3 cm) above lower edge and 1¾" (4.5 cm) from vertical line.

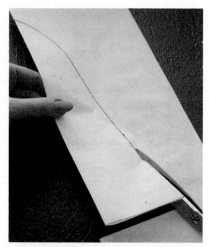

2 Connect points to perpendicular lines, curving the line slightly. Fold on vertical line; cut on the marked lines. Unfold paper.

3 Draw line 3½" (9 cm) above lower edge, perpendicular to vertical line. Cut off lower portion on marked line; this section is pattern for lower body of elf. Remaining section is pattern for upper body and also for hat. Transfer the patterns to paper, adding ¼" (6 mm) seam allowances.

4 Cut body pieces from fabric (opposite). Apply paper-backed fusible web to scrap of fabric for face, following manufacturer's directions. Cut an oval for face, about 2" (5 cm) long and 2¼" (6 cm) wide, from paper-backed fabric.

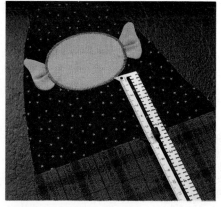

5 Align upper and lower front body sections, right sides together; stitch ¼" (6 mm) seam. Repeat for the back body sections, leaving a 3" (7.5 cm) opening in center of seam.

6 Stitch ⅛" (3 mm) seam around the ears, using short stitch length; leave straight edges open. Turn ears right side out, and press. Using cotton swab, rub pink blush in center of ears.

7 Remove paper backing from face. Make ⅛" (3 mm) tuck along the straight edge of each ear; baste to wrong side of face. Center face on upper body, with the face about 2¼" (6 cm) above the body seam. Fuse in place. Stitch around the face, using a narrow zigzag stitch.

(Continued)

8 Fold rectangle for sleeve in half, right sides together, matching short edges; stitch ¼" (6 mm) seam. Press seam open; turn tube right side out. Center the seam down front of tube. Make four ⅛" (3 mm) tucks, spaced evenly along upper edge of tube, so width is about 1½" (3.8 cm).

9 Pin tucked end of sleeve, seam side down, to right side of front upper body; match raw edges, and position sleeve about 1" (2.5 cm) above body seam. Baste. Repeat for other sleeve.

10 Fold rectangle for pants leg, right sides together, matching short edges; stitch ¼" (6 mm) seam. Press seam open; turn tube right side out. Center seam down back of tube. Repeat for other pants leg. Pin upper edge of pants legs to lower edge of front body section, centering them and matching raw edges; baste.

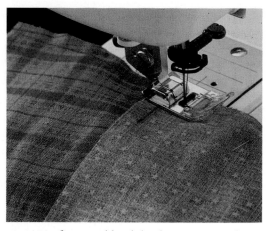

11 Pin front and back body sections right sides together. Stitch ¼" (6 mm) seam around body, taking care not to catch sleeves, pants legs, and ears in stitching.

12 Push in lower corners of elf, from right side, to shape the box corners. Slipstitch, or turn inside out and machine-stitch, across corners; turn right side out.

13 Roll up sleeves and pants legs. Thread needle with heavy-duty thread; secure thread to body, centered inside one pants leg. Thread a 2¾" (7 cm) strand of buttons, then thread back through the opposite holes of buttons; adjust the strand so top button of strand dangles about 3" (7.5 cm) below body. Secure thread. Repeat for other leg.

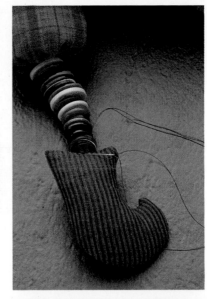

14 Stuff pants legs lightly with polyester fiberfill. On each pants leg, fold lower ¼" (6 mm) to the inside. Using hand running stitches, stitch close to the fold and tightly gather pants legs above buttons; secure thread.

15 Stitch ⅛" (3 mm) seam around the boot, using short stitch length; leave upper edge open. Clip inner curve. Turn right side out; stuff with polyester fiberfill. On each boot, fold upper ¼" (6 mm) to inside; slipstitch closed. Stitch the center of each boot to lower button of each button strand for legs.

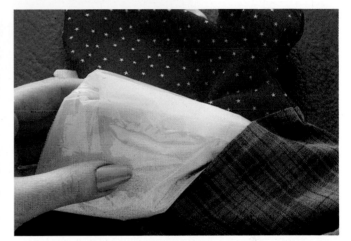

16 Secure heavy-duty thread to body, centered inside one sleeve. Thread a 3" (7.5 cm) strand of buttons; secure thread inside other sleeve, allowing button strand to dangle from body about 2" (5 cm) at each side. Stuff sleeves and gather above buttons as in step 14.

17 Place about ⅔ cup (150 mL) sand in plastic bag. Tape bag closed, allowing space inside for sand to shift easily; this makes it easier for elf to sit. Insert the bag into the lower portion of body. Stuff remainder of body with polyester fiberfill; slipstitch opening closed.

18 Sew on buttons for the eyes; insert needle from back of body, and pull thread taut for a slight indentation. Rub pink blush on the face, for cheeks. Make jute hair, if desired, as on page 12, step 15; remove jute from dowel. Cut lengths of jute, and glue around face for the hair and beard.

19 Pin the hat pieces right sides together; stitch ¼" (6 mm) seam around curved sides. Turn right side out. Sew on buttons as desired at top of hat. Fold lower ¼" (6 mm) of hat to inside. Using hand running stitches, stitch close to fold; gather hat to fit head. Glue the hat to the elf. Secure any additional embellishments.

Pose a pair of carolers, complete with a lamppost, on a table or mantel to spread holiday cheer. Crafted using wooden dowels and ball knobs, each piece is easy to assemble. The garments are assembled using simple rectangular fabric pieces, requiring no patterns and minimal sewing.

The carolers can be made in a variety of styles, depending on the fabrics chosen. For a country look, select fabrics such as corduroy or flannel. For a more elegant look, use fabrics such as velvet or taffeta. Floral wire in each arm allows the figures to be posed, holding a variety of embellishments.

MATERIALS (for pair of carolers and lamppost)

- Three wooden plaques, for base of each piece.
- Two 2" (5 cm) wooden balls, for heads.
- Four 1" (2.5 cm) wooden ball knobs, for feet.
- One 2¼" (6 cm) wooden ball knob, for lamppost.
- Four 18 mm wooden beads, for hands.
- Four 8" (20.5 cm) lengths of ⅝" (1.5 cm) dowel, for legs.
- One 11" (28 cm) length of ¾" (2 cm) dowel, for lamppost.
- Drill; ⅟₁₆" and ⅛" drill bits.
- Six 6 × 1⅝" (4 cm) drywall screws.
- One ³⁄₁₆ × 2" (5 cm) dowel screw; four 19 × ½" (1.3 cm) wire nails.
- 22-gauge paddle floral wire.
- Fabric scraps, for pants, shirt, and dress.

- Buttons, for shirt.
- Scrap of Ultrasuede® or felt, for cap.
- Scrap of ribbing, for leggings.
- ½ yd. (0.5 m) trim, such as gimp trim or ribbon, for pants.
- ⅝ yd. (0.6 m) eyelet or lace, at least 6" (15 cm) wide, for slip.
- ⅜ yd. (0.35 m) eyelet or lace, about 1" (2.5 cm) wide, for neck trim of dress.
- ¼" (6 mm) pom-pom, for cap.
- Doll hair; polyester fiberfill.
- Craft glue; adhesive felt.
- Acrylic gloss enamel paints; artist's brushes.
- Embellishments, such as miniature evergreen garland, ribbon, and small cones, for lamppost.

CUTTING DIRECTIONS

For the boy caroler, cut two 5½" (14 cm) squares from the fabric for the pants. For the shirt, cut one 4" × 12" (10 × 30.5 cm) rectangle for the body of the shirt and two 5" × 6" (12.5 × 15 cm) rectangles for the sleeves. For the scarf, cut one 1" × 14" (2.5 × 35.5 cm) rectangle. For the cap, cut one 1½" (3.8 cm) circle and one 4" (10 cm) circle from felt or Ultrasuede; cut the smaller circle in half for the brim.

For the girl caroler, cut one 6" × 20" (15 × 51 cm) rectangle for the slip. For the dress, cut one 12" × 20" (30.5 × 51 cm) rectangle. Cut two 5" × 6" (12.5 × 15 cm) rectangles for the sleeves of the dress. For the leggings, cut two 3" × 4" (7.5 × 10 cm) rectangles from ribbing, placing the rib of the fabric on the longest edge.

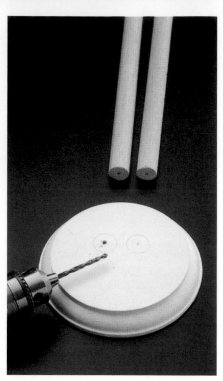

1 Paint 1" (2.5 cm) ball knobs for feet as desired. Paint 2" (5 cm) ball knob for head and 18 mm beads for hands flesh color. Paint or stain base plaque as desired.

2 Position dowels and ball knobs for feet on the plaque for desired placement, with dowels 1/4" (6 mm) apart. Mark the position for dowels, using a pencil as shown.

3 Mark placement for screw in the center of each marking for dowel; mark center of each dowel at one end. Predrill holes at marks, using 1/8" drill bit.

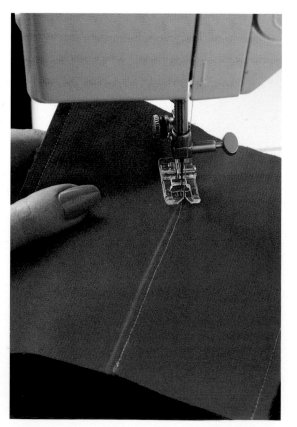

4 Secure dowels to base plaque, inserting screws from bottom of plaque.

5 Mark a 4" (10 cm) line, centered as shown, on wrong side of one pants piece, for pants inseam. Place pants pieces right sides together. Stitch 1/4" (6 mm) side seams. Stitch inseam, stitching 1/8" (3 mm) from marked line and tapering stitches to line at top. With the needle down, rotate fabric and repeat stitching on remaining side of marked line.

6 Cut inseam on marked line; press seam allowances on sides open. Turn pants right side out. Using hand running stitches and double-threaded needle, stitch close to upper edge of pants, leaving thread tails. Repeat at lower edge of each pants leg.

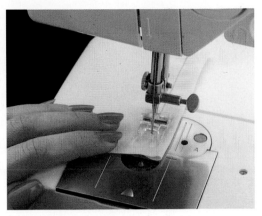

7 Fold rectangle for body of shirt, wrong sides together, matching the short edges; stitch ½" (1.3 cm) from the folded edge to make center tuck.

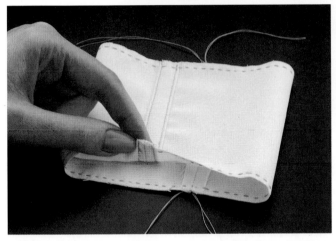

8 Press tuck, centering over seam; edgestitch on both sides through all layers. Fold the rectangle right sides together, matching short edges; stitch ¼" (6 mm) seam. Press seam allowances open, and turn tube right side out. Using hand running stitches and double-threaded needle, stitch close to upper edge of shirt, leaving thread tails. Repeat at lower edge.

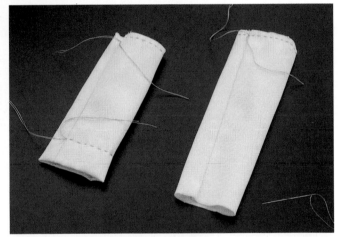

9 Fold rectangle for sleeve, right sides together, matching long edges; stitch ¼" (6 mm) seam. Press seam allowances open; turn tube right side out. Stitch row of hand running stitches close to upper edge. Fold under 1" (2.5 cm) at lower edge; stitch row of running stitches ¾" (2 cm) from folded edge. Repeat for other sleeve.

10 Slip pants over the dowels, inserting one dowel in each leg of pants. Gather lower edge of each leg, and knot thread. Slip shirt over dowels; gather and knot lower edge of shirt, centering tuck and back seam. Glue lower edge of shirt to dowels; allow upper edge of shirt to extend slightly above top of the dowels.

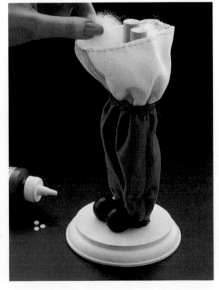

11 Gather and knot upper edge of the pants; secure with glue. Secure gimp at waist and ankles. Glue feet to base. Lightly stuff body of the shirt with polyester fiberfill as necessary. Gather and knot the upper edge of the shirt; glue to dowels. Glue buttons to shirt.

(Continued)

12 Cut wire about 16" (40.5 cm) in length. Secure the wire to the ends of dowels by wrapping wire around a wire nail inserted into each dowel; to prevent splitting the wood, predrill, using 1/16" drill bit.

13 Thread bead onto wire; wrap end of wire as shown so length of arm is about 3½" (9 cm). Repeat for opposite side.

14 Slip sleeve over wire arm. Gather and knot the upper edge of sleeve, centering seam down inside of arm; glue sleeve to upper edge of shirt. Lightly stuff the sleeve with polyester fiberfill. Tightly gather lower edge of sleeve; secure with knot. Repeat for second sleeve.

15 Glue head to top of dowels. Cut and glue individual lengths of doll hair to head for hair, working in sections; for the bangs, glue short pieces across front of head.

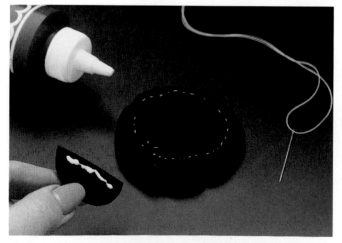

16 Stitch row of hand running stitches close to edge of 4" (10 cm) circle for beret. Gather circle to measure about 2¾" (7 cm) in diameter; knot the thread. Glue brim in place.

17 Stuff the cap lightly with polyester fiberfill. Glue the pom-pom to center of cap. Glue cap to caroler. Cut fringe on ends of scarf; tie scarf around neck.

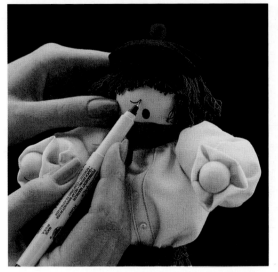

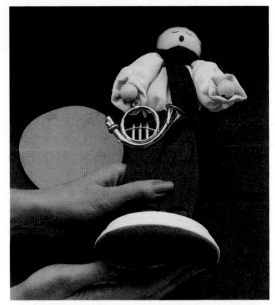

18 Draw eyes and mouth as shown, using fine-point permanent-ink marker.

19 Place caroler on paper side of adhesive felt; trace around the base. Cut felt just inside the marked lines. Remove the paper backing, and secure felt to the bottom of the base. Secure any embellishments as desired.

HOW TO MAKE A GIRL CAROLER

1 Follow page 136, steps 1 to 4. Fold rectangle for leggings right sides together, matching long edges; stitch ¼" (6 mm) seam. Turn tube right side out. Repeat for other legging. Slip one legging over each dowel leg, with seam centered down back of leg. Secure at lower edge with craft glue. Glue feet to base.

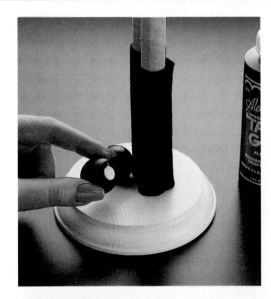

2 Fold the lace for slip right sides together, matching short ends; stitch ¼" (6 mm) seam. Press seam open. Repeat for dress.

3 Fold the dress lengthwise, with wrong sides together and raw edges even; lightly press folded edge. Pin-mark lower edge of the dress 2⅜" (6.2 cm) to each side of dress center front and center back.

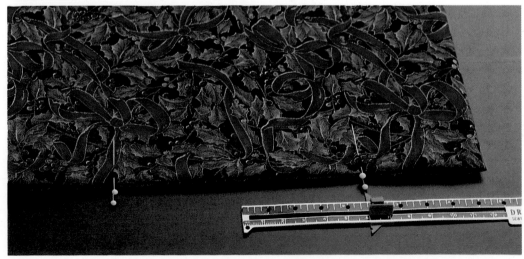

(Continued)

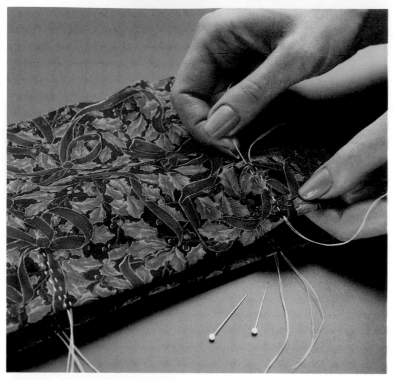

4 Stitch from pin mark at edge of dress to 1½" (3.8 cm) from the edge, using double-threaded needle. Stitch back to edge of skirt ⅛" (3 mm) from previous stitching as shown; leave thread tails. Repeat at remaining pin marks.

5 Place slip, right side out, inside dress, with raw edges even. Using hand running stitches, stitch close to the upper raw edges, stitching through all layers and leaving thread tails.

6 Gather the lower edge of dress at stitching, to create scalloped edge; knot threads to secure. Glue or stitch ribbon rose at peak of each scallop.

7 Assemble sleeves as on page 137, step 9. Slip the dress over dowels. Tightly gather upper edge, and knot the thread; glue dress to dowels at upper edge.

8 Attach wire arms and sleeves as on page 138, steps 12 to 14.

9 Glue on head and hair as on page 138, step 15. Stitch hand running stitches in heading of lace for neck trim. Gather and glue the lace around the neck, positioning raw edges at back of caroler. Complete caroler, following page 139, steps 18 and 19.

HOW TO MAKE A LAMPPOST

1 Paint or stain base plaque as desired. Paint ¾" (2 cm) dowel black for post. Paint 2¼" (6 cm) ball knob antique white for light globe.

2 Position the dowel as desired on base plaque; mark position, using pencil. Secure dowel to base as on page 136, steps 3 and 4. Predrill screw hole for dowel screw into upper end of dowel, using ⅛" drill bit; secure the dowel screw.

3 Secure the ball knob to dowel. Wrap the lampost with garland, securing with hot glue. Embellish the light globe as desired. Attach felt to base as on page 139, step 19.

BIAS-TRIMMED STOCKINGS

Large stockings, waiting to be filled with candy and trinkets, set the mood for the holiday season. A bias-trimmed stocking can be made in a variety of styles, depending on the choice of fabric and types of embellishments used. For a simple stocking, choose fabric that is distinctive and add embellishments such as purchased appliqués, ribbons, and buttons.

Make the binding from matching or contrasting fabric; a striped or plaid fabric can be used to create interesting effects. The stocking is lined and has a layer of fleece for added body.

MATERIALS

- ¾ yd. (0.7 m) outer fabric.
- ¾ yd. (0.7 m) lining fabric.
- ½ yd. (0.5 m) fabric, for bias binding.
- Polyester fleece.
- Embellishments, such as purchased appliqués, ribbon, or buttons.

CUTTING DIRECTIONS

Make the stocking pattern (below). With the right sides of the fabric together, cut two stocking pieces from the outer fabric and two from the lining. Also cut two stocking pieces from polyester fleece. Cut bias fabric strips, 2½" (6.5 cm) wide, for the binding, cutting two 10" (25.5 cm) strips for the upper edges of the stocking and one 60" (152.5 cm) strip for the sides. Piece the strips as necessary, as on page 80, step 7.

HOW TO MAKE A STOCKING PATTERN

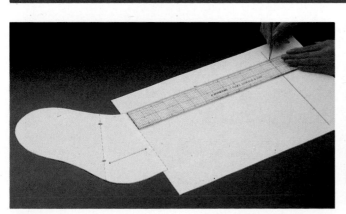

1 Transfer partial pattern pieces A and B (page 315) to paper. Tape pieces together, matching notches. Tape a large piece of paper to upper edge of partial stocking. Draw a line parallel to and 13" (33 cm) above dotted line, to mark upper edge of stocking. Align quilter's ruler to dotted line at side; mark point on line for upper edge. Repeat for the other side.

2 Measure out ⅞" (2.2 cm) from the marked points; mark. Connect the outer points at the upper edge to sides at ends of dotted line, to make full-size stocking pattern.

HOW TO SEW A BIAS-TRIMMED STOCKING

1 Layer the stocking front, fleece, and lining, right sides out. Baste layers together a scant ¼" (6 mm) from raw edges. Repeat for stocking back.

2 Position flat embellishments on the stocking as desired; pin or glue-baste in place. Stitch close to edges of trims.

3 Press the binding strips in half lengthwise, wrong sides together. Pin one 10" (25.5 cm) binding strip to upper edge of stocking front, right sides together, matching raw edges; stitch scant ⅜" (1 cm) seam.

4 Wrap binding around upper edge, covering stitching line on back of stocking; pin. Stitch in the ditch on the right side of stocking, catching binding on stocking back. Trim ends of binding even with stocking. Apply binding to upper edge of stocking back.

5 Align stocking front and back, with lining sides together; pin. Pin the binding to the stocking front, matching raw edges, with right sides together and ends extending ¾" (2 cm) on toe side of the stocking and 6" (15 cm) on the heel side; excess binding on the heel side becomes the hanger. Stitch scant ⅜" (1 cm) from raw edges; ease binding at heel and toe.

6 Fold the short end of the binding over upper edge of stocking. Wrap the binding around edge of stocking, covering stitching line on back; pin.

7 Fold up ½" (1.3 cm) on the end of the extended binding. Press up ¼" (6 mm) on raw edges of the extended binding. Fold the binding in half lengthwise, encasing the raw edges; pin. Edgestitch along pinned edges of the binding, for hanger. Stitch in the ditch around remainder of binding as in step 4.

8 Fold the extended binding strip to the back of stocking, forming a loop for hanger. Hand-stitch in place.

9 Hand-stitch ribbons, bows, or other embellishments to stocking front, if desired.

MORE IDEAS FOR BIAS-TRIMMED STOCKINGS

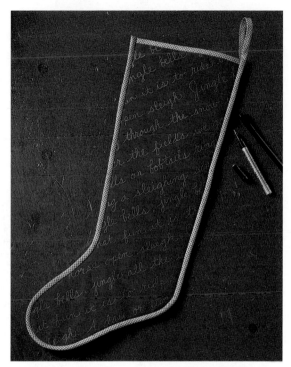

Written verses from "Jingle Bells" cover the front of this stocking. The verses are written using fine-point permanent-ink markers.

Buttons, stitched to the top of the stocking, give the appearance of a cuff.

Tea-dyed fabrics give a homespun look to this stocking. Fused appliqués are applied to the stocking front, using paper-backed fusible web as on pages 78 and 80. Fabric paint is used to personalize the stocking.

WOOLEN STOCKINGS

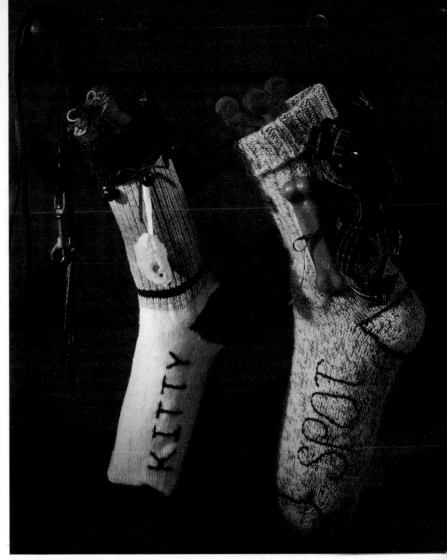

Turn woolen socks into personalized, one-of-a-kind Christmas stockings. Right at home hanging on a mantel, they also make a fun accent hung from an armoire.

Choose trims that complement the homespun look of the stockings. Add patches of flannel or wool fabric, and trims such as buttons, bells, or fringe. For a cuff, simply turn down the top of the sock. Or hand-stitch a fabric cuff to the top of the stocking. Most items can be stitched in place using a darning needle and narrow ribbon, yarn, or pearl cotton.

Wool socks are available at stores specializing in outdoor clothing. For extra-long stockings, purchase cross-country ski socks.

Woolen stockings can be decorated for a variety of looks. Opposite, a stocking is embellished with sprigs of greenery and cones. Another features a snowman design, stitched in place using blanket stitches. Above, stockings are custom-designed for family pets.

TIPS FOR MAKING WOOLEN STOCKINGS

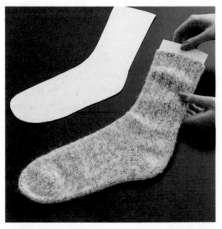

Insert a cardboard liner, cut slightly larger than the sock, into the sock before decorating with hand stitching; the liner will prevent catching stitches in the back of the sock.

Stitch letters, using yarn and back-stitches; secure stitches by taking one or two concealed small stitches.

Knot a loop of ribbon through top of sock for a hanger. Stuff finished stocking with tissue paper or with polyester fiberfill.

DECORATING
MANTELS

Family photographs *from previous Christmases are grouped on a mantel for a nostalgic look. Honeysuckle vine and dried hydrangeas are used to embellish the artificial garland.*

Mantels are the perfect place to showcase Christmas decorations. Evergreen boughs or garlands displayed on a mantel can serve as a backdrop for a collection of family photos, Santas, unique ornaments, or hand-crafted Christmas items. For interest, mix a few dried or artificial floral elements with traditional Christmas accessories.

Safety note: *Do not leave any open flame, including candles, unattended.*

Gilded reindeer
and candles in brass
candlesticks (above)
are arranged on an
ornate mantel with
greenery, cones,
and berries. The
papier-mâché
reindeer were gilded
with metallic paint.

Amaryllis (right)
are set on each
side of a picture,
dominating this
Christmas display.

Countdown calendar (below) is made by hanging twenty-four tea-dyed stocking ornaments (page 15), filled with
holiday candies, along a fresh garland. A star ornament hangs at the end of the garland for Christmas Day.

Honeysuckle vine *encircles an artificial wreath. A gilded reindeer and gold bow are elegant highlights. Artichokes, cones, hydrangea, and pomegranates add textural interest.*

Wreaths can be embellished for a variety of looks. For the base, select a fresh or artificial evergreen wreath, or a grapevine wreath. Embellish the base with items such as ribbons, ornaments, and floral materials to create a wreath that reflects your personal style.

Artificial evergreen wreaths are especially easy to decorate, because many items can be secured by simply twisting the branches around the embellishments. Items can also be secured to wreaths using floral wire or hot glue.

Embellish wreaths with one material at a time, spacing the items evenly to achieve a balanced look. Add large items first and fill in any bare areas with smaller ones. Secure embellishments to the surface as well as to the wreath base, to give a sense of depth.

Artificial evergreen garland *is wrapped around a grapevine wreath. A natural look is created by adding birch bark and twig birdhouses, artificial birds, and stems of rose hips.*

Santa's elf *(page 130) is wired to the center area of this fresh wreath to create a focal point. Dried fruit slices, cinnamon sticks, and paper twist are added to give this wreath a country look.*

Wire-mesh bow *(page 9) and metal ornaments (page 23) are used to embellish a fresh evergreen wreath. The mesh strips for the bow measure about 4" (10 cm) wide and 24" (61 cm) long. Lights were added to the wreath before it was decorated.*

Village house *becomes the focal point of an artificial wreath. Additional sprigs of greenery, cones, and berries are added for texture and fullness. For a snowy effect, aerosol artificial snow is sprayed over polyester fiberfill.*

TIPS FOR EMBELLISHING WREATHS

Attach wire to a cone by wrapping the wire around bottom layers of cone. Attach wire to a cinnamon stick by inserting it through length of stick; wrap wire around stick, and twist the ends at the middle.

Make floral or berry clusters by grouping items together. Attach wire to the items as necessary. Wrap stems and wires with floral tape.

Add texture to a wreath by inserting sprigs of other evergreen varieties. Secure sprigs to the wreath base, using wire.

Display Christmas collectibles, such as village houses and ornaments, on a wreath for visual impact. Wire items securely to the wreath base.

Gild embellishments, such as twigs, cones, artichokes, and sprigs of greenery, by applying gold aerosol acrylic paint.

Embellish wreath with ribbon by weaving it through the wreath; create twists and turns for depth. Secure the ribbon as necessary with hot glue.

Wrap honeysuckle vine loosely over a wreath, for added texture. Secure the vine with floral wire or hot glue.

Wrap artificial garland around a grapevine wreath to add color and dimension.

Add battery-operated lights to a wreath by weaving the cords into the wreath boughs.

Embellish bows with additional loops of contrasting ribbon. Fold length of ribbon in half to form loop the same size as loops on the existing bow; wrap ends tightly with wire. Secure to the center of bow, using hot glue.

A candy wreath is a festive holiday decoration full of little gifts. In one version, brightly wrapped Christmas candies nestle among coils of curled ribbon. For a fringed fabric wreath, candies are tied with raffia between knotted strips of cotton fabric. Small scissors hanging from the wreath invite each guest to snip out a piece of candy.

MATERIALS

- Metal ring, 8" (20.5 cm) in diameter.
- 50 to 70 yd. (46 to 64.4 m) curling ribbon in choice of colors, for ribbon wreath.
- ¼ yd. (0.25 m) each of three cotton print fabrics, for fringed fabric wreath.
- Raffia, for fringed fabric wreath.
- Wrapped Christmas candies.
- Small scissors.

HOW TO MAKE A CANDY & RIBBON WREATH

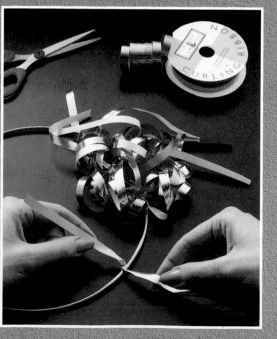

1 Cut a 12" (30.5 cm) length of curling ribbon. Wrap ribbon around metal ring; knot, leaving tails of equal length. Repeat, alternating ribbon colors as desired; cover about 4" (10 cm) of the metal ring.

2 Curl ribbon tails with blade of scissors. Tie pieces of wrapped candy to wreath; space evenly. Pack knotted ribbons tightly.

3 Repeat steps 1 and 2 until the entire wreath is covered. Fold 40" (102 cm) length of curling ribbon in half; wrap folded end around metal ring at top of wreath. Knot, allowing 2" (5 cm) loop for hanger.

4 Insert tails of ribbon through handle of small scissors; knot, allowing scissors to hang just below wreath. Curl ribbon tails.

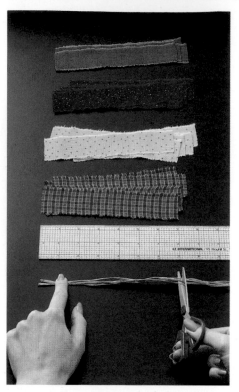

1 Cut selvages from fabrics. Tear fabric crosswise into strips, 1½" (3.8 cm) wide. Cut strips into 7" (18 cm) lengths. Cut raffia into 7" (18 cm) lengths.

2 Wrap length of fabric around metal ring; knot, leaving tails of equal length. Wrap length of raffia around metal ring next to knotted fabric; knot, leaving tails of equal length. Repeat until entire ring is covered, alternating fabrics and packing knots close together.

3 Tie wrapped candies to wreath where desired, using raffia tails.

4 Fold 36" (91.5 cm) length of raffia in half; wrap the folded end around the metal ring at top of wreath. Knot, allowing 2" (5 cm) loop for the hanger. Insert tails of raffia through the handle of a small pair of scissors; knot, allowing the scissors to hang just below wreath.

WALL TREES

Make a stunning wall accent from a miniature artificial pine tree. The branches of the tree are bent to the front, creating a flat surface in the back. This allows the tree to be displayed flat against a wall. The wall tree is embellished with a variety of fruit and is topped with a large bow.

MATERIALS

- Artificial pine tree with attached trunk, about 24" (61 cm) tall.
- Four or five varieties of fruit, including apples, pears, grape clusters, and berries.
- Preserved leaves on stems.
- 3 yd. (2.75 m) wired ribbon, for bow.
- Floral wire.

1 Bend branches of artificial tree around to one side. Place flat on table, and arrange branches.

2 Secure pears to tree with hot glue, forming a curved diagonal line as shown.

3 Gild leaves as on page 97, step 1. Secure thin layer of gilded leaves along sides of pears, using hot glue. Lift pine boughs to surround the row of pears and leaves. Insert second variety of fruit and another row of gilded leaves, following the same line as the pears; secure with hot glue.

4 Continue to secure alternating rows of fruit and gilded leaves, until the entire tree is covered. Arrange pine boughs between rows of fruit and leaves.

5 Form large loops from wired ribbon as shown **(a).** Continue to make six loops. Make small loop at center. Bend wire around ribbon at center; twist wire tightly, gathering ribbon **(b).** Separate and shape the loops.

6 Secure bow to top of tree, using wire. Twist excess wire into loop at back, for hanging tree. Tuck ends of ribbon into sides of tree.

Make a classic topiary tree to accent your fireplace or display on a sideboard for the holidays. This finished tree measures about 24" (61 cm) tall. Embellish the top of this miniature tree with artificial fruit, floral materials, and decorative ribbon. The tree is set in a terra-cotta pot.

MATERIALS

- 4" (10 cm) Styrofoam® ball.
- Artificial pine boughs.
- Wired ribbon.
- Latex grape clusters and small pears.
- Dried yarrow.
- Small red-leaf preserved foliage; artificial green leaves.
- 7" (18 cm) terra-cotta pot.
- Floral foam, for silk arranging.
- Several dogwood stems.
- Hot glue gun and glue sticks.

1 Trim floral foam with a knife to fit pot snugly; secure with hot glue. Cut dogwood stems about 14" (35.5 cm) long. Insert several stems into center of the pot; secure with hot glue.

HOW TO MAKE A TOPIARY TREE

(Continued)

161

2 Secure the opposite ends of the stems to one side of the Styrofoam® ball, using hot glue.

3 Cut pine boughs into pieces about 3" (7.5 cm) long. Insert the pine stems into ball and foam in pot until the surfaces are covered.

4 Cut apart the grape stems and pears; insert as desired, securing with hot glue. Insert a large grape cluster into pot, allowing it to cascade over edge.

5 Cut red-leaf foliage into 4" (10 cm) stems. Secure leaf stems and yarrow pieces to ball with hot glue. Tuck the ribbon into ball; secure with hot glue, if necessary.

HANGING PINE BALLS

A holiday pine ball is created by decorating a Styrofoam® ball with pine stems, preserved leaves, and artificial berries. Display the pine ball indoors by hanging it from either a window or door frame, using a decorative ribbon and an upholstery tack. The pine ball can also be hung outdoors, offering a festive welcome to holiday guests.

MATERIALS

- 4" (10 cm) Styrofoam ball.
- Artificial pine boughs.
- Small-leaf preserved foliage.
- Artificial berries.
- Ribbon; floral wire.

HOW TO MAKE A HANGING PINE BALL

1 Cut several pieces of pine into 1½" (3.8 cm) lengths. Insert pine lengths into ball until surface is covered. Insert short pieces of small-leaf foliage into the ball, interspersing them among pine lengths. Cut sprigs of berries, and insert berries as desired.

2 Make six ribbon loops; secure with glue at center as shown. Cut ribbon to desired length for hanger. Cut 8" (20.5 cm) length of wire. Hold end of ribbon over wire; secure with glue. Bend wire ends down; insert wire ends into the foam ball over ribbon loops.

163

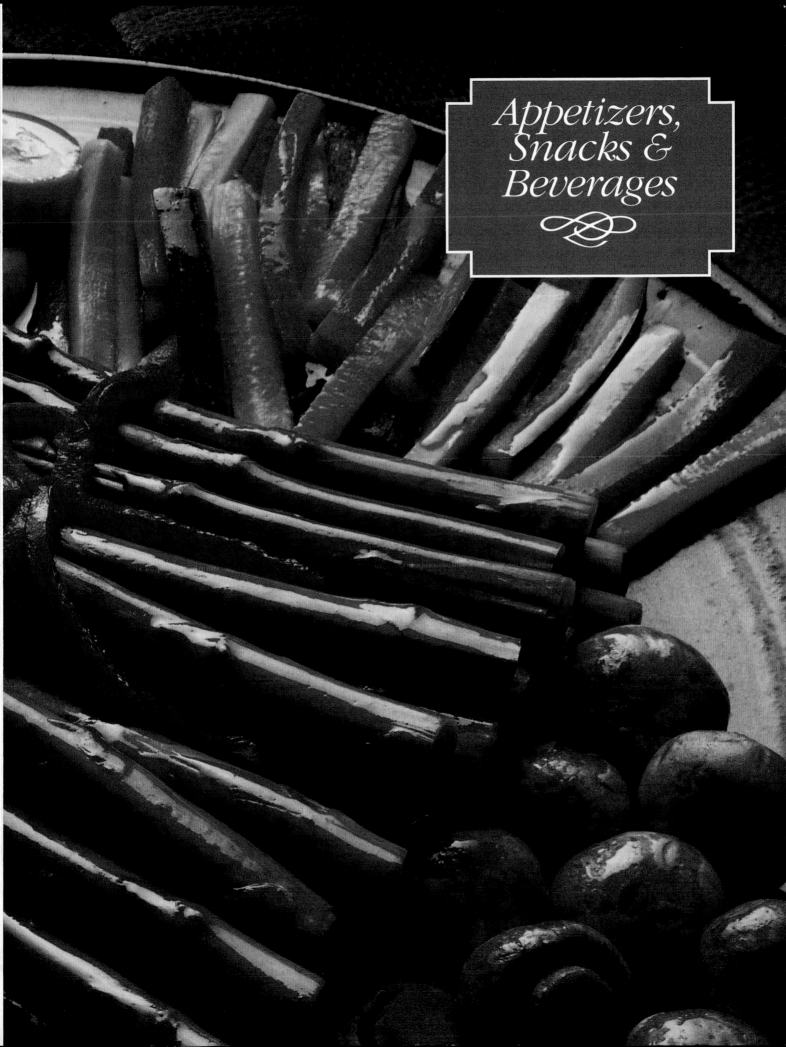

Appetizers,
Snacks &
Beverages

APPETIZERS

SHRIMP IN BEER ↓

- 2 pkgs. (12 oz./ 375 g each) frozen quick-cooking shrimp
- 1 can (12 oz./ 341 mL) beer
- 1 teaspoon (5 mL) garlic powder
- 1 teaspoon (5 mL) chopped chives

10 to 12 servings

Combine all ingredients in 2-qt. (2 L) casserole; cover. Microwave at High 8 to 13 minutes, or until shrimp are opaque, stirring 2 or 3 times. Drain all but ½ cup (125 mL) liquid before serving. Serve with cocktail picks.

↑ SPICED SHRIMP

- 2 lbs. (1 kg) raw shrimp, peeled and deveined
- ¼ cup (50 mL) butter or margarine
- 2 tablespoons (25 mL) all-purpose flour
- 2 teaspoons (10 mL) snipped fresh parsley or 1 teaspoon (5 mL) dried parsley flakes
- ½ teaspoon (2 mL) ground coriander
- ½ teaspoon (2 mL) ground cumin
- ¼ teaspoon (1 mL) salt
- ¼ teaspoon (1 mL) pepper
- ¼ teaspoon (1 mL) ground nutmeg
- Pinch ground cloves
- 1¼ cups (300 mL) milk

6 to 8 servings

1 Place shrimp in 1½-qt. (1.5 L) casserole. Microwave, covered, at High 5 to 8 minutes, or until shrimp are opaque, stirring 2 or 3 times. Do not overcook. Set aside.

2 Place butter in 4-cup (1 L) measure. Microwave at High 45 to 60 seconds, or until melted. Blend in flour, parsley, coriander, cumin, salt, pepper, nutmeg and cloves. Blend in milk. Microwave at High 3 to 6 minutes, or until thick and bubbly, stirring with wire whip 2 or 3 times. Drain shrimp; stir in sauce. Serve with cocktail picks.

← SHRIMP WRAP-UPS

- 8 slices bacon
- 8 large raw shrimp, peeled, deveined and cut in half
- 1 large green pepper, cut into 16 pieces
- 2 tablespoons (25 mL) soy sauce
- 2 tablespoons (25 mL) white wine or water
- 2 tablespoons (25 mL) chili sauce
- 2 tablespoons (25 mL) plum or grape jelly

6 servings

1 Place 3 layers of paper towel directly on microwave oven floor. Arrange 4 bacon slices on towel; cover with another towel. Arrange remaining 4 bacon slices on top; cover with towel. Microwave at High 4 to 5 minutes, or until bacon is slightly brown but not fully cooked.

2 Cut bacon slices in half. Wrap a piece of shrimp and green pepper in each bacon piece. Secure with a cocktail pick. Place in 9" x 9" (2.5 L) glass baking dish.

3 In 2-cup (500 mL) measure, mix remaining ingredients. Pour over wrap-ups. Cover. Refrigerate no longer than 8 hours or overnight, stirring once or twice. To serve, microwave at High 3 to 4 minutes, or until shrimp is cooked.

POLYNESIAN APPETIZERS →

- 1 tablespoon (15 mL) packed brown sugar
- 2 teaspoons (10 mL) cornstarch
- Pinch ground ginger
- Pinch garlic powder
- 1 tablespoon (15 mL) water
- 1 tablespoon (15 mL) soy sauce
- 1 can (8 oz./227 mL) pineapple chunks, drained and ⅓ cup (75 mL) juice reserved
- 8 oz. (250 g) frozen fully cooked brown and serve sausages

2 servings

In 1-qt. (1 L) casserole, blend brown sugar, cornstarch, ginger, garlic powder, water, soy sauce and pineapple juice. Cut each sausage into thirds. Stir into casserole with pineapple chunks. Microwave at High 3 to 7 minutes, or until sauce is thickened, stirring 2 or 3 times.

STUFFED CHERRY TOMATOES

- 1 pint (500 mL) cherry tomatoes
- ½ cup (125 mL) herbed cream cheese spread
- ⅓ cup (75 mL) shredded Cheddar cheese
- 4 slices bacon, cooked crisp, crumbled
- Snipped fresh parsley (optional)

6 to 8 servings

1 Cut thin slice from stem end of tomato. With small spoon or melon baller, scoop out pulp. Discard pulp and tops of tomatoes. Place tomatoes cut-sides-down on paper towel to drain.

2 Combine remaining ingredients in small mixing bowl. Mix well. Stuff tomatoes with cheese mixture. Arrange tomatoes on paper-towel-lined plate, with smaller tomatoes in center. Microwave at High 1½ to 2½ minutes, or until mixture is hot, rotating plate once. Sprinkle tomatoes lightly with snipped fresh parsley, if desired.

SAUSAGE-STUFFED MUSHROOMS

- 12 large fresh mushrooms (2" to 2½"/5 to 6 cm)
- ¼ lb. (125 g) bulk pork sausage
- 1 teaspoon (5 mL) instant minced onion
- 1 teaspoon (5 mL) dried parsley flakes
- 2 tablespoons (25 mL) seasoned dry bread crumbs
- 1 tablespoon (15 mL) grated Parmesan cheese

4 to 6 servings

1 Trim small portion of stem from each mushroom. Wipe caps clean with damp paper towel. Remove stems. Set caps aside. Finely chop enough stems to equal ¼ cup (50 mL). Place chopped stems in 1-quart (1 L) casserole. Discard remaining stems, or save for later use. Crumble sausage over chopped mushrooms. Sprinkle with onion and parsley. Cover. Microwave at High 1½ to 2½ minutes, or until sausage is no longer pink, stirring once to break apart. Mix in remaining ingredients.

2 Stuff sausage mixture evenly into mushroom caps. Arrange stuffed mushrooms on paper-towel-lined plate. Microwave at High 3 to 6 minutes, or until mushrooms are hot, rotating plate once.

SALMON-CUCUMBER CANAPÉS

- 2 cucumbers (8"/20 cm)
- 3 tablespoons (50 mL) chopped celery
- 2 tablespoons (25 mL) chopped onion
- 1 can (6¾ oz./192 g) skinless, boneless salmon, drained
- 2 tablespoons (25 mL) sour cream
- 1 teaspoon (5 mL) lemon juice
- ½ teaspoon (2 mL) grated lemon peel
- Pinch pepper
- Paprika

1 dozen canapés

1 Slice each cucumber crosswise into 6 equal pieces. With small spoon or melon baller, scoop out center of each piece, leaving ¼" (5 mm) shell. Flatten ends of rounded pieces by cutting thin slices from green ends. Place pieces hollowed-sides-down on paper towel to drain.

2 In small mixing bowl, combine celery and onion. Cover with plastic wrap. Microwave at High 1 to 2 minutes, or until vegetables are tender. Add remaining ingredients, except paprika. Mix well. Fill cucumber cups evenly with salmon mixture. Arrange canapés on plate. Microwave at High 3 to 6 minutes, or until canapés are warm, rotating plate once. Sprinkle with paprika to serve. (Canapés may also be refrigerated and served chilled.)

FLORENTINE CANAPÉS

- 2 pkgs. (9 oz./255 g each) frozen creamed spinach
- ¼ cup (50 mL) grated Parmesan cheese
- ¼ cup (50 mL) seasoned dry bread crumbs
- ¼ cup (50 mL) chopped tomato
- 2 teaspoons (10 mL) instant minced onion
- ¼ teaspoon (1 mL) ground nutmeg
- Melba cracker rounds

4 to 5 dozen

Place spinach in 2-qt. (2 L) casserole. Microwave at High 4 to 8 minutes, or until defrosted, breaking apart with fork once or twice. Drain. Stir in cheese, bread crumbs, tomato, minced onion and nutmeg. Spread on crackers. Place 12 crackers on paper-towel-lined plate. Microwave at High 1 to 1½ minutes, or until hot, rotating plate once. Repeat with remaining canapés.

Advance preparation: *Prepare spinach spread the day before. Cover and refrigerate. Canapés can be assembled 2 to 3 hours in advance and refrigerated. Add 15 to 20 seconds to microwaving time if spread is cold.*

CRAB CANAPÉS

- 1 can (6 oz./170 g) crab meat, rinsed, drained and cartilage removed
- ⅓ cup (75 mL) all-purpose flour
- 1 egg
- ¼ cup (50 mL) finely chopped green onion
- 1 jar (2 oz./57 g) chopped pimiento, drained
- 1 teaspoon (5 mL) lemon juice
- 1 teaspoon (5 mL) Worcestershire sauce
- ¼ teaspoon (1 mL) salt
- Pinch pepper
- 36 melba sesame rounds

3 dozen

1 Mix all ingredients, except melba rounds, in medium bowl. Drop by teaspoonfuls onto wax-paper-lined baking sheet. Cover and freeze overnight. Pack in freezer container; label. Freeze no longer than 2 weeks.

2 To serve, place 18 melba rounds around edge of paper-towel-lined 12" (30 cm) serving plate. Top each with frozen crab mixture. Microwave at 70% (Medium-High) 1¾ to 3 minutes, or until heated, rearranging after half the time. Repeat with remaining canapés as needed.

CHICKEN LIVER PÂTÉ

- 1½ lbs. (750 g) chicken livers
- 1 teaspoon (5 mL) instant chicken bouillon granules
- ½ cup (125 mL) water
- 1 hard-cooked egg
- ¼ cup (50 mL) butter or margarine, softened
- 2 tablespoons (25 mL) finely chopped onion
- 1 clove garlic, minced
- 1 teaspoon (5 mL) salt
- 1 teaspoon (5 mL) dry mustard

10 to 12 servings

In 1½-qt. (1.5 L) casserole, combine chicken livers, bouillon granules and water; cover. Microwave at High 8 to 12 minutes, or until livers are no longer pink, stirring after half the time. Drain. Purée livers and egg in meat grinder or food processor. In medium bowl, blend purée with remaining ingredients. Pour into well-oiled 2-cup (500 mL) mold. Chill at least 6 hours or overnight. Unmold onto serving plate. Garnish with chopped tomatoes and cucumbers, if desired.

← PICKLED SAUSAGES

- ¾ cup (175 mL) sugar
- 1 teaspoon (5 mL) pickling spice
- 1 teaspoon (5 mL) salt
- ¼ teaspoon (1 mL) peppercorns
- ½ cup (125 mL) water
- ½ cup (125 mL) cider vinegar
- 1 lb. (500 g) knockwurst or ring bologna
- 1½ cups (375 mL) pearl onions, or chunks of white onion

10 to 12 servings

In 2-qt. (2 L) casserole, mix sugar, pickling spice, salt, peppercorns, water and vinegar; cover. Microwave at High 1 to 3 minutes, or until boiling. Cut knockwurst lengthwise in half, then cut into ½" (1 cm) pieces. Add knockwurst and onions to sugar-vinegar mixture; cover. Refrigerate 4 to 7 days, stirring occasionally. Remove knockwurst and onions to serving dish with slotted spoon. Serve with cocktail picks.

CRAB-STUFFED ZUCCHINI ↑

- ¾ cup (175 mL) chopped fresh mushrooms
- 3 tablespoons (50 mL) butter or margarine
- 2 tablespoons (25 mL) all-purpose flour
- ¾ cup (175 mL) half-and-half
- ½ cup (125 mL) chopped green onion
- ¼ teaspoon (1 mL) paprika

- ¼ teaspoon (1 mL) salt
- Pinch pepper
- 2 tablespoons (25 mL) sherry
- 2 cans (6 oz./170 g each) crab meat, rinsed, drained and cartilage removed
- 1¼ to 1½-lb. (625 to 750 g) small zucchini, cut into ¾" (2 cm) pieces

4 to 4½ dozen

Advance preparation:
Prepare recipe as directed below, but do not sprinkle with paprika. Cover each plate with plastic wrap. Refrigerate no longer than 8 hours. Uncover. Sprinkle with paprika. Microwave one plate at a time at 70% (Medium-High) 2 to 5 minutes, or until heated, rotating once or twice.

1 Combine mushrooms and butter in 1-qt. (1 L) casserole. Microwave at High 1 to 2 minutes, or until butter is melted and mushrooms are tender. Stir in flour. Blend in half-and-half until smooth. Stir in onion, paprika, salt, pepper and sherry.

2 Microwave at High 2 to 4 minutes, or until very thick, blending with wire whip once or twice. Stir in crab meat. Set aside. With a spoon, hollow out each zucchini piece about halfway down leaving ⅛" to ¼" (3 to 5 mm) on sides. Spoon crab mixture into zucchini pieces.

3 Place on two paper-towel-lined plates. Sprinkle with additional paprika. Reduce power to 70% (Medium-High). Microwave one plate at a time 1 to 3 minutes, or until heated, rotating plate once or twice. Repeat with remaining plate.

SPINACH BALLS

- 1 pkg. (10 oz./300 g) frozen, chopped spinach
- ¾ cup (175 mL) shredded Swiss cheese
- ¼ cup (50 mL) dry bread crumbs
- 2 tablespoons (25 mL) grated Parmesan cheese
- 1 tablespoon (15 mL) grated onion
- ½ teaspoon (2 mL) salt
- 1 egg, beaten

2 dozen

1 Place package of spinach in microwave oven. Microwave at High 4 to 5 minutes, or until defrosted. Drain, pressing out excess liquid. Mix with remaining ingredients. Shape into 1" (2.5 cm) balls, about 1½ teaspoons (7 mL) each. Place on wax-paper-lined baking sheet; cover. Freeze overnight. Pack in freezer container; label. Freeze no longer than 2 weeks.

2 To serve, place all spinach balls on paper-towel-lined baking sheet. Microwave at High 2 minutes. Reduce power to 50% (Medium). Microwave 4½ to 6 minutes, or until hot and just set, rearranging once or twice.

SAUSAGE BALLS

- 1 pkg. (12 oz./375 g) bulk pork sausage
- ¾ cup (175 mL) seasoned bread crumbs
- ¼ cup (50 mL) grated Parmesan cheese
- Pinch ground red pepper
- 1 tablespoon (15 mL) dried parsley flakes
- 2 eggs

4 dozen

1 Crumble sausage into 2-qt. (2 L) casserole. Microwave at High 2 to 4 minutes, or until sausage is no longer pink, stirring to break apart; drain. Stir in remaining ingredients. Shape into balls, about 1 teaspoon (5 mL) each. Place on wax-paper-lined baking sheet; cover. Freeze overnight. Pack in freezer container; label. Freeze no longer than 2 weeks.

2 To serve, place 24 balls around edge of paper-towel-lined 12" (30 cm) serving plate. Microwave at High 1½ to 3½ minutes, or until heated and firm to the touch, rearranging once. Repeat with remaining sausage balls.

SPICED NUTS ↑

- ¼ cup (50 mL) butter or margarine
- 2 tablespoons (25 mL) Worcestershire sauce
- ¾ teaspoon (4 mL) seasoned salt
- ½ teaspoon (2 mL) garlic powder
- ¼ teaspoon (1 mL) cayenne
- 2 cans (12 oz./375 g each) mixed nuts

4 cups (1 L)

Place butter in 3-qt. (3 L) casserole. Microwave at High 45 to 60 seconds, or until melted. Mix in remaining ingredients except nuts. Add nuts, stirring to coat. Microwave at High 7 to 9 minutes, or until butter is absorbed, stirring 2 or 3 times during cooking. Spread on paper-towel-lined baking sheet to dry. Store nuts in tightly covered container.

HAM SALAD FINGER ROLLS

- 1 can (6½ oz./184 g) chunked ham
- ¼ cup (50 mL) mayonnaise or salad dressing
- 2 tablespoons (25 mL) sweet pickle relish
- 1 teaspoon (5 mL) grated onion

- 6 slices whole wheat bread
- ¼ cup (50 mL) butter or margarine
- 1 egg
- ¼ cup (50 mL) sesame seed

3 dozen

1 In small bowl, mix ham, mayonnaise, pickle relish and onion. Set aside. Trim crusts from bread. Roll to ¼" (5 mm) thickness with rolling pin. Spread each with ham mixture; roll up jelly roll style.

2 Place butter in shallow dish. Microwave at High 45 to 60 seconds, or until melted. Beat egg into butter. Roll sandwich rolls in butter-egg mixture, then in sesame seed to coat generously. Wrap, label and freeze. Freeze no longer than 2 weeks.

3 To serve, cut each roll into 6 pieces. Place around edges of two 12" (30 cm) plates. Microwave each plate at High 3 to 6 minutes, or until hot, rotating plate once or twice.

BAKED POTATO SKINS ↓

- 3 small russet potatoes (6 to 7 oz./ 175 to 200 g each)
- ½ teaspoon (2 mL) salt
- ¼ teaspoon (1 mL) ground cumin

- ⅓ cup (75 mL) finely chopped seeded tomato
- 3 tablespoons (50 mL) sliced green onions
- 1 jalapeño pepper, seeded and finely chopped

- 1 tablespoon (15 mL) snipped fresh cilantro (optional)
- ¼ cup (50 mL) nonfat or low-fat sour cream

6 servings

1 Heat oven to 425°F/220°C. Pierce potatoes several times with fork. Place potatoes on rack in oven. Bake for 45 to 50 minutes, or until tender. Cut each potato in half lengthwise. Scoop out pulp, leaving ½" (1 cm) shells. (Reserve pulp for other uses.)

2 Spray baking sheet with nonstick vegetable cooking spray. Arrange shells, skinsides-up, on baking sheet. Spray shells with nonstick vegetable cooking spray. Bake for 10 to 13 minutes, or until skins are crisp. Turn shells over. Sprinkle inside of shells evenly with salt and cumin.

3 Combine tomato, onions, pepper and cilantro in small mixing bowl. Spoon tomato mixture evenly into shells. Top each shell with 2 teaspoons (10 mL) sour cream.

Arrangement is the secret of microwaving several foods with different cooking times. Place longer-cooking items around the edge of the platter. Make a second ring of vegetables with medium cooking times. Quick-cooking vegetables go in the center, where they receive less energy. The vegetables cook evenly and look beautiful.

← ## GARDEN BOUQUET VEGETABLE PLATTER

- 1 lb. (500 g) fresh asparagus, trimmed
- 4 oz. (125 g) fresh whole mushrooms, 1" (2.5 cm) diameter
- ½ lb. (250 g) yellow squash, cut into ½" (1 cm) slices
- 1 medium zucchini, cut into 2½" x ¼" (6 cm x 5 mm) strips
- 1 medium carrot, cut into 2½" x ¼" (6 cm x 5 mm) strips
- 2 tablespoons (25 mL) water
- 1 whole pimiento
- Browned butter

6 to 8 servings

1 Arrange asparagus spears in center of 12" to 14" (30 to 35 cm) round microwave-safe platter. Arrange mushrooms, squash, zucchini and carrots around spears, alternating colors and types of vegetables. Sprinkle with water. Cover with plastic wrap.

2 Microwave at High 8 to 9 minutes, or until tender-crisp, rotating platter 2 times during cooking. Feel through wrap to test doneness; vegetables should feel soft to the touch and pliable. Let stand 5 minutes. Cut pimiento into spiral strip and form a bow. Garnish asparagus spears with pimiento bow. Prepare browned butter. Serve with vegetables.

ELEGANT VEGETABLE PLATTER ↑

- 1 artichoke
- ½ lb. (250 g) fresh carrots, cut into 2½" x ¼" (6 cm x 5 mm) strips
- 4 cups (1 L) fresh cauliflowerets
- 8 oz. (250 g) fresh Brussels sprouts, trimmed and cut in half
- 2 tablespoons (25 mL) water
- Cheese Sauce (page 183)

6 to 8 servings

1 Trim artichoke 2" (5 cm) from top and close to base so it will stand upright. Snap off small lower leaves. Snip tips of outer leaves. Rinse; shake off excess water. Wrap in plastic wrap. Microwave at High 3 minutes. Remove plastic and place artichoke at one end of microwave-safe platter.

2 Place carrots in center of platter. Arrange cauliflowerets and Brussels sprouts around edge, alternating clusters of vegetables for color effect. Sprinkle water over vegetables. Cover platter with plastic wrap. Microwave at High 8 to 11 minutes, or until tender-crisp, rotating platter 2 times. Feel through wrap to test doneness; vegetables should feel soft to the touch and pliable. Let stand 5 minutes. Prepare Cheese Sauce as directed. Serve with vegetable platter.

WHOLE CAULIFLOWER

Wash a 1-lb. (500 g) head of cauliflower. Shake off water. Wrap in plastic wrap. Place on serving plate upside down. Microwave at High 3 minutes. Turn over. Microwave at High 2½ to 4½ minutes, or until base is fork tender. Let stand, covered, 3 minutes. Serve with Cheese Sauce, page 183.

TOMATO & FETA PITA PIZZAS

- 3 Roma tomatoes, finely chopped
- 1 tablespoon (15 mL) crumbled feta cheese
- 1 green onion, finely chopped
- 2 teaspoons (10 mL) balsamic vinegar
- 1 teaspoon (5 mL) olive oil
- ¼ teaspoon (1 mL) dried oregano leaves
- ¼ teaspoon (1 mL) pepper
- 4 whole soft pitas

8 servings

1 Combine all ingredients, except pitas, in small mixing bowl. Cover with plastic wrap. Let stand 20 minutes.

2 Heat oven to 350°F/180°C. Arrange pitas on baking sheet. Spread tomato mixture evenly over pitas. Bake for 10 to 12 minutes, or until hot. Cut each pita into 4 wedges to serve.

TIP: *These pizzas can also be served as a main dish.*

BBQ CHICKEN PITA PIZZAS

- 1 cup (250 mL) cubed cooked chicken breast (no skin; ½"/1 cm cubes)
- ¼ cup (50 mL) prepared barbecue sauce
- 4 whole soft pitas
- ¼ cup (50 mL) shredded reduced-fat Cheddar cheese

8 servings

1 Heat oven to 350°F/180°C. In small mixing bowl, combine chicken and barbecue sauce. Set aside.

2 Arrange pitas on baking sheet. Spread chicken mixture evenly over pitas. Sprinkle cheese evenly over top. Bake for 10 to 12 minutes, or until pitas are hot and cheese is melted.

- ½ cup (125 mL) ready-to-serve chicken broth, divided
- 1 large onion, sliced into ¼" (5 mm) rings
- 4 whole soft pitas
- 4 teaspoons (20 mL) shredded fresh Parmesan cheese
- 1 teaspoon (5 mL) snipped fresh rosemary leaves

8 servings

1 Heat ¼ cup (50 mL) broth in 10" (25 cm) nonstick skillet over medium-low heat until bubbly. Add onion. Cook for 35 to 40 minutes, or until onion is dark golden brown, stirring occasionally. Sprinkle only enough of remaining ¼ cup (50 mL) broth over onion as needed to prevent burning. (Adding too much broth at one time will make onions soggy and prevent browning.)

2 Heat oven to 350°F/180°C. Arrange pitas on baking sheet. Spread onion evenly over pitas. Sprinkle cheese and rosemary evenly over top. Bake for 10 to 12 minutes, or until pitas are hot and cheese is melted.

ANTIPASTO KABOBS

- 1 pkg. (9 oz./255 g) fresh cheese tortelloni or ravioli
- 1 can (14 oz./398 mL) quartered artichoke hearts in water, rinsed and drained
- 1 small red pepper, seeded and cut into 40 chunks
- 20 small fresh mushrooms, cut in half
- 10 jumbo pitted black olives, cut in half
- 10 large pimiento-stuffed green olives, cut in half
- 20 wooden skewers (10"/25 cm)
- 1 bottle (16 oz./500 mL) fat-free Italian dressing

20 kabobs

1 Prepare tortelloni as directed on package. Rinse with cold water. Drain.

2 Cut large artichoke heart quarters in half lengthwise in order to get 20 pieces. Thread ingredients on skewers as follows: pepper chunk, mushroom half, tortelloni, black olive half, artichoke heart, green olive half, tortelloni, mushroom half and pepper chunk.

3 Arrange kabobs in a shallow dish. Pour dressing evenly over kabobs, turning to coat. Cover. Chill at least 2 hours, turning kabobs occasionally. Drain dressing from kabobs before serving.

TIP: *Drained dressing may be reserved for other uses.*

EASY SNACK MIX

Seasoning Mix:

- 4 teaspoons (20 mL) dry buttermilk powder
- 1 teaspoon (5 mL) dry dill weed
- ½ teaspoon (2 mL) onion powder
- ¼ teaspoon (1 mL) garlic powder
- ¼ teaspoon (1 mL) paprika
- Pinch cayenne

- 4 cups (1 L) mixed cereals, pretzels and/or crackers (mini shredded wheat, nonfat low-sodium pretzels, corn squares, toasted oat cereal, oyster crackers)
- Butter-flavored nonstick vegetable cooking spray

4 servings

Combine seasoning mix ingredients in large plastic food-storage bag. Set aside. Spread cereal mixture on large baking sheet. Spray well with cooking spray (about 8 seconds). Stir mixture. Spray again (about 5 seconds). Pour mixture into bag. Seal bag. Shake to coat cereal mixture.

FRUITY POPCORN MIX

- 7 cups (1.75 L) unsalted air-popped popcorn
- 1½ cups (375 mL) miniature knot pretzels
- 2 tablespoons (25 mL) margarine
- ⅓ cup (75 mL) light corn syrup
- 1 pkg. (3 oz./85 g) fruit-flavored gelatin powder (any flavor)
- ¼ teaspoon (1 mL) baking soda

8 servings

1 Heat oven to 200°F/100°C. Spray 15½" x 10½" (40 x 25 cm) jelly roll pan with nonstick vegetable cooking spray. Combine popcorn and pretzels in prepared pan. Set aside.

2 Melt margarine over low heat in 2-quart (2 L) saucepan. Stir in corn syrup. Bring to full boil over medium heat. Remove from heat. Add gelatin. Stir until gelatin is dissolved. Add baking soda. Mix well. Immediately pour over popcorn mixture, stirring to coat.

3 Spread mixture evenly in pan. Bake for 1 hour, stirring after every 15 minutes. Remove from oven. Stir. Cool completely, stirring frequently to break popcorn mix apart. Store in airtight container in cool place.

ANIMAL CRACKERS

- 1½ cups (375 mL) whole wheat or graham flour
- ½ cup (125 mL) all-purpose flour
- ¼ cup (50 mL) sugar
- 2 tablespoons (25 mL) ground cinnamon
- ½ teaspoon (2 mL) baking powder
- ½ teaspoon (2 mL) baking soda
- ¼ teaspoon (1 mL) salt
- ⅓ cup (75 mL) light corn syrup
- ⅓ cup (75 mL) plain nonfat or low-fat yogurt
- 3 tablespoons (50 mL) vegetable oil
- ½ teaspoon (2 mL) vanilla

18 servings

1 Heat oven to 350°F/180°C. Spray baking sheets with nonstick vegetable cooking spray. Set aside. In large mixing bowl, combine flours, sugar, cinnamon, baking powder, baking soda and salt. In 1-cup (250 mL) measure, combine corn syrup, yogurt, oil and vanilla.

2 Add corn syrup mixture to flour mixture. Beat at low speed of electric mixer just until dry ingredients are moistened (dough will be crumbly). Form dough into ball. On lightly floured surface, knead dough for 3 to 5 minutes, or until smooth (adding additional flour as necessary to reduce stickiness). Divide dough in half. Wrap one half in plastic wrap. Set aside.

3 Roll remaining dough to ¼" (5 mm) thickness on lightly floured surface. Using 1½" (4 cm) assorted animal cookie cutters, cut shapes into dough. Place shapes 1" (2.5 cm) apart on prepared baking sheets. Repeat with remaining dough. Bake, one sheet at a time, for 7 to 9 minutes, or just until edges of crackers begin to brown.

Variation: Prepare dough as directed. Roll all dough into 16" x 8" (40 x 20 cm) rectangle (¼"/5 mm thick). Using pastry wheel or sharp knife, cut dough into 1" (2.5 cm) squares. Place squares 1" (2.5 cm) apart on prepared baking sheets. Bake, one sheet at a time, for 7 to 9 minutes, or just until edges of crackers begin to brown.

TIP: *Roll dough to ⅛" (3 mm) thickness for a crisper cracker.*

Microwaved nuts heat quickly and brown evenly. Remove from oven as soon as they start to color; they brown as they stand.

ROASTED PEANUTS

- 1 cup (250 mL) shelled raw peanuts
- 1 teaspoon (5 mL) vegetable oil

1 cup (250 mL)

Place peanuts in 9" (23 cm) pie plate. Add oil, tossing to coat nuts. Microwave at High 5 to 7 minutes, or until barely light brown, stirring every 2 minutes. Peanuts may be browner on inside and will continue to roast after they are removed from oven. Cool on double thickness of paper towels. Salt, if desired.

SAVORY SNACK MIX

- 3 cups (750 mL) thin pretzel sticks
- 1 cup (250 mL) Spanish peanuts
- 2 tablespoons (25 mL) butter or margarine
- 2 teaspoons (10 mL) Worcestershire sauce
- ½ teaspoon (2 mL) chili powder
- Pinch garlic salt
- ¼ teaspoon (1 mL) red pepper sauce

4 cups (1 L)

In large bowl, combine pretzels and peanuts. Set aside. In 1-cup (250 mL) measure, combine butter, Worcestershire sauce, chili powder, garlic salt and red pepper sauce. Microwave at High 45 to 60 seconds, or until butter melts. Stir. Pour over pretzels and peanuts, tossing to coat. Microwave at High 3 to 5 minutes, or until mixture is hot and butter is absorbed, stirring after each minute. Spread on paper towels to cool.

Variation: Substitute ½ cup (125 mL) cashews for ½ cup (125 mL) of the Spanish peanuts.

SUN-DRIED TOMATO & GARLIC SPREAD

- 1 whole bulb garlic
- 1 cup (250 mL) boiling water
- 2 oz. (60 g) dry-pack sun-dried tomatoes (about 1 cup/250 mL)
- 2 tablespoons (25 mL) pine nuts, toasted*
- 2 tablespoons (25 mL) shredded fresh Parmesan cheese
- 2 teaspoons (10 mL) snipped fresh basil leaves
- 1 fresh baguette (8 oz./250 g), cut into 24 slices, toasted

8 servings

To toast pine nuts, cook in a dry skillet over medium-low heat, stirring frequently to prevent burning.

1 Heat oven to 350°F/180°C. Remove outer peel of garlic bulb without separating cloves. Cut off and discard top 1/3 of each clove. Place garlic in center of 12" x 9" (30 x 23 cm) sheet of foil. Fold opposite edges of foil together, crimping edges to seal. Place foil packet on rack in oven. Bake for 1 hour. Let packet stand 10 to 15 minutes, or until garlic is cool enough to handle. Squeeze soft garlic from each clove peel. Set roasted garlic aside.

2 Meanwhile, in small mixing bowl, combine water and tomatoes. Let stand 30 minutes. Drain, reserving liquid. In food processor or blender, combine tomatoes, roasted garlic, pine nuts, Parmesan cheese and basil. Process until smooth, adding enough of reserved liquid to make smooth spread. Transfer spread to small mixing bowl. Cover with plastic wrap. Refrigerate overnight to blend flavors. To serve, spread tomato and garlic spread evenly on toast slices.

LAYERED
CHEESE LOAF →

- ½ pkg. (8 oz./250 g) cream cheese
- 2 tablespoons (25 mL) butter or margarine
- ½ teaspoon (2 mL) dried basil leaves or dry mustard
- 3 slices Colby cheese, 3½" x 3½" (9 x 9 cm)
- 3 slices brick cheese, 3½" x 3½" (9 x 9 cm)
- 1 slice (¾ oz./21 g) salami
- 2 tablespoons (25 mL) snipped fresh parsley

One ¾-lb. (375 g) loaf

Place cream cheese and butter in small bowl. Microwave at 30% (Medium-Low) 15 to 60 seconds, or until softened, rotating every 15 seconds. Blend in basil. On serving plate, layer cheese slices and salami, spreading about 2 teaspoons (10 mL) of cream cheese mixture between each layer. Use remaining cream cheese mixture to spread on top and sides. Sprinkle with parsley, pressing gently to coat loaf. Refrigerate at least 3 hours before serving. Serve with crackers, if desired.

CHEESE SAUCE

- 2 tablespoons (25 mL) butter or margarine
- Pinch salt
- 2 tablespoons (25 mL) all-purpose flour
- 1 cup (250 mL) milk
- 1 cup (250 mL) shredded cheese (jalapeño, caraway, onion, garlic or dill)

1½ cups (375 mL)

Place butter and salt in 4-cup (1 L) measure. Microwave at High 30 to 45 seconds, or until butter melts. Blend in flour; stir in milk. Microwave at High 3 to 4 minutes, or until thickened, stirring with fork or wire whip after each minute. Add cheese, stirring until melted. Serve hot over cooked vegetables, or cover and chill to serve as a dip for raw vegetables.

HOT ARTICHOKE DIP

- 6 whole wheat pitas
- ½ to ¾ cup (125 to 175 mL) skim milk, divided
- 1 teaspoon (5 mL) olive oil
- ½ cup (125 mL) finely chopped leek
- 2 cloves garlic, minced
- 1 tablespoon (15 mL) all-purpose flour
- 1 can (14 oz./398 mL) artichoke hearts in water, rinsed, drained and coarsely chopped
- ½ cup (125 mL) plain nonfat or low-fat yogurt
- ½ cup (125 mL) low-fat cream cheese
- 2 tablespoons (25 mL) snipped fresh parsley
- ½ teaspoon (2 mL) Worcestershire sauce
- Pinch cayenne
- Pinch freshly ground pepper

1 Heat oven to 350°F/180°C. Cut each pita into 8 wedges. Arrange wedges on large baking sheet. Bake for 11 to 13 minutes, or until wedges are crisp. Set wedges aside.

2 Combine ½ cup (125 mL) milk and the oil in 2-quart (2 L) saucepan. Heat over medium heat until bubbly. Stir in leek and garlic. Cook for 2 to 3 minutes, or until leek is tender, stirring frequently. Stir in flour. Cook for 2 minutes, stirring constantly.

3 Reduce heat to low. Stir in remaining ingredients, except remaining milk. Cook for 4 to 5 minutes, or until dip is heated through, stirring frequently. Stir in just enough of remaining ¼ cup (50 mL) milk for desired consistency. Garnish with additional snipped fresh parsley, if desired. Serve dip with baked pita wedges.

12 servings

HUMMUS

- 2 cans (15 oz/426 mL each) garbanzo beans, rinsed and drained
- ¼ cup (50 mL) fresh lemon juice
- 2 tablespoons (25 mL) snipped fresh parsley
- 2 tablespoons (25 mL) water
- 1 tablespoon (15 mL) extra-virgin olive oil
- 2 cloves garlic, minced
- ¼ teaspoon (1 mL) cayenne
- 5 whole wheat pitas, each cut into 8 wedges

20 servings

1 Combine all ingredients, except pitas, in food processor or blender. Process until smooth. Transfer hummus to serving dish.

2 Place dish in center of serving plate. Arrange pita wedges around dish. Garnish hummus with parsley sprig, if desired.

TIP: *For a thinner hummus, add additional water, 1 tablespoon (15 mL) at a time, while processing, until desired consistency is reached.*

185

SEASONED CHIPS WITH LONE STAR CAVIAR

- 2 medium tomatoes, seeded and chopped (2 cups/500 mL)
- 1 can (15 oz./426 mL) black-eyed peas, rinsed and drained
- 1 medium green pepper, chopped (1⅓ cups/325 mL)
- ½ cup (125 mL) sliced green onions
- ½ cup (125 mL) snipped fresh cilantro leaves
- 2 tablespoons (25 mL) lemon juice
- 2 serrano peppers, seeded and finely chopped
- 1 to 2 jalapeño peppers, seeded and finely chopped
- 2 cloves garlic, minced
- 2¼ teaspoons (11 mL) ground cumin, divided
- ½ teaspoon (2 mL) salt
- 2 teaspoons (10 mL) chili powder
- 1 teaspoon (5 mL) garlic powder
- 16 whole wheat flour tortillas (6"/15 cm)

16 servings

1 Combine tomatoes, peas, green pepper, onions, cilantro, juice, serrano peppers, jalapeño peppers, garlic, ¼ teaspoon (1 mL) cumin and the salt in medium mixing bowl. Cover with plastic wrap. Chill Lone Star Caviar at least 4 hours to blend flavors, stirring occasionally.

2 Heat oven to 375°F/ 190°C. In large plastic food-storage bag, combine remaining 2 teaspoons (10 mL) cumin, the chili powder and garlic powder. Set aside. Spray both sides of each tortilla with non-stick vegetable cooking spray. Cut each tortilla into 8 wedges. Place wedges in bag. Secure bag. Shake to coat.

3 Arrange 32 wedges in single layer on baking sheet. Bake for 7 to 9 minutes, or until light golden brown. Repeat with remaining tortilla wedges. Cool completely. Serve chips with Lone Star Caviar.

MICROWAVE TIP: *Arrange 16 seasoned wedges in single layer on paper-towel-lined plate. Microwave at High 4 to 5 minutes, or until crisp, rotating plate once. Loosen chips from paper towel immediately. Repeat with remaining tortilla wedges. Continue as directed.*

LAYERED BEAN DIP

Garbanzo Bean Layer:

- 1 can (15 oz./426 mL) garbanzo beans, rinsed and drained
- 1 to 2 tablespoons (15 to 25 mL) fresh lemon juice
- 1 tablespoon (15 mL) olive oil
- 2 cloves garlic, minced
- ½ teaspoon (2 mL) ground cumin
- ¼ teaspoon (1 mL) salt

Black Bean Layer:

- 1 can (15 oz./426 mL) black beans, rinsed and drained
- ½ cup (125 mL) chopped freshly roasted red pepper or roasted red peppers in marinade, rinsed and drained
- 1 tablespoon (15 mL) snipped fresh cilantro
- 1 tablespoon (15 mL) finely chopped green onion

Yogurt Layer:

- 1 cup (250 mL) nonfat yogurt cheese
- 1 to 2 tablespoons (15 to 25 mL) snipped fresh cilantro
- 2 to 3 teaspoons (10 to 15 mL) snipped fresh mint leaves
- 1 to 2 teaspoons (5 to 10 mL) fresh lemon juice

- 1 cup (250 mL) finely shredded lettuce
- 1 Roma tomato, chopped
- 1 tablespoon (15 mL) chopped black or Kalamata olives (optional)

12 servings

1 Combine garbanzo bean layer ingredients in food processor or blender. Process until smooth. Spread the mixture evenly in bottom of 9" (23 cm) pie plate. Set aside.

2 Combine black bean layer ingredients in medium mixing bowl. Spread mixture evenly over garbanzo bean layer to within 1" (2.5 cm) of edge. In small mixing bowl, combine yogurt layer ingredients. Spoon yogurt mixture evenly over black bean layer. Cover with plastic wrap. Chill at least 1 hour.

3 Arrange lettuce and tomato around edges of dip. Garnish with olives. Serve dip with pita bread, chips or raw vegetable sticks, if desired.

TIP: To roast fresh peppers, first pierce the skin several times with a fork. If roasting over a gas burner, spear pepper with long-handled fork and hold over flame, turning until skin is blackened. If using a broiler, place peppers on broiler pan as close to heat as possible, turning until skin is blackened. Place peppers in closed paper bag for about 10 minutes; then peel and use.

SPINACH-FILLED BREAD

- 1 loaf (16 oz./500 g) round crusty bread
- 2 pkgs. (10 oz./300 g each) frozen chopped spinach
- 2 pkgs. (8 oz./250 g each) cream cheese
- 3 tablespoons (50 mL) milk
- 1 teaspoon (5 mL) lemon juice
- ½ teaspoon (2 mL) salt
- Pinch pepper (optional)
- Pinch ground nutmeg

8 servings

Advance preparation:
Prepare filling 1 day ahead; refrigerate. To serve, microwave filling at High 30 seconds to 1¼ minutes, or until warm. Fill bread. Microwave as directed.

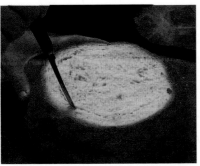

1 Cut 1½" to 2" (4 to 5 cm) slice from top of bread. Cut a circle 1½" (4 cm) from the outer edge of crust.

2 Remove the center, leaving at least 2" (5 cm) of bread on bottom. Cut center and top into pieces for dipping. Set aside.

3 Place packages of spinach in microwave oven. Microwave at High 4½ to 6½ minutes, or until heated, rearranging once. Drain, pressing out excess liquid.

4 Place cream cheese in medium bowl. Microwave at High 30 to 45 seconds, or until softened. Mix in remaining ingredients.

5 Spoon into bread shell. Place on paper-towel-lined plate.

6 Microwave at High 45 seconds to 1¼ minutes, or until bread is warm. Serve with bread pieces for dipping.

FRESH ZUCCHINI DIP (a)

- 1½ cups (375 mL) shredded zucchini (1 medium)
- ¼ cup (50 mL) finely chopped onion
- ¼ cup (50 mL) finely chopped green pepper
- 1 tablespoon (15 mL) butter or margarine
- ¼ cup (50 mL) mayonnaise or salad dressing
- ¾ cup (175 mL) dairy sour cream
- 1 teaspoon (5 mL) garlic salt
- 1 teaspoon (5 mL) Worcestershire sauce
- Pinch cayenne

2 cups (500 mL)

Place shredded zucchini between layers of paper towel. Press to remove excess moisture. In 1-qt. (1 L) casserole, combine onion, green pepper and butter. Microwave at High 1 to 3 minutes, or until onion is tender. Stir in zucchini and remaining ingredients. Chill at least 2 hours.

CHIPPED BEEF DIP (b)

- ¼ cup (50 mL) chopped green onion
- 1 clove garlic, minced
- 1 tablespoon (15 mL) butter or margarine
- 1 pkg. (8 oz./250 g) cream cheese
- ½ cup (125 mL) dairy sour cream
- ¼ cup (50 mL) half-and-half or milk
- 1 pkg. (2½ oz./75 g) dried beef, chopped
- 2 tablespoons (25 mL) snipped fresh parsley
- 1 tablespoon (15 mL) prepared horseradish
- 1 tablespoon (15 mL) lemon juice

About 2 cups (500 mL)

In 1-qt. (1 L) casserole, combine green onion, garlic and butter. Microwave at High 30 to 60 seconds, or until butter melts. Add cream cheese. Microwave at High 45 seconds to 1½ minutes, or until cream cheese is softened. Mix in remaining ingredients. Chill at least 2 hours or overnight.

JALAPEÑO CHEESE DIP (c)

- 1 medium onion, chopped
- 1 tablespoon (15 mL) vegetable oil
- 2 cups (500 mL) shredded Monterey Jack cheese
- 2 cups (500 mL) shredded Cheddar cheese
- ½ cup (125 mL) half-and-half
- 2 tablespoons (25 mL) chopped jalapeño peppers

10 to 12 servings

Place onion and oil in 1½-qt. (1.5 L) casserole. Cover. Microwave at High 2 to 3 minutes, or until onion is tender. Stir in remaining ingredients. Reduce power to 50% (Medium). Microwave 3 to 6 minutes, or until heated and smooth, stirring every 2 minutes. Serve with taco chips, if desired.

CHEESE BALL

- ¼ cup (50 mL) chopped green pepper
- ¼ cup (50 mL) chopped green onion
- 1 teaspoon (5 mL) butter or margarine
- 1 pkg. (8 oz./250 g) cream cheese
- 2 cups (500 mL) shredded Cheddar cheese
- 1 pkg. (4 oz./125 g) blue cheese, crumbled
- 1 tablespoon (15 mL) chopped pimiento
- 2 teaspoons (10 mL) prepared horseradish
- 2 teaspoons (10 mL) Worcestershire sauce
- 1 clove garlic, minced
- ½ cup (125 mL) chopped pecans

10 to 12 servings

In small bowl, combine green pepper, onion and butter; cover. Microwave at High 30 to 45 seconds, or until vegetables are tender-crisp, stirring once. Place cream cheese in large bowl. Reduce power to 50% (Medium). Microwave 1 to 1½ minutes, or until softened. Stir in vegetables and remaining ingredients except pecans. Shape into ball. Wrap in plastic wrap. Chill 2 to 3 hours. Unwrap; roll in pecans. Serve with assorted crackers, if desired.

CURRY DIP (d)

- 1 pkg. (8 oz./250 g) cream cheese
- 3 tablespoons (50 mL) milk
- ½ teaspoon (2 mL) curry powder
- ½ teaspoon (2 mL) garlic salt
- 1 cup (250 mL) dairy sour cream
- 8 to 10 cups (2 to 2.5 L) raw vegetables (carrot and celery sticks, cauliflowerets, broccoli flowerets, zucchini strips)

6 to 8 servings

Place cream cheese in small bowl. Microwave at High 20 to 45 seconds, or until softened. Mix in milk, curry powder and garlic salt. Microwave at High 30 to 60 seconds, or until warm. Stir to blend. Mix in sour cream. Serve with raw vegetables.

Advance preparation: *Prepare the day before or the morning of the party. Cover and refrigerate. Before serving, microwave dip at High 45 seconds to 1½ minutes, or until softened, stirring once or twice. Add 1 to 2 teaspoons (5 to 10 mL) milk if needed for smoother consistency.*

CHEESY SEAFOOD SNACK DIP

- 2 pkgs. (8 oz./250 g each) cream cheese, cut into 1" (2.5 cm) cubes
- ¾ cup (175 mL) cocktail sauce
- 1 can (6 oz./170 g) crab meat, rinsed, drained and cartilage removed
- 1 can (4 oz./113 g) medium shrimp, rinsed and drained
- 2 tablespoons (25 mL) sliced green onion

6 to 8 servings

Arrange cream cheese cubes in single layer on 12" (30 cm) round platter. Microwave at 50% (Medium) 1½ to 3 minutes, or until cheese softens, rotating platter once or twice. Spread cream cheese into even layer on platter, to within 1" (2.5 cm) of edges. Top evenly with cocktail sauce. Sprinkle with remaining ingredients. Serve dip with assorted crackers.

MEXICAN SNACK DIP

- 2 pkgs. (8 oz./250 g each) cream cheese, cut into 1" (2.5 cm) cubes
- 1 cup (250 mL) refried beans
- ¾ cup (175 mL) taco sauce
- 1 cup (250 mL) shredded Cheddar cheese
- ½ cup (125 mL) seeded chopped tomato
- ¼ cup (50 mL) sliced black olives
- 2 tablespoons (25 mL) sliced green onion

6 to 8 servings

1 Arrange cream cheese cubes in single layer on 12" (30 cm) platter. Microwave at 50% (Medium) 1½ to 3 minutes, or until cheese softens, rotating platter once or twice.

2 Spread cream cheese into even layer on platter, to within 1" (2.5 cm) of edges. Spread refried beans in even layer over the cream cheese, to within ½" (1 cm) of edges. Top with taco sauce. Sprinkle with remaining ingredients. Serve snack platter with corn or tortilla chips.

CHEESE DIP ↑
IN PEPPER

1 In small mixing bowl, microwave 1 pkg. (3 oz./ 85 g) cream cheese at High 15 to 30 seconds, or until softened. Add ⅓ cup (75 mL) pasteurized process cheese spread and 2 tablespoons (25 mL) sliced green onion. Mix well and set aside.

2 Cut thin slice from top of large pepper (red, green or yellow). Set top aside. Remove and discard core and seeds. Spoon cheese mixture into pepper. Place pepper in a 6-oz. (175 mL) custard cup. Microwave at 70% (Medium High) 2½ to 4 minutes, or until pepper is warm and cheese mixture is melted, rotating 2 or 3 times. Stir cheese. If desired, place pepper in the center of the raw vegetable platter to serve. Replace top of pepper, if desired.

SAVORY
PEPPER WEDGES

- 4 teaspoons (20 mL) butter or margarine
- 1½ cups (375 mL) cooked rice
- ½ cup (125 mL) grated carrot
- ¼ cup (50 mL) finely chopped zucchini
- ¼ teaspoon (1 mL) dried thyme leaves
- ¼ teaspoon (1 mL) salt
- Pinch pepper
- 1 medium red pepper
- 1 medium yellow pepper

4 servings

1 In small mixing bowl, microwave butter at High 45 seconds to 1 minute, or until melted. Add remaining ingredients, except red and yellow peppers. Set aside.

2 Remove and discard core and seeds. Cut each pepper lengthwise into quarters and fill pepper quarters evenly with rice mixture.

3 Arrange pepper wedges on plate. Cover with wax paper. Microwave at High 5 to 7 minutes, or until rice mixture is hot and peppers are tender-crisp, rotating plate once. If desired, top peppers with snipped parsley to serve.

SEAFOOD & AVOCADO DIP ↑

- 1 large ripe avocado
- Lemon juice
- 1 pkg. (3 oz./85 g) cream cheese
- 1 tablespoon (15 mL) sliced green onion
- 1 small clove garlic, minced
- ½ cup (125 mL) shredded seafood sticks or rinsed and drained crab meat
- 1 teaspoon (5 mL) lime juice
- ¼ teaspoon (1 mL) Worcestershire sauce
- Pinch cayenne

6 to 8 servings

1 Cut avocado in half lengthwise and remove the pit. With small spoon, scoop out pulp, leaving ¼" (5 mm) shell. Chop avocado pulp and set aside. Brush surfaces of avocado shells with lemon juice. Set aside.

2 In small mixing bowl, place cream cheese, green onion and garlic. Microwave at High 15 to 30 seconds, or until cheese softens. Mix in chopped avocado pulp and remaining ingredients. Stuff seafood mixture evenly into avocado shells. Place one shell on plate. Microwave at High 30 seconds to 1 minute, or until dip is warm. Repeat with second avocado shell if needed. Serve dip with corn or tortilla chips, or assorted crackers.

TIP: Dip is conveniently served in its own natural container. Microwave one avocado shell, and refrigerate second shell until more warm dip is needed.

MIXED FRUIT WARMER →

- 4 cups (1 L) cranberry-raspberry drink
- 2 cups (500 mL) water
- 1 can (6 oz./170 mL)* frozen orange juice concentrate, defrosted
- ⅓ cup (75 mL) packed brown sugar
- 8 thin orange slices
- 1 stick cinnamon

8 servings

Combine all ingredients in 3-quart (3 L) saucepan. Stir until sugar is dissolved. Cook over Medium-High heat for 10 to 14 minutes, or until mixture is hot and flavors are blended, stirring occasionally. (Do not boil.) Remove and discard cinnamon stick before serving.

MICROWAVE TIP: In 8-cup (2 L) measure, combine all ingredients. Stir until sugar is dissolved. Microwave at High 10 to 16 minutes, or until mixture is hot and flavors are blended, stirring once or twice.

*If 6-oz. (170 mL) can not available, use half of 12-oz. (341 mL) can.

BEVERAGES

MEXICAN HOT COCOA

- ⅔ cup (150 mL) sugar
- ½ cup (125 mL) unsweetened cocoa
- ½ cup (125 mL) hot water
- 4 cups (1 L) skim milk
- 2 sticks cinnamon
- 1 teaspoon (5 mL) vanilla

5 servings

1 Combine sugar and cocoa in 2-quart (2 L) saucepan. Add water. Stir with whisk until smooth. Cook over medium heat for 3 to 5 minutes, or just until edges of mixture begin to bubble, stirring constantly.

2 Blend in milk. Add cinnamon sticks. Cook for additional 10 to 12 minutes, or until mixture is hot, stirring frequently. (Do not boil.) Remove from heat. Stir in vanilla.

TIP: *For stronger cinnamon flavor, let cocoa stand additional 10 minutes.*

Serving suggestion: *Place 1 stick cinnamon in each serving glass and garnish with a dollop of nonfat whipped topping.*

TEXAS MARY

- 1 can (46 oz./1.3 L) no-salt-added tomato juice
- 1 can (11½ oz./327 mL) vegetable juice
- ¼ to ½ cup (50 to 125 mL) fresh lime juice
- 2 tablespoons (25 mL) Worcestershire sauce
- 1½ teaspoons (7 mL) red pepper sauce
- 1 teaspoon (5 mL) prepared horseradish
- 1 teaspoon (5 mL) ground cumin
- ½ teaspoon (2 mL) freshly ground pepper
- Pinch celery seed, crushed
- 8 fresh asparagus spears, trimmed (optional)

8 servings

1 Combine all ingredients, except asparagus, in 8-cup (2 L) measure. Add asparagus spears to juice mixture. Cover with plastic wrap. Refrigerate overnight.

2 Pack serving glasses with ice. Pour mixture over ice. Add 1 asparagus spear to each glass.

RUSSIAN TEA

- 1 teaspoon (5 mL) ground cloves
- 1 teaspoon (5 mL) ground cinnamon
- 8 cups (2 L) water
- ½ cup (125 mL) sugar
- 2 single-serving black tea bags
- ¼ cup (50 mL) frozen orange juice concentrate, defrosted
- ¼ cup (50 mL) fresh lemon juice

8 servings

1 Cut 4-inch (10 cm) square cheesecloth. Place cloves and cinnamon in center of square. Bring corners of cheesecloth together to form bag. Secure spice bag with string.

2 Combine spice bag, water, sugar and tea bags in 3-quart (3 L) saucepan. Bring to boil over high heat, stirring to dissolve sugar. Remove from heat. Let stand for 5 minutes. Remove and discard spice bag and tea bags. Stir in concentrate and juice. Serve immediately. Serve with cinnamon sticks, if desired.

IRISH COFFEE

- ¼ cup (50 mL) packed light brown sugar
- 7 teaspoons (35 mL) instant coffee crystals
- 5½ cups (1.375 L) hot water
- 1¼ to 1½ cups (300 to 375 mL) Irish whiskey
- Sweetened whipped cream

6 to 8 servings

In 2-qt. (2 L) measure or bowl, combine brown sugar, coffee crystals and hot water; cover. Microwave at High 5 to 8 minutes, or until very hot. Stir to dissolve brown sugar. Stir in whiskey. Pour into individual cups. Top with sweetened whipped cream.

CAPPUCCINO FOR TWO

- 2 to 3 teaspoons (10 to 15 mL) packed light brown sugar
- 2 teaspoons (10 mL) instant coffee crystals
- 1⅓ cups (325 mL) hot water
- ¼ cup (50 mL) orange liqueur
- Sweetened whipped cream

2 servings

In 2-cup (500 mL) measure, combine brown sugar, coffee crystals, and hot water. Cover. Microwave at High 2 to 4 minutes, or until hot. Stir to dissolve sugar. Stir in liqueur. Pour into individual cups. Top with sweetened whipped cream.

CAPPUCCINO FOR EIGHT

- 2 to 3 tablespoons (25 to 50 mL) packed light brown sugar
- 2 tablespoons (25 mL) instant coffee crystals
- 4 cups (1 L) hot water
- ¾ cup (175 mL) orange liqueur
- Sweetened whipped cream

8 servings

In 1½- to 2-qt. (1.5 to 2 L) measure or bowl, combine brown sugar, coffee crystals and hot water. Cover. Microwave at High 4 to 6½ minutes, or until hot. Stir to dissolve sugar. Stir in liqueur. Pour into individual cups. Top with sweetened whipped cream.

ORANGE LIQUEUR

- 3 oranges
- 1 cup (250 mL) sugar
- 1 stick cinnamon
- 2 cups (500 mL) brandy

About 3 cups (750 mL)

1 Remove the peel from one orange with vegetable peeler or zester. Do not include white membrane. Cut oranges in half; squeeze juice. (Yields 1 cup/250 mL). In 4-cup (1 L) measure, combine orange peel, orange juice, sugar and cinnamon. Microwave at High 3 to 4 minutes, or until boiling, stirring after each minute. Boil 30 seconds. Watch closely; stir if necessary to prevent boilover. Cool to room temperature.

2 Remove cinnamon stick. Strain cooled juice mixture through cheesecloth. Add brandy to the strained liquid. Pour into bottle; cap. Let stand in a cool, dark place 1 month before serving. Shake bottle occasionally to mix.

CREME DE MENTHE

- 1½ cups (375 mL) sugar
- 1 cup (250 mL) water
- 1½ cups (375 mL) vodka or gin
- 1 teaspoon (5 mL) mint flavor
- ¼ teaspoon (1 mL) green food coloring

About 4 cups (1 L)

1 In 4-cup (1 L) measure or large bowl, combine sugar and water. Microwave at High 4 to 5 minutes, or until boiling. Boil 5 minutes. Watch closely; stir if necessary to prevent boilover.

2 Cool to room temperature. Skim any foam from top. Stir in remaining ingredients.

3 Pour into bottle; cap. Let stand in a cool, dark place 1 month before serving. Shake bottle occasionally to mix.

ANISE LIQUEUR

- 1½ cups (375 mL) light corn syrup
- ½ cup (125 mL) water
- ¼ teaspoon (1 mL) instant unflavored, unsweetened tea powder
- 1½ cups (375 mL) vodka
- ¾ teaspoon (4 mL) anise extract
- ½ teaspoon (2 mL) vanilla
- 2 drops yellow food coloring

3½ cups (875 mL)

1 In 4-cup (1 L) measure or large bowl, combine corn syrup, water and tea powder. Microwave at High 4 to 5½ minutes, or until boiling. Watch closely; stir if necessary to prevent boilover. Cool to room temperature.

2 Skim any foam from top. Stir in vodka, anise extract, vanilla and yellow food coloring. Pour into bottle; cap. Let stand in a cool, dark place 1 month before serving. Shake bottle occasionally to mix.

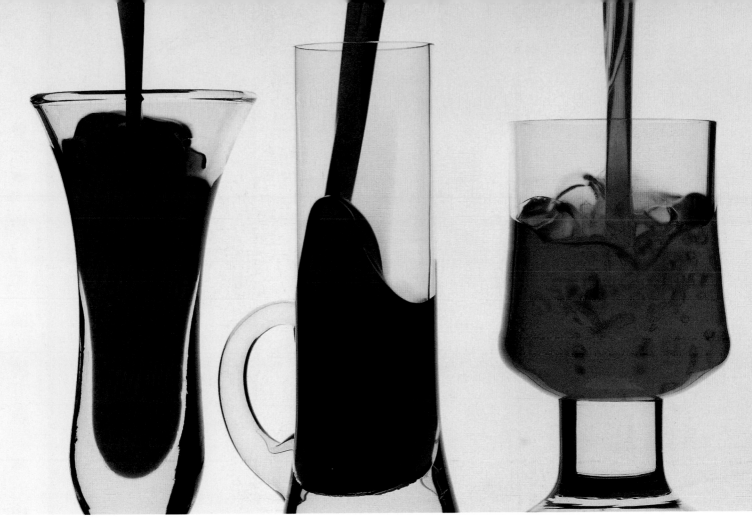

RASPBERRY LIQUEUR

- 2 pkgs. (10 oz./300 g each) frozen raspberries in syrup
- 1½ cups (375 mL) sugar
- 1½ cups (375 mL) vodka

3 cups (750 mL)

1 Remove raspberries from packages and place in large bowl. Microwave at 50% (Medium) 4 to 5 minutes, or until partially defrosted. Gently separate with fork. Let stand to complete defrosting. Drain juice into 8-cup (2 L) measure or large bowl. Set raspberries aside.

2 Add sugar to juice. Microwave at High 3 to 5 minutes, or until sugar dissolves and mixture boils, stirring every 2 minutes. Cool to room temperature. Skim any foam from top. Add reserved raspberries and vodka. Pour into bottle; cap. Let stand in a cool, dark place 1 month before serving. Shake bottle occasionally to mix. Strain through cheesecloth before serving. Serve raspberries over ice cream.

COFFEE LIQUEUR

- 1½ cups (375 mL) sugar
- 1 cup (250 mL) water
- ¼ cup (50 mL) instant coffee crystals
- 1½ cups (375 mL) vodka
- 1 vanilla bean or 1 teaspoon (5 mL) vanilla extract

2½ cups (625 mL)

1 In 4-cup (1 L) measure or large bowl, combine sugar and water. Microwave at High 4 to 5 minutes, or until boiling. Boil 5 minutes. Watch closely; stir if necessary to prevent boilover.

2 Stir in coffee crystals until dissolved. Cool to room temperature. Skim any foam from top. Add vodka and vanilla bean.

3 Pour into bottle; cap. Let stand in a cool, dark place 1 month before serving. Shake bottle occasionally to mix.

APRICOT BRANDY

- 1 pkg. (6 oz./175 g) dried apricots
- 1½ cups (375 mL) white wine
- 1 cup (250 mL) sugar
- 1 cup (250 mL) brandy

About 3 cups (750 mL)

1 If desired, chop apricots. In 4-cup (1 L) measure, combine apricots, wine and sugar. Cover with plastic wrap. Microwave at High 4 to 6 minutes, or until sugar dissolves and mixture boils, stirring every 2 minutes. Cool to room temperature. Skim any foam from top. Add brandy.

2 Pour into bottle; cap. Let stand in a cool, dark place 1 month before serving. Shake bottle occasionally to mix. Strain through cheesecloth before serving. Serve apricots over ice cream.

TIP: *Serve liqueurs in Chocolate Liqueur Cups, page 269; stir into softened ice cream, or give as gifts.*

Christmas
Cookies

CHRISTMAS COOKIE BASICS

This collection of Christmas cookies has recipes from a variety of countries. Austrian bakers get the credit for creating rich, buttery Florentines. These chocolate-glazed specialties are traditionally a mixture of honey, butter, sugar and candied fruit. Pfeffernüsse, or "peppernuts," are spicy cookies that are served at Christmastime in Germany. And Fattigmands are a crispy fried Scandinavian specialty, also a Christmas favorite. Italian Biscotti can be served any time. These intensely flavored cookies are twice-baked, making them crunchy and perfect for dipping in coffee or a sweet dessert wine.

Some of these recipes require specialized equipment, which is available at specialty cooking or kitchen stores.

Madeleine pans: These pans have special scallop-shell indentations for the cookies' signature look.

Cookie cutters: In a few recipes, we call for special cookie cutters. These can be found in many stores, or you can make your own.

Madeleine pan

Rosette iron

Special cookie cutters

Rosette irons: A heatproof handle is attached to one or two long metal rods. Various decorative forms can be attached to the rods. The forms are dipped in batter, then lowered into hot oil.

Krumkake and pizzelle irons: Krumkake and pizzelles are baked on the stovetop in hinged irons that leave designs on the thinly pressed cookies. Freshly made krumkake are shaped around a special cone. Pizzelles are served flat.

Krumkake iron

Krumkake cone

Pizzelle iron

← SOUR CREAM CUTOUTS

- 2 cups (500 mL) sugar
- 1 cup (250 mL) sour cream
- 3 eggs
- ½ cup (125 mL) butter or margarine, softened
- ½ cup (125 mL) vegetable shortening
- 5½ cups (1.375 L) all-purpose flour
- 2 teaspoons (10 mL) baking powder
- 2 teaspoons (10 mL) baking soda
- 1 teaspoon (5 mL) vanilla
- 1 teaspoon (5 mL) almond extract
- ¼ teaspoon (1 mL) salt
- Decorator Frosting (page 242)

About 10 dozen cookies

1 In large mixing bowl, combine sugar, sour cream, eggs, butter and shortening. Beat at medium speed of electric mixer until light and fluffy. Add flour, baking powder, baking soda, vanilla, almond extract and salt. Beat at low speed until soft dough forms. Cover with plastic wrap. Chill 1 to 2 hours, or until firm.

2 Heat oven to 350°F/180°C. On well-floured surface, roll dough to ¼" (5 mm) thickness. Using 3" (8 cm) cookie cutters, cut desired shapes into dough. Place shapes 2" (5 cm) apart on ungreased cookie sheets. Bake for 6 to 8 minutes, or until edges are light golden brown. Prepare frosting as directed. Decorate cookies as desired. Let dry completely before storing.

SPECIAL-OCCASION SUGAR COOKIES

- 1 cup (250 mL) sugar
- ¾ cup (175 mL) butter or margarine, softened
- 1 egg
- 3 tablespoons (50 mL) whipping cream
- 1 teaspoon (5 mL) vanilla
- 1 teaspoon (5 mL) almond extract
- 3 cups (750 mL) all-purpose flour
- 1½ teaspoons (7 mL) baking powder
- ½ teaspoon (2 mL) salt
- Granulated sugar
- Decorator Frosting (page 242)

5½ dozen cookies

1 In large mixing bowl, combine 1 cup (250 mL) sugar, the butter, egg, whipping cream, vanilla and almond extract. Beat at medium speed of electric mixer until light and fluffy. Add flour, baking powder and salt. Beat at low speed until soft dough forms. Cover with plastic wrap. Chill 1 to 2 hours, or until firm.

2 Heat oven to 400°F/200°C. On floured surface, roll dough to ¼" (5 mm) thickness. Using 3" (8 cm) cookie cutters, cut desired shapes into dough. Place shapes 2" (5 cm) apart on ungreased cookie sheets. Sprinkle shapes with sugar. Bake for 4 to 6 minutes, or until edges are light golden brown. Prepare frosting as directed. Decorate cookies as desired. Let dry completely before storing.

HOLIDAY MERINGUE COOKIES

- 3 egg whites
- ½ teaspoon (2 mL) white vinegar
- Pinch salt
- 1¼ cups (300 mL) sugar
- ½ teaspoon (2 mL) vanilla
- Any combination cinnamon candies, multicolored shot, chocolate-flavored candy sprinkles, etc.

About 1 dozen cookies

1 Heat oven to 300°F/150°C. Line cookie sheets with parchment paper. Set aside. In small mixing bowl, combine egg whites, vinegar and salt.

2 Beat at high speed of electric mixer until soft peaks form. Add sugar, 1 tablespoon (15 mL) at a time, beating at high speed. Beat until stiff peaks form. Beat in vanilla.

3 Fill pastry bag with meringue mixture. Using open star tip, pipe holiday designs 1" (2.5 cm) apart on prepared cookie sheets. Decorate as desired with candies, shot, sprinkles, etc.

4 Bake for 23 to 25 minutes, or until light golden brown. Cool completely before removing from parchment paper.

HOLIDAY HORNS

- ½ cup (125 mL) butter or margarine, softened
- 1 pkg. (3 oz./85 g) cream cheese, softened
- 1⅓ cups (325 mL) all-purpose flour
- 2 tablespoons (25 mL) sugar
- 1 tablespoon (15 mL) milk
- ½ teaspoon (2 mL) vanilla
- ½ cup (125 mL) favorite red jelly
- ½ cup (125 mL) finely chopped pistachios

4 dozen cookies

1 In small mixing bowl, combine butter and cream cheese. Beat at medium speed of electric mixer until light and fluffy. Add flour, sugar, milk and vanilla. Beat at low speed until soft dough forms. Cover with plastic wrap. Chill 4 to 5 hours, or until firm.

2 Heat oven to 325°F/160°C. Lightly grease cookie sheets. Set aside. Divide dough into quarters. On floured surface, roll one quarter dough to ⅛" (3 mm) thickness. Using 2" (5 cm) round cookie cutter, cut circles into dough. Place circles 2" (5 cm) apart on prepared cookie sheets.

3 Spoon ¼ teaspoon (1 mL) jelly onto center of each circle. Sprinkle ½ teaspoon (2 mL) pistachios over jelly on each circle. Lightly brush edges with water.

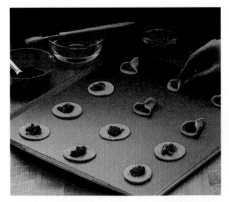

4 Fold opposite edges over filling and pinch together to form cone. Repeat with remaining dough, jelly and pistachios. Bake for 13 to 15 minutes, or until golden brown. Cool completely before storing.

TIP: *If dough becomes too sticky to roll, refrigerate until firm.*

COCOA PEPPERMINT PRETZELS →

- 1 cup (250 mL) powdered sugar
- 1 cup (250 mL) butter or margarine, softened
- 1 egg
- 1½ teaspoons (7 mL) vanilla
- 2½ cups (625 mL) all-purpose flour

- ½ cup (125 mL) unsweetened cocoa
- ½ teaspoon (2 mL) salt
- ½ cup (125 mL) vanilla baking chips
- 1 teaspoon (5 mL) vegetable shortening
- 12 hard peppermint candies, crushed

4 dozen cookies

1 In large mixing bowl, combine sugar, butter, egg and vanilla. Beat at medium speed of electric mixer until light and fluffy. Add flour, cocoa and salt. Beat at low speed until soft dough forms. Cover with plastic wrap. Chill 2 to 3 hours, or until firm.

2 Heat oven to 375°F/190°C. Shape level measuring tablespoons (15 mL) dough into 9"-long (23 cm) ropes. Twist ropes into pretzel shapes. Place pretzels 2" (5 cm) apart on ungreased cookie sheets. Bake for 8 to 9 minutes, or until set. Cool completely.

3 Line cookie sheets with wax paper. Set aside. In 1-quart (1 L) saucepan, combine chips and shortening. Melt over low heat, stirring constantly. Dip one end of each pretzel into melted chips, then roll dipped ends into crushed candies. Place pretzels on prepared cookie sheets. Let dry completely before storing.

MICROWAVE TIP: *In small mixing bowl, melt chips and shortening at 50% (Medium) for 2 to 4 minutes, stirring after every minute. Continue as directed.*

← MINT TRUFFLE COOKIES

- 1¼ cups (300 mL) sugar
- 1 cup (250 mL) butter or margarine, softened
- 2 eggs
- 1 teaspoon (5 mL) vanilla
- 2½ cups (625 mL) all-purpose flour
- ¼ cup (50 mL) unsweetened cocoa
- 1 teaspoon (5 mL) baking powder
- ¼ teaspoon (1 mL) salt

- 1 pkg. (4.67 oz./132 g) chocolate sandwich mints, coarsely chopped

Glaze

- 8 oz. (250 g) white candy coating
- 1 teaspoon (5 mL) vegetable shortening
- 1 or 2 drops green food coloring

4 dozen cookies

1 In large mixing bowl, combine sugar, butter, eggs and vanilla. Beat at medium speed of electric mixer until light and fluffy. Add flour, cocoa, baking powder and salt. Beat at low speed until soft dough forms. Stir in mints. Cover with plastic wrap. Chill 2 to 3 hours, or until firm.

2 Heat oven to 375°F/190°C. Lightly grease cookie sheets. Shape dough into 1" (2.5 cm) balls. Place balls 2" (5 cm) apart on prepared cookie sheets. Bake for 8 to 10 minutes, or until set. Cool completely.

3 In 1-quart (1 L) saucepan, combine candy coating and shortening. Melt over low heat, stirring constantly. Stir in food coloring. Pipe or drizzle glaze over cookies to form stripes. Let dry completely before storing.

MICROWAVE TIP: *In small mixing bowl, melt candy coating and shortening at 50% (Medium) for 2 to 4 minutes, stirring after every minute. Continue as directed.*

← POPPY SEED PINWHEELS

- ½ cup (125 mL) butter or margarine, softened
- ¼ cup (50 mL) granulated sugar
- 1 egg
- 1 teaspoon (5 mL) grated orange peel
- 1 teaspoon (5 mL) vanilla
- 1½ cups (375 mL) all-purpose flour
- ½ teaspoon (2 mL) baking soda
- 1 cup (250 mL) poppy seed filling, divided
- Powdered sugar (optional)

4 dozen cookies

1 In large mixing bowl, combine butter, granulated sugar, egg, peel and vanilla. Beat at medium speed of electric mixer until light and fluffy. Add flour and bak-ing soda. Beat at low speed until soft dough forms. Divide dough in half. Cover with plastic wrap. Chill 30 minutes to 1 hour, or until firm.

2 Roll half of dough between 2 sheets of wax paper into 12" x 10" (30 x 25 cm) rectangle. Repeat with remaining dough. Chill 30 minutes.

3 Heat oven to 350°F/180°C. Lightly grease cookie sheets. Set aside. Discard top sheet of wax paper from first half dough. Spread ½ cup (125 mL) fill-ing to within ¼" (5 mm) of edges. Roll dough jelly roll style, starting with long side. (Peel off wax paper when rolling.) Pinch edge to seal. Repeat with remaining dough and ½ cup (125 mL) filling.

4 Cut rolls into ½" (1 cm) slices. Place slices 2" (5 cm) apart on prepared cookie sheets. Bake for 10 to 12 minutes, or until edges are light golden brown. Cool completely. Sprinkle pinwheels with powdered sugar.

Optional Glaze:

- 1 cup (250 mL) powdered sugar
- 1 to 2 tablespoons (15 to 25 mL) orange juice

In small mixing bowl, combine sugar and juice. Stir until smooth. Drizzle over cooled pinwheels.

← HOLIDAY THUMBPRINT COOKIES

- 1 cup (250 mL) butter or margarine, softened
- ½ cup (125 mL) packed brown sugar
- 2 eggs, separated
- 2 cups (500 mL) all-purpose flour
- 1 teaspoon (5 mL) water
- 1½ cups (375 mL) finely chopped pecans
- 3 tablespoons (50 mL) currant jelly or other tart jelly

3 dozen cookies

1 Heat oven to 300°F/150°C. In large mixing bowl, combine butter, sugar and egg yolks. Beat at medium speed of electric mixer until light and fluffy. Add flour. Beat at low speed until soft dough forms. Set aside.

2 In small mixing bowl, beat egg whites and water at high speed until foamy. Set aside.

3 Shape dough into 1" (2.5 cm) balls. Dip balls into egg white mixture. Roll balls in pecans. Place balls 2" (5 cm) apart on ungreased cookie sheets. Indent top of each cookie with thumb. Bake for 18 to 20 minutes, or until set.

4 Immediately indent cookies again. Spoon ¼ teaspoon (1 mL) jelly into each thumbprint. Cool completely before storing. (Do not stack cookies.)

TIP: *Use end of spoon to make indentation in hot cookies.*

BRANDIED GINGER SNAPS

- ½ cup (125 mL) granulated sugar
- ½ cup (125 mL) butter or margarine
- ⅓ cup (75 mL) dark molasses
- 1 tablespoon (15 mL) apricot-flavored brandy
- 1¾ to 2 cups (425 to 500 mL) all-purpose flour, divided
- 1 teaspoon (5 mL) pumpkin pie spice
- Pinch salt

Frosting:

- 2 cups (500 mL) powdered sugar
- ¼ cup (50 mL) caramel ice cream topping
- 1 to 2 teaspoons (5 to 10 mL) milk
- ½ teaspoon (2 mL) vanilla

About 3½ dozen cookies

1 Heat oven to 350°F/180°C. Lightly grease cookie sheets. Set aside. In 1-quart (1 L) saucepan, combine gran-ulated sugar, butter and molasses. Bring to boil over medium heat, stirring constantly. Boil for 1 minute. Remove from heat. Stir in brandy. Set aside.

2 In large mixing bowl, combine 1¼ cups (300 mL) flour, the pumpkin pie spice and salt. Add butter mixture. Beat at medium speed of electric mixer until well blended. Stir or knead in enough of remaining ¾ cup (175 mL) flour to form stiff dough.

3 On prepared cookie sheet, roll out two-thirds dough to ⅛" to ¼" (3 to 5 mm) thickness. Using 3" (8 cm) star-shaped cookie cutter, cut shapes into dough at ½" (1 cm) intervals. Remove scraps and knead into remaining dough. Repeat with remain-ing dough on additional prepared cookie sheets. Bake for 7 to 8 minutes, or until set. Cool completely.

4 In small mixing bowl, combine frosting ingredients. Beat at high speed of electric mixer until smooth. Pipe star outline on cookies, or frost cookies with thin layer of frosting. Let dry completely before storing.

APPLIQUÉD ALMOND COOKIES

- ¾ cup (175 mL) butter or margarine, softened
- ⅓ cup (75 mL) almond paste
- 1 cup (250 mL) granulated sugar
- 1 egg
- 3 tablespoons (50 mL) milk
- 1 teaspoon (5 mL) almond extract

- 3 cups (750 mL) all-purpose flour
- 1½ teaspoons (7 mL) baking powder
- ½ teaspoon (2 mL) salt
- Food coloring
- Coarse sugar crystals

6 dozen cookies

1 In large mixing bowl, combine butter and almond paste. Beat at medium speed of electric mixer until smooth. Add granulated sugar, egg, milk and almond extract. Beat at medium speed until well blended. Add flour, baking powder and salt. Beat at low speed until soft dough forms. Divide dough into thirds. Cover ⅔ dough with plastic wrap. Add food coloring, one drop at a time, to remaining ⅓ dough, kneading dough until color is equally distributed and dough is desired shade. Cover with plastic wrap. Chill all dough 2 to 3 hours, or until firm.

2 Heat oven to 400°F/200°C. On floured surface, roll half of uncolored dough to ⅛" (3 mm) thickness. Using 2¼" (6 cm) round cookie cutter, cut circles into dough. Place circles 2" (5 cm) apart on ungreased cookie sheets. Set aside.

3 On floured surface, roll half of colored dough to ⅛" (3 mm) thickness. Using 2" (5 cm) cutter of desired shape (see Decorating Tip), cut shapes into dough. Place one colored shape on top of each uncolored circle. Repeat with remaining colored and uncolored dough. Sprinkle shapes with sugar crystals. Bake for 5 to 7 minutes, or until edges are golden brown. Cool completely before storing.

LEMON BLOSSOM SPRITZ ↑

- 1 cup (250 mL) butter or margarine, softened
- ½ cup (125 mL) granulated sugar
- ½ cup (125 mL) packed brown sugar
- 1 egg
- 1 teaspoon (5 mL) grated lemon peel
- 1 tablespoon (15 mL) fresh lemon juice
- 1 teaspoon (5 mL) vanilla
- 2½ cups (625 mL) all-purpose flour

- ¼ teaspoon (1 mL) baking soda
- ¼ teaspoon (1 mL) salt

Frosting:

- 1¼ cups (300 mL) powdered sugar
- ½ teaspoon (2 mL) grated lemon peel
- 2 to 4 teaspoons (10 to 20 mL) fresh lemon juice
- ½ teaspoon (2 mL) vanilla

About 5 dozen cookies

1 In large mixing bowl, combine butter, granulated sugar, brown sugar, egg, 1 teaspoon (5 mL) peel, 1 tablespoon (15 mL) juice and 1 teaspoon (5 mL) vanilla. Beat at medium speed of electric mixer until light and fluffy. Add flour, baking soda and salt. Beat at low speed until soft dough forms. Cover with plastic wrap. Chill 1 to 2 hours, or until firm.

2 Heat oven to 400°F/200°C. Place dough in cookie press. Using flower-patterned plate, press cookies 2" (5 cm) apart onto ungreased cookie sheets. Bake for 5 to 7 minutes, or until edges are light golden brown. Cool completely.

3 In small mixing bowl, combine frosting ingredients. Beat at low speed of electric mixer until smooth. Spread frosting evenly on cookies. Let dry completely before storing.

FATTIGMANDS

- Vegetable oil
- 3 tablespoons (50 mL) sour cream
- 3 tablespoons (50 mL) granulated sugar
- 3 egg yolks
- ½ teaspoon (2 mL) almond extract
- ¼ teaspoon (1 mL) ground cloves
- ¼ teaspoon (1 mL) salt
- 1¼ cups (300 mL) all-purpose flour, divided
- Powdered sugar

About 1½ dozen cookies

1 In deep-fat fryer, heat 3" (8 cm) vegetable oil to 375°F/190°C. In small mixing bowl, combine sour cream, granulated sugar, egg yolks, almond extract, cloves and salt. Beat at medium speed of electric mixer until smooth. Add 1 cup (250 mL) flour. Beat at low speed until soft dough forms. Knead in enough of remaining ¼ cup (50 mL) flour to form stiff dough.

2 On lightly floured surface, roll dough into ¹⁄₁₆" to ⅛"-thick (1.5 to 3 mm) rectangle. Using pastry wheel or sharp knife, cut dough into 2" (5 cm) strips. Cut strips diagonally at 4" (10 cm) intervals to form diamonds.

3 Cut 1" (2.5 cm) slit in center of each diamond. Pull one end of diamond completely through slit.

4 In hot oil, fry diamonds for 30 to 40 seconds, or until golden brown, turning over once. Drain on paper-towel-lined plate. Before serving, sprinkle fattigmands with powdered sugar.

MADELEINES

- 2 eggs
- Pinch salt
- ½ cup (125 mL) sugar
- 1 teaspoon (5 mL) grated lemon peel
- ½ teaspoon (2 mL) vanilla
- ½ cup (125 mL) plus 2 tablespoons (25 mL) all-purpose flour
- ½ cup (125 mL) butter or margarine, melted

2 dozen cookies

1 Heat oven to 400°F/200°C. Heavily grease 12-form madeleine pan. Set aside. In medium mixing bowl, combine eggs and salt. Beat at high speed of electric mixer until foamy. Add sugar, peel and vanilla. Beat at high speed for 10 to 12 minutes, or until light and airy, scraping sides of bowl frequently. Using whisk, gently fold in flour, 2 tablespoons (25 mL) at a time. Gently fold in butter, 1 tablespoon (15 mL) at a time.

2 Spoon 1 measuring tablespoon (15 mL) batter into each madeleine form. Bake for 5 to 7 minutes, or until edges are golden brown. Let cool for 3 minutes before removing from pan. Carefully remove madeleines from pan. Cool flat-sides-down on wire racks.

← CHOCOLATE ALMOND ROSETTES

- Vegetable oil
- 1 cup (250 mL) all-purpose flour
- ¼ cup (50 mL) unsweetened cocoa
- 3 tablespoons (50 mL) granulated sugar
- ½ teaspoon (2 mL) salt
- 1 cup (250 mL) milk
- 2 eggs
- 2 tablespoons (25 mL) vegetable oil
- ½ teaspoon (2 mL) almond extract
- Powdered sugar

4 dozen cookies

1 In deep-fat fryer, heat 3" (8 cm) vegetable oil to 375°F/190°C. In medium mixing bowl, combine flour, cocoa, granulated sugar and salt. Add milk, eggs, oil and almond extract. Beat at medium speed of electric mixer until smooth.

2 Heat rosette iron forms in hot oil for 30 seconds. Shake excess oil from forms. Dip hot forms into batter, making sure batter does not coat top side of forms. Immerse forms completely in hot oil. Fry for 30 to 40 seconds, or until edges begin to brown. (Rosettes may release from forms. If so, remove from oil with slotted spoon.)

3 Drain on paper-towel-lined plate. Repeat with remaining batter. Before serving, sprinkle rosettes with powdered sugar.

Optional Glaze:

   3 cups (750 mL) powdered sugar

   3 to 4 tablespoons (50 mL) milk

   ½ teaspoon (2 mL) almond extract

In small bowl, combine glaze ingredients. Stir until smooth. Dip tops of cooled rosettes into glaze.

← ROSETTES

- Vegetable oil
- 1 cup (250 mL) whipping cream
- 2 eggs
- 1 tablespoon (15 mL) granulated sugar
- 1 teaspoon (5 mL) vanilla
- ½ teaspoon (2 mL) ground cinnamon
- ½ teaspoon (2 mL) salt
- ¾ cup (175 mL) all-purpose flour
- Powdered sugar

About 4½ dozen cookies

1 In deep-fat fryer, heat 3" (8 cm) vegetable oil to 375°F/190°C. In medium mixing bowl, combine whipping cream, eggs, granulated sugar, vanilla, cinnamon and salt. Beat at low speed of electric mixer until smooth. Add flour. Beat at low speed until smooth.

2 Heat rosette iron forms in hot oil for 30 seconds. Shake excess oil from forms. Dip hot forms into batter, making sure batter does not coat top side of forms. Immerse forms completely in hot oil. Fry for 25 to 35 seconds, or until golden brown. (Rosettes may release from forms. If so, remove from oil with slotted spoon.)

3 Drain on paper-towel-lined plate. Repeat with remaining batter. Before serving, sprinkle rosettes with powdered sugar.

TIPS: *If batter does not adhere to forms, batter may be too thin (add additional flour, 1 tablespoon/15 mL at a time), or oil may be too hot or too cold. If rosettes adhere to forms after they are browned, rap top of forms gently with knife handle. If batter begins to thicken, thin with small amount of whipping cream.*

ORANGE-SPICED KRUMKAKE

- 1 cup (250 mL) sugar
- ½ cup (125 mL) butter or margarine, softened
- 2 eggs
- 1 teaspoon (5 mL) grated orange peel
- ¼ teaspoon (1 mL) ground cloves
- ¼ teaspoon (1 mL) ground cardamom
- 1½ cups (375 mL) all-purpose flour
- 1 cup (250 mL) milk

5 dozen cookies

1 In medium mixing bowl, combine sugar, butter, eggs, peel, cloves and cardamom. Beat at medium speed of electric mixer until smooth. Gradually add flour, alternating with milk, beating at low speed until smooth batter forms, scraping sides of bowl frequently.

2 Brush inside of krumkake iron with small amount of vegetable shortening. Heat iron over medium-low heat (if using gas stove) or medium heat (if using electric stove).

3 Place 1 measuring tablespoon (15 mL) batter in the center of open iron. Close the iron and firmly hold together. Cook for 5 to 20 seconds, or until light golden brown, turning iron over once. (Watch carefully to prevent burning.)

4 Remove the krumkake with spatula, and immediately roll into cone. Repeat with remaining batter. (The krumkake iron does not need to be rebrushed with shortening after the first krumkake is made.)

220

PIZZELLES

- 2 cups (500 mL) all-purpose flour
- 1 cup (250 mL) sugar
- 4 eggs
- ¾ cup (175 mL) butter or margarine, melted and slightly cooled
- ¼ cup (50 mL) finely ground hazelnuts
- 1 tablespoon (15 mL) anise extract

About 3½ dozen cookies

1 In medium mixing bowl, combine all ingredients. Beat at low speed of electric mixer until smooth batter forms, scraping sides of bowl frequently.

2 Brush inside of pizzelle iron with small amount of vegetable shortening. Heat iron over medium heat (if using gas stove) or medium-high heat (if using electric stove).

3 Place 1 measuring tablespoon (15 mL) batter in center of open iron. Close iron. (Do not squeeze shut.) Cook for 30 seconds to 1 minute 30 seconds, or until light golden brown, turning iron over once. (Watch carefully to prevent burning.)

4 With spatula, immediately remove pizzelle. Repeat with remaining batter. (The pizzelle iron does not need to be rebrushed with shortening after the first pizzelle is made.)

5 Cool pizzelles completely before storing. If desired, trim edges of cooled pizzelles with scissors.

TIP: *To recrisp pizzelles, bake at 250°F/120°C for 3 to 5 minutes.*

← ORANGE SNOWBALLS

- 2¾ cups (675 mL) finely crushed vanilla wafers
- 1 cup (250 mL) powdered sugar
- 1 cup (250 mL) finely chopped almonds
- ⅓ cup (75 mL) butter or margarine, melted
- ¼ cup (50 mL) frozen orange juice concentrate, defrosted
- Flaked coconut

3½ dozen cookies

1 Line airtight container with wax paper. Set aside. In large mixing bowl, combine wafers, sugar, almonds, butter and concentrate. Stir until well blended (mixture will be crumbly).

2 Shape mixture into ¾" (2 cm) balls. Roll balls in coconut. Place balls in prepared container. Store in refrigerator.

CHOCO-BRANDY → BALLS

- 2½ cups (625 mL) finely crushed chocolate wafers, divided
- 1¼ cups (300 mL) granulated sugar
- ½ cup (125 mL) butter or margarine, melted
- ½ cup (125 mL) finely chopped pecans
- ¼ cup (50 mL) brandy
- Powdered sugar

2½ dozen cookies

1 Line airtight container with wax paper. Set aside. In large mixing bowl, combine 2 cups (500 mL) wafers, the granulated sugar, butter, pecans, and brandy. Stir until well blended (mixture will be crumbly).

2 Shape mixture into 1" (2.5 cm) balls. Roll balls in remaining ½ cup (125 mL) wafers or powdered sugar. Place balls in prepared container. Store in refrigerator.

CHOCOLATE-GINGER → ROCKING HORSE

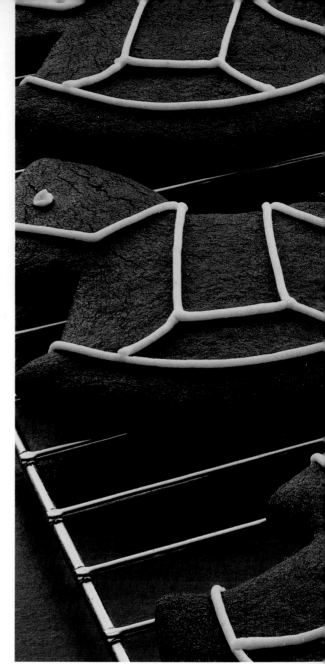

- 2¼ cups (550 mL) all-purpose flour
- ¾ cup (175 mL) unsweetened cocoa
- 1 teaspoon (5 mL) baking soda
- 1 teaspoon (5 mL) ground ginger
- ½ teaspoon (2 mL) baking powder
- ½ teaspoon (2 mL) ground allspice
- ¼ teaspoon (1 mL) ground cardamom
- ¼ teaspoon (1 mL) salt
- 1 cup (250 mL) sugar
- ½ cup (125 mL) butter or margarine, softened
- ½ cup (125 mL) light molasses
- 1 egg
- ½ teaspoon (2 mL) vanilla
- Decorator Frosting (page 242)

About 3 dozen cookies

1 In medium mixing bowl, combine flour, cocoa, baking soda, ginger, baking powder, allspice, cardamom and salt. Set aside.

2 In large mixing bowl, combine sugar, butter, molasses, egg and vanilla. Beat at medium speed of electric mixer until well blended. Add flour mixture. Beat at low speed until soft dough forms. Cover with plastic wrap. Chill 2 to 3 hours, or until firm.

3 Heat oven to 350°F/180°C. Lightly grease cookie sheets. Set aside. Divide dough in half. On lightly floured surface, roll half of dough to ⅛" to ¼" (3 to 5 mm) thickness. Using 3½" (9 cm) rocking horse cookie cutter, cut shapes into dough.

4 Place shapes 2" (5 cm) apart on prepared cookie sheets. Repeat with remaining dough. Bake for 8 to 10 minutes, or until set. Cool completely. Prepare frosting as directed. Decorate cookies as desired. Let dry completely before storing.

CANDY-FILLED CHOCOLATE WHEELS →

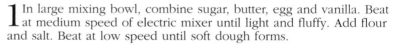

- 1½ cups (375 mL) powdered sugar
- 1 cup (250 mL) butter or margarine, softened
- 1 egg
- 1 teaspoon (5 mL) vanilla
- 2⅔ cups (650 mL) all-purpose flour
- ¼ teaspoon (1 mL) salt
- ¼ cup (50 mL) unsweetened cocoa
- 1 tablespoon (15 mL) milk
- ¼ cup (50 mL) finely crushed fruit-flavored hard candies

4 dozen cookies

1 In large mixing bowl, combine sugar, butter, egg and vanilla. Beat at medium speed of electric mixer until light and fluffy. Add flour and salt. Beat at low speed until soft dough forms.

2 Divide dough in half. Add cocoa and milk to half of dough. Beat at low speed until well blended. Roll chocolate dough between 2 sheets of wax paper into 12" x 8" (30 x 20 cm) rectangle. Discard top sheet of wax paper. Set dough aside.

3 Stir crushed candies into remaining half dough. Shape candied dough into 12"-long (30 cm) log. Place log lengthwise on long edge of rectangle. Roll chocolate dough jelly roll style around log. (Peel off wax paper when rolling.) Pinch edge to seal. Wrap in plastic wrap or wax paper. Chill 1 to 2 hours, or until firm.

4 Heat oven to 375°F/190°C. Cut roll into ¼" (5 mm) slices. Place slices 2" (5 cm) apart on ungreased cookie sheets. Bake for 8 to 10 minutes, or until set. Let cool 1 minute before removing from cookie sheets. Cool completely before storing.

← CHOCOLATE-DIPPED HAZELNUT BISCOTTI

- 1 cup (250 mL) slivered almonds
- 1½ cups (375 mL) sugar
- ½ cup (125 mL) unsalted butter, softened
- 2 tablespoons (25 mL) hazelnut liqueur
- 3 eggs
- 3¾ cups (925 mL) all-purpose flour
- 2 teaspoons (10 mL) baking powder
- Pinch salt
- 1 cup (250 mL) milk chocolate chips
- 2 teaspoons (10 mL) vegetable shortening
- 1½ cup (125 mL) finely chopped hazelnuts

3½ dozen cookies

1 Heat oven to 350°F/180°C. Lightly grease cookie sheets. Set aside. Place almonds in 8" (2 L) square baking pan. Bake for 10 to 12 minutes, or until light golden brown, stirring occasionally. Coarsely chop almonds. Set aside.

2 In large mixing bowl, combine sugar, butter and liqueur. Beat at medium speed of electric mixer until light and fluffy. Add eggs, one at a time, beating after each addition. Add flour, baking powder and salt. Beat at low speed until soft dough forms. Stir in almonds.

3 Divide dough into quarters. On lightly floured surface, shape each quarter into 2"-diameter (5 cm) log. Place logs 2" (5 cm) apart on prepared cookie sheet. Bake for 30 to 35 minutes, or until golden brown.

4 Immediately cut logs diagonally into ¾" (2 cm) slices. Place slices 1" (2.5 cm) apart on prepared cookie sheets. Bake for additional 10 to 15 minutes, or until dry and golden brown. Cool completely.

5 In 1-quart (1 L) saucepan, combine chips and shortening. Melt over low heat, stirring constantly. Remove from heat. Dip one end of each cookie diagonally into melted chocolate. Sprinkle hazelnuts evenly over dipped ends. Let dry completely before storing.

← STAINED GLASS COOKIES

- 1 cup (250 mL) sugar
- ½ cup (125 mL) butter or margarine, softened
- ⅓ cup (75 mL) vegetable shortening
- 2 eggs
- 1 teaspoon (5 mL) grated orange peel
- 1 teaspoon (5 mL) vanilla
- 2¾ cups (675 mL) all-purpose flour
- 1 teaspoon (5 mL) baking powder
- 1 teaspoon (5 mL) salt
- 5 rolls (.9 oz./22 g each) ring-shaped hard candies (assorted flavors)

4 dozen cookies

1 In large mixing bowl, combine sugar, butter and shortening. Beat at medium speed of electric mixer until light and fluffy. Add eggs, peel and vanilla. Beat at medium speed until well blended. Add flour, baking powder and salt. Beat at low speed until soft dough forms. Cover with plastic wrap. Chill 1 to 2 hours, or until firm.

2 Heat oven to 350°F/180°C. Line cookie sheets with foil. Set aside. Divide dough into thirds. On well-floured surface, roll one third dough to ¼" (5 mm) thickness. Using 3" (8 cm) cookie cutters, cut desired shapes into dough. Place shapes 2" (5 cm) apart on prepared cookie sheets.

3 Using smaller cookie cutters, straws or a sharp knife, cut desired shapes out of cookies on cookie sheets. (If cookies are to be hung as ornaments, make a small hole at the top of each cookie for string.) Repeat with remaining dough.

4 Place like-colored candies in small plastic bags. Coarsely crush candies by tapping each bag with back of large spoon. Fill cutout areas of cookies to the top with candies. Bake for 7 to 9 minutes, or until edges are light golden brown and candies are melted. Cool completely before removing from foil. Gently pull cookies off foil.

POPPY-RASPBERRY KOLACHKES →

- ½ cup (125 mL) butter or margarine, softened
- 1 pkg. (3 oz./85 g) cream cheese, softened
- ¼ cup (50 mL) granulated sugar
- ½ teaspoon (2 mL) vanilla
- 1½ cups (375 mL) all-purpose flour
- 1½ teaspoons (7 mL) poppy seed
- ⅓ cup (75 mL) raspberry jam

Glaze:

- ½ cup (125 mL) powdered sugar
- 4 to 5 teaspoons (20 to 25 mL) half-and-half
- ¼ teaspoon (1 mL) almond extract

About 3 dozen cookies

1 Heat oven to 375°F/190°C. In large mixing bowl, combine butter, cream cheese, granulated sugar and vanilla. Beat at medium speed of electric mixer until light and fluffy. Add flour and poppy seed. Beat at low speed until soft dough forms. Divide dough in half. On lightly floured board, roll half of dough to ⅛" to ¼" (3 to 5 mm) thickness. Using 2½" (6 cm) round cookie cutter, cut circles into dough. Place circles 2" (5 cm) apart on ungreased cookie sheets.

2 Spoon about ¼ teaspoon (1 mL) raspberry jam onto center of each circle. Fold top half of circle over bottom half. Press edges with fork dipped in flour to seal. Repeat with remaining dough and jam. Bake for 7 to 9 minutes, or until edges are light golden brown. Cool completely.

3 In small mixing bowl, combine glaze ingredients. Stir until smooth. Drizzle glaze over cookies. Let dry completely before storing.

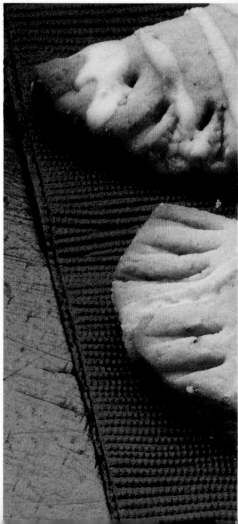

← VIENNESE KISS COOKIES

- 1½ cups (375 mL) all-purpose flour
- ¾ cup (175 mL) butter or margarine, chilled and cut into 1" (2.5 cm) pieces
- ¼ cup (50 mL) sugar
- 3 tablespoons (50 mL) sour cream
- 1 teaspoon (5 mL) vanilla
- 24 chocolate kisses

2 dozen cookies

1 Heat oven to 350°F/180°C. Grease two 12-cup miniature muffin pans (1¾"/4.5 cm diameter). Set aside. In large mixing bowl, combine flour, butter and sugar. Beat at medium speed of electric mixer until mixture resembles coarse crumbs. Add sour cream and vanilla. Beat at low speed until soft dough forms.

2 Shape dough into 1" (2.5 cm) balls. Place 1 ball in each prepared muffin cup. Bake for 20 to 25 minutes, or until edges are golden brown. Immediately press kiss into center of each cookie. Let cool 1 minute before removing from pans. Cool completely before storing.

FRUITFUL FLORENTINES

- ½ cup (125 mL) butter or margarine, softened
- ⅓ cup (75 mL) honey
- ¼ cup (50 mL) sugar
- ½ teaspoon (2 mL) vanilla
- 1 cup (250 mL) uncooked quick-cooking oats
- ⅔ cup (150 mL) all-purpose flour
- 1 cup (250 mL) chopped candied fruit

Glaze:

- ¼ cup (50 mL) semisweet chocolate chips
- 2 tablespoons (25 mL) butter or margarine

2½ dozen cookies

1 Heat oven to 350°F/180°C. Lightly grease cookie sheets. Set aside. In large mixing bowl, combine ½ cup (125 mL) butter, the honey, sugar and vanilla. Beat at medium speed of electric mixer until well blended. Add oats and flour. Beat at low speed until soft dough forms. Stir in candied fruit.

2 Drop dough by heaping teaspoons 2" (5 cm) apart onto prepared cookie sheets. Flatten dough slightly with back of spoon. Bake for 10 to 12 minutes, or until edges are golden brown. Let cool 2 minutes before removing from cookie sheets. Cool completely.

3 In 1-quart (1 L) saucepan, combine glaze ingredients. Melt over low heat, stirring constantly. Drizzle glaze over cookies. Let dry completely before storing. Store in refrigerator.

MICROWAVE TIP: *In small mixing bowl, melt glaze ingredients at 50% (Medium) 2 to 4 minutes, stirring after every minute. Continue as directed.*

GREEK AMARETTO COOKIES

- 2 tablespoons (25 mL) honey
- 3½ teaspoons (17 mL) amaretto, divided
- 1 jar (6 oz./170 g) red maraschino cherries, drained (reserve juice)
- 1 jar (6 oz./170 g) green maraschino cherries, drained
- ¾ cup (175 mL) chopped pecans
- 2 tablespoons (25 mL) strawberry jelly
- 2 cups (500 mL) all-purpose flour
- ¼ teaspoon (1 mL) salt
- ¾ cup (175 mL) butter or margarine, chilled, cut into small pieces
- 5 to 6 tablespoons (75 to 90 mL) ice water

2 dozen cookies

1 Heat oven to 400°F/200°C. Lightly grease cookie sheets. Set aside. In 1-cup (250 mL) measure, combine honey and 2 teaspoons (10 mL) amaretto. Set glaze aside.

2 Cut 12 red and 12 green cherries in half. Set aside. Chop remaining cherries. In medium mixing bowl, combine remaining 1½ teaspoons (7 mL) amaretto, the chopped cherries, reserved red cherry juice, pecans and jelly. Set cherry mixture aside.

3 In large mixing bowl, combine flour and salt. Using pastry blender, cut in butter until mixture resembles coarse crumbs. Sprinkle with water, 1 tablespoon (15 mL) at a time, mixing with fork until particles are moistened and cling together. Form dough into ball. Divide dough in half. Wrap half of dough in plastic wrap. Chill.

4 On lightly floured surface, roll remaining dough to ⅛" (3 mm) thickness. Using 3" (8 cm) round cookie cutter, cut circles into dough.

5 Place heaping measuring teaspoon (5 mL) cherry mixture onto center of each circle. Overlap two opposite sides to form cylinders. Brush edges with water. Press edges to seal.

6 Place cylinders 2" (5 cm) apart on prepared cookie sheets. Repeat with remaining dough and cherry mixture. Insert 1 red and 1 green cherry half into opposite ends of each cylinder. Bake for 17 to 19 minutes, or until light golden brown. Immediately brush half of honey glaze over top and sides of cookies. Cool completely. Brush remaining glaze over cookies. Let dry completely before storing.

RUM BALLS

- 2 cups (500 mL) finely crushed vanilla wafers
- 1 cup (250 mL) granulated sugar
- ½ cup (125 mL) finely chopped walnuts
- ⅓ cup (75 mL) butter or margarine, melted
- ¼ cup (50 mL) light rum
- Powdered sugar

2½ dozen cookies

1 Line airtight container with wax paper. Set aside. In large mixing bowl, combine wafers, granulated sugar and walnuts. Add butter and rum. Stir until well blended (mixture will be crumbly).

2 Shape mixture into 1" (2.5 cm) balls. Roll balls in powdered sugar. Place on ungreased cookie sheets. Let stand 1 hour. Reroll balls in powdered sugar before placing in prepared container. Store in refrigerator.

TIP: *Flavor of rum balls improves after a few weeks' storage.*

CHOCOLATE SNOWBALLS

- 2½ cups (625 mL) all-purpose flour
- ½ cup (125 mL) unsweetened cocoa
- 2 teaspoons (10 mL) baking powder
- Pinch salt
- 3 cups (750 mL) sugar, divided
- 4 eggs
- ½ cup (125 mL) vegetable shortening
- 4 teaspoons (20 mL) vanilla, divided
- Granulated sugar
- 5 to 6 cups (1.25 to 1.5 L) flaked coconut
- 3 or 4 drops red food coloring
- 3 envelopes (.25 oz./7 g each) unflavored gelatin
- ⅔ cup (150 mL) ice water
- 1⅓ cups (325 mL) light corn syrup

8 dozen cookies

1 In medium mixing bowl, combine flour, cocoa, baking powder and salt. Set aside. In large mixing bowl, combine 2 cups (500 mL) sugar, the eggs, shortening and 2 teaspoons (10 mL) vanilla. Beat at medium speed of electric mixer until creamy. Add flour mixture. Beat at low speed until soft dough forms. Cover with plastic wrap. Chill 1 to 2 hours, or until firm.

2 Heat oven to 350°F/180°C. Lightly grease cookie sheets. Set aside. Shape dough into ½" (1 cm) balls. Place balls 2" (5 cm) apart on prepared cookie sheets. Flatten balls to 2"-diameter (5 cm) circles with bottom of drinking glass, dipping glass in granulated sugar to prevent sticking. Bake for 12 to 15 minutes, or until set. Cool completely.

3 Place coconut and food coloring in 1-gallon (4 L) sealable freezer bag. Shake to coat. Set aside. In top of double boiler, combine gelatin and ice water. Stir until gelatin is dissolved. Add remaining 1 cup (250 mL) sugar. In bottom of double boiler, bring additional water to boil. Place top of double boiler over boiling water. Cook gelatin mixture over medium heat until sugar is dissolved, stirring occasionally. Remove from heat.

4 In large mixing bowl, combine gelatin mixture, corn syrup and remaining 2 teaspoons (10 mL) vanilla. Beat at high speed of electric mixer for 15 minutes, or until topping is light and fluffy. Spoon about 1 tablespoon (15 mL) topping onto back of each cookie. Sprinkle topping with colored coconut. Let dry completely before storing.

TIP: *Chocolate cookie can be made in advance and frozen in airtight container.*

APRICOT-DATE BALLS (top)

- ¾ cup (175 mL) sugar
- ½ cup (125 mL) chopped dried apricots
- ½ cup (125 mL) chopped dates
- 2 eggs, beaten
- 1 cup (250 mL) finely chopped walnuts
- 1 teaspoon (5 mL) vanilla
- Granulated sugar

4 dozen cookies

1 Line airtight container with wax paper. Set aside. In 2-quart (2 L) saucepan, combine ¾ cup (175 mL) sugar, the apricots, dates and eggs. Cook over low heat for 6 to 8 minutes, or until mixture pulls away from side of pan, stirring constantly.

2 Remove from heat. Stir in walnuts and vanilla. Let stand for 45 to 50 minutes, or until mixture is cool enough to handle.

3 Shape mixture into 1" (2.5 cm) balls. Roll balls in sugar. Place balls in prepared container. Store in refrigerator.

SPICY GREEK JEWELS (bottom)

- 2 cups (500 mL) powdered sugar
- 1 cup (250 mL) butter or margarine, softened
- 1 egg
- 2½ cups (625 mL) all-purpose flour
- 1½ cups (375 mL) ground almonds
- 1½ teaspoons (7 mL) apple pie spice
- ¼ teaspoon (1 mL) salt
- Powdered sugar
- 24 red candied cherries, halved
- 12 green candied pineapple chunks, each cut into 8 pieces

4 dozen cookies

1 Heat oven to 350°F/180°C. In large mixing bowl, combine 2 cups (500 mL) powdered sugar, the butter and egg. Beat at medium speed of electric mixer until light and fluffy. Add flour, almonds, apple pie spice and salt. Beat at low speed until soft dough forms.

2 Shape dough into 1" (2.5 cm) balls. Place balls 2" (5 cm) apart on ungreased cookie sheets. Flatten to ¼" (5 mm) thickness with bottom of drinking glass, dipping glass in powdered sugar to prevent sticking.

3 Decorate each cookie with 1 cherry half and 2 pineapple pieces, pressing fruit lightly into dough. Bake for 12 to 14 minutes, or until edges are golden brown. Cool completely before storing.

MEXICAN BISCOCHITAS

- 3 cups (750 mL) all-purpose flour
- 1½ teaspoons (7 mL) baking powder
- ¼ teaspoon (1 mL) salt
- 1 cup (250 mL) sugar, divided
- 1 cup (250 mL) vegetable shortening
- 1 egg
- 1 tablespoon (15 mL) anise seed
- ¼ cup (50 mL) brandy
- 1 teaspoon (5 mL) ground cinnamon

About 4 dozen cookies

1 Heat oven to 350°F/180°C. In medium mixing bowl, combine flour, baking powder and salt. Set aside. In large mixing bowl, combine ¾ cup (175 mL) sugar, the shortening, egg and anise seed. Beat at medium speed of electric mixer until light and fluffy. Gradually add flour mixture, alternating with brandy, beating at low speed until soft dough forms.

2 On lightly floured surface, roll dough to ¼" to ½" (5 mm to 1 cm) thickness. Using 2½" (6 cm) flower-shaped or round cookie cutter, cut shapes into dough. Place shapes 2" (5 cm) apart on ungreased cookie sheets. Set aside.

3 In small bowl, combine remaining ¼ cup (50 mL) sugar and the cinnamon. Sprinkle shapes evenly with sugar mixture. Bake for 9 to 11 minutes, or until light golden brown. Cool completely before storing.

FRENCH LACE COOKIE CUPS

- 1 cup (250 mL) all-purpose flour
- 1 cup (250 mL) finely chopped almonds
- ½ cup (125 mL) packed brown sugar
- ½ cup (125 mL) butter or margarine
- ⅓ cup (75 mL) light corn syrup
- ½ teaspoon (2 mL) almond extract

4 dozen cookies

1 Heat oven to 350°F/180°C. Lightly grease cookie sheets and outsides of 4 inverted 6-oz. (175 mL) custard cups. Set aside. In medium mixing bowl, combine flour and almonds. Set aside.

2 In 1-quart (1 L) saucepan, combine sugar, butter and corn syrup. Bring to boil over medium heat, stirring constantly. Remove from heat. Gradually stir in flour mixture. Stir in extract.

3 Drop batter by measuring tablespoons (15 mL) onto prepared cookie sheets, spreading batter into 4" (10 cm) circles (4 circles per sheet). Bake for 5 to 6 minutes, or until edges are golden brown. Let cool 1 minute before removing from cookie sheets.

4 Place cookies over inverted custard cups, molding around cups and pinching edges to shape. Let cookie cups cool before removing from custard cups. To serve, fill cookie cups with cut-up fruit or ice cream.

GREEK HOLIDAY COOKIES

- 1 cup (250 mL) butter or margarine, softened
- ½ cup (125 mL) granulated sugar
- 1 egg
- ½ teaspoon (2 mL) vanilla
- ½ teaspoon (2 mL) brandy extract
- 2½ cups (625 mL) all-purpose flour
- 1 teaspoon (5 mL) baking powder
- ¼ teaspoon (1 mL) ground cloves
- ¼ teaspoon (1 mL) salt
- Whole cloves
- Powdered sugar

4½ dozen cookies

1 Heat oven to 350°F/180°C. In large mixing bowl, combine butter, granulated sugar, egg, vanilla and brandy extract. Beat at medium speed of electric mixer until light and fluffy. Add flour, baking powder, ground cloves and salt. Beat at low speed until soft dough forms.

2 Shape heaping teaspoons dough into crescent or S shapes. Place shapes 2" (5 cm) apart on ungreased cookie sheets. Press 2 whole cloves into each shape.

3 Bake for 9 to 11 minutes, or until set. Let cool 1 minute before removing from cookie sheets. Sprinkle cookies with powdered sugar. Cool completely before storing. Remove whole cloves before eating.

TIP: *Flavor of cookies improves after a few days' storage.*

CHOCOLATE-DIPPED PALMIERS

- 1 pkg. (1 lb./454 g) frozen puff pastry dough, defrosted, divided
- ½ cup (125 mL) sugar
- 2 cups (500 mL) semisweet chocolate chips
- 3 teaspoons (15 mL) vegetable shortening, divided
- 1½ cups (375 mL) vanilla baking chips

6 dozen cookies

1 Heat oven to 375°F/190°C. Lightly grease cookie sheets. Set aside. On lightly sugared surface, roll 1 sheet pastry into 12" x 10" (30 x 25 cm) rectangle.

2 Fold long sides of pastry toward center line, leaving ¼" (5 mm) gap in center.

3 Fold pastry in half lengthwise to form 12" x 2½" (30 x 6 cm) strip. Lightly press edges together to seal.

4 Cut dough crosswise into ¼" (5 mm) slices. Place slices 2" (5 cm) apart on prepared cookie sheets. Bake for 8 to 10 minutes, or until light golden brown, rotating cookie sheet after 5 minutes. Repeat with remaining pastry. Cool completely.

5 In 1-quart (1 L) saucepan, combine chocolate chips and 2 teaspoons (10 mL) shortening. Melt over low heat, stirring constantly. Repeat with vanilla chips and remaining 1 teaspoon (5 mL) shortening. Dip one end of each palmier in melted chocolate. Let dry on cooling rack. Dip again in melted vanilla chips. Let dry completely before storing.

THREE-CORNERED HATS

- 1½ cups (375 mL) butter or margarine, softened
- ½ cup (125 mL) sugar
- 1 egg
- ¼ cup (50 mL) evaporated milk
- ½ teaspoon (2 mL) vanilla
- 2¾ cups (675 mL) all-purpose flour, divided

Filling:

- 1 pkg. (12 oz./341 g) pitted dried prunes
- ½ cup (125 mL) finely chopped walnuts
- 2 tablespoons (25 mL) sugar
- 1 to 2 teaspoons (5 to 10 mL) grated orange peel
- 1 egg yolk beaten with 1 tablespoon (15 mL) water

About 3 dozen cookies

1 In large mixing bowl, combine butter, ½ cup (125 mL) sugar and the egg. Beat at medium speed of electric mixer until light and fluffy. Add milk and vanilla. Beat at medium speed until well blended. Add 1¾ cups (425 mL) flour. Beat at low speed until soft dough forms. Stir in remaining 1 cup (250 mL) flour to form stiff dough. Cover with plastic wrap. Chill 30 minutes to 1 hour, or until firm.

2 In food processor or blender, process prunes until smooth. In medium mixing bowl, combine processed prunes and remaining filling ingredients. Set aside.

3 Heat oven to 350°F/180°C. Lightly grease cookie sheets. Set aside. On lightly floured surface, roll dough to ⅛" to ¼" (3 to 5 mm) thickness. Using 3" (8 cm) round cookie cutter, cut circles into dough. Place circles 2" (5 cm) apart on prepared cookie sheets.

4 Place heaping measuring teaspoon (5 mL) filling onto center of each circle. Lightly brush edges with water. Bring sides of dough up and pinch together to form triangle, leaving top of triangle open to show filling. Lightly brush top and sides of dough with egg yolk mixture. Bake for 14 to 16 minutes, or until set. Cool completely before storing.

GERMAN PFEFFERNÜSSE

- 1 cup (250 mL) granulated sugar
- ¾ cup (175 mL) butter or margarine, softened
- 1 cup (250 mL) dark corn syrup
- 3 tablespoons (50 mL) hot water
- 2 teaspoons (10 mL) anise seed
- 1 teaspoon (5 mL) black pepper
- 1 teaspoon (5 mL) baking soda
- ¼ teaspoon (1 mL) ground allspice
- ¼ teaspoon (1 mL) ground cardamom
- ¼ teaspoon (1 mL) ground cloves
- ¼ teaspoon (1 mL) salt
- 4 to 5 cups (1 to 1.25 L) all-purpose flour, divided
- Powdered sugar

About 9 dozen cookies

1 In large mixing bowl, combine granulated sugar and butter. Beat at medium speed of electric mixer until light and fluffy. Add corn syrup, water, anise, pepper, baking soda, allspice, cardamom, cloves and salt. Beat at low speed until well blended.

2 Gradually add 4 cups (1 L) flour, beating at low speed. Stir or knead in enough of remaining 1 cup (250 mL) flour to form stiff dough. Cover with plastic wrap. Chill 3 to 4 hours, or until firm.

3 Heat oven to 350°F/180°C. Divide dough into 8 pieces. Roll each piece into ½" to ¾"-thick (1 to 2 cm) rope. Cut ropes diagonally into 1" to 1½" (2.5 to 4 cm) lengths. Place the lengths 2" (5 cm) apart on ungreased cookie sheets. Bake for 10 to 15 minutes, or until golden brown. Cool completely. Roll in powdered sugar before storing.

DECORATING WITH FROSTING

The quickest and easiest way to decorate cookies is with frosting. Here is a recipe for a basic decorator frosting that can be used for spreading or piping on cookies.

DECORATOR FROSTING

- ½ cup (125 mL) butter or margarine, softened
- ½ cup (125 mL) vegetable shortening
- 1 teaspoon (5 mL) vanilla
- 4 cups (1 L) powered sugar
- 3 to 4 tablespoons (50 mL) milk
- Food coloring (optional)

3 cups (750 mL)

In large mixing bowl, combine butter, shortening and vanilla. Beat at medium speed of electric mixer until creamy. Add sugar, 1 cup (250 mL) at a time, beating at low speed until well blended. Add milk. Beat at medium speed until light and fluffy. Beat in food coloring, 1 drop at a time, until frosting is desired color.

TIP: *One-half teaspoon (2 mL) almond extract, mint extract or other flavored extract can be substituted for vanilla.*

Dip corner or part of cookie in slightly thinned frosting. If desired, sprinkle with chopped nuts, coconut or other decorative topping (see page 246). Cookies can also be dipped in melted chocolate or vanilla chips, or in melted candy coating.

Place stencil over freshly frosted cookie, and lightly dust with sifted powdered sugar.

Pull fork tines through lines of frosting to create a marbled look.

242

Drizzle thinned frosting over the cookies with a spoon.

Use a small frosting spatula or table knife to spread frosting evenly on cookies. (Do not spread frosting too thick.) Frost cookies that are completely cooled, so the frosting does not melt. Also, warm cookies are more fragile and might break during the handling that is required.

Paint thinned frosting on cookies for a detailed look, or use a paintbrush to make designs and textures in frosting.

Thin frosting by beating in milk, 1 tablespoon (15 mL) at a time (for small amounts, ½ teaspoon/2 mL at a time), until desired consistency.

243

DECORATING WITH A PASTRY BAG

Use a pastry bag to pipe frosting on cookies. These bags are available at specialty kitchen stores and some supermarkets. Inexpensive metal or plastic decorating tips are also available at these stores. A coupler allows you to change decorating tips without emptying the pastry bag.

Pictured are six of the more common decorating tips.

#2 Writing tip

#5 Writing tip

#67 Leaf tip

#13 Open star tip

#27 Closed star tip

#18 Open star tip

HOW TO USE A PASTRY BAG

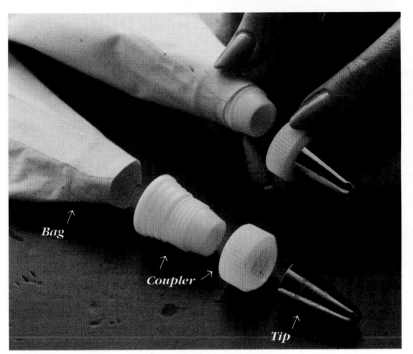

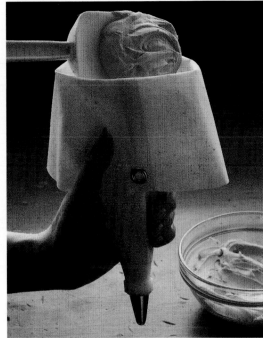

1 Place large part of coupler in bag, making sure bag fits snugly around coupler. Place tip through small part of coupler, then screw both halves of coupler together.

2 Scoop frosting into rolled-down pastry bag until bag is about two-thirds full. (Roll up bag while filling.)

HOW TO MAKE A PASTRY BAG

3 Twist or roll down the top of the bag to keep steady pressure on the frosting as you squeeze. Before decorating, hold the bag closed and squeeze out a small amount of frosting to eliminate air bubbles in the bag.

Fill a heavy, resealable food-storage bag half full of frosting; seal the bag. Snip off the tip (arrow) of one corner to create a writing tip that produces a line. Start with a small hole, and enlarge it, if necessary. A coupler and decorating tips can also be used with food-storage bags.

Decorative toppings can be sprinkled over or pressed on frostings, as shown below. Add toppings to cookies before frosting dries, so toppings will stay in place. Or put toppings on cookies before baking, and leave the cookies unfrosted. Toppings like dried fruit, candies or nuts can sometimes be pressed into cookies fresh from the oven.

Colored sugar is tinted granulated sugar and is available in several colors and granule sizes.

Decorating or coarse sugar has granules about four times larger than those of regular granulated sugar. Dragées are tiny, round hard candies that come in sizes ranging from pinhead to ¼" (5 mm). Shot, confetti and sprinkles are commonly available decorative toppings.

Candies, dried fruit, nuts, miniature chocolate chips, licorice, coconut and grated citrus peel can also be used as cookie toppings.

Gumdrops

Cinnamon candies

Dragées

Whole nuts

Candied fruits

Shot

Chopped nuts

Miniature chips

Candy-coated chocolate pieces

Licorice

Confetti

Jelly beans

Colored sugar

Grated citrus peel

Sprinkles

Coarse sugar

Shredded coconut

MORE DECORATING IDEAS

Here are some additional ideas for decorating home-baked cookies or cookies you buy at the store:

Cut *dried fruit, gumdrops and licorice strings to make designs, eyes, hats, etc.*

Place *a small amount of fairly stiff frosting or a gumdrop in a garlic press. Carefully press out strands for "hair" or a textured look.*

Smooth *thin frosting base on cookies. Let it dry, then pipe outline or design on top. Decorative toppings can be added to complete the design.*

HOW TO TINT COCONUT

Color *coconut by placing it in a large, resealable food-storage bag. Add a few drops of food color to get the desired color.*

Seal *the bag and shake until coconut is uniform in color. Spread coconut on wax paper and let stand for a few minutes before using.*

247

Desserts
& Sweets

PLUM PUDDING

- 2 cups (500 mL) soft bread cubes (about 3 slices, trimmed)
- ½ cup (125 mL) all-purpose flour
- ½ cup (125 mL) currants
- ½ cup (125 mL) raisins
- 2 tablespoons (25 mL) packed dark brown sugar
- ½ teaspoon (2 mL) baking soda
- ½ teaspoon (2 mL) ground cinnamon
- ¼ teaspoon (1 mL) ground nutmeg
- ¼ teaspoon (1 mL) salt
- ¼ cup (50 mL) butter or margarine
- ½ cup (125 mL) half-and-half
- 2 tablespoons (25 mL) sherry
- 1½ tablespoons (20 mL) molasses
- 1 egg
- 2 tablespoons (25 mL) brandy

4 to 6 servings

1 Grease 2-cup (500 mL) measure. Cut two 1½"-wide (4 cm) strips of wax paper long enough to cover bottom and sides of measure, with 1" (2.5 cm) of overhang on each side. Overlap strips in base of measure. Set aside.

2 Combine all ingredients except brandy in medium bowl. Beat at medium speed of electric mixer, until well blended, scraping bowl frequently. Pour batter into prepared measure. Cover with plastic wrap. Place in oven on inverted saucer.

3 Microwave at 50% (Medium) 8 to 12 minutes, or until no uncooked batter appears through sides and cake feels springy to the touch, rotating every 2 minutes. Let stand, covered, 5 minutes. Remove plastic wrap. Loosen edges with small spatula. Invert measure, pulling wax-paper strips to remove pudding to serving plate. To serve, place brandy in small bowl. Microwave at High about 20 seconds, or until heated. Pour into large spoon or ladle; ignite and spoon flaming brandy over pudding.

HOLIDAY FRUITCAKE

Homemade fruitcake needn't take days or weeks to make. This recipe is uncomplicated and produces a fruitcake that's sure to become a family tradition.

- 1 cup (250 mL) chopped dried apricots
- 1 cup (250 mL) chopped dried figs or raisins
- ¾ cup (175 mL) brandy
- 1 cup (250 mL) unbleached white flour
- 1 cup (250 mL) granulated sugar
- 1 teaspoon (5 mL) salt
- ½ teaspoon (2 mL) baking powder
- 2 eggs plus 2 egg whites, slightly beaten (or ¾ cup/175 mL liquid egg substitute)

- ½ cup (125 mL) frozen orange juice concentrate, defrosted
- 1 10-oz. (284 mL) jar maraschino cherries, drained and patted dry
- 1 cup (250 mL) chopped pecans
- 1 cup (250 mL) chopped walnuts

Glaze:

- ½ cup (125 mL) powdered sugar
- 2 teaspoons (10 mL) frozen orange juice concentrate, defrosted
- 1 teaspoon (5 mL) water

TIPS:

If desired, omit brandy in step 1.

Use scissors to cut up dried fruit.

For easy cleanup, place wax paper under cooling rack before drizzling glaze over cake.

15 servings

1 Place apricots and figs or raisins in a small bowl. Cover with plastic wrap. Let stand overnight at room temperature. Drain. Set aside.

2 Preheat oven to 300°F/150°C. In a large mixing bowl, combine flour, granulated sugar, salt and baking powder. Stir in eggs or egg substitute and ½ cup (125 mL) orange juice concentrate. Stir in cherries, pecans, walnuts, apricots and figs or raisins. Mix well. Pour batter into a 9" x 5" (2 L) loaf pan that has been sprayed with vegetable cooking spray.

3 Bake fruitcake for 2 hours. Cover cake with foil. Bake for 15 minutes more, or until toothpick inserted in center comes out clean. Let cake cool 15 minutes before removing from pan. Remove cake from pan and place on wire rack to cool.

4 Meanwhile, combine glaze ingredients in a small bowl. Drizzle glaze over cake while cake is still hot. Cool completely. Wrap cooled cake in plastic wrap, then in foil. Store in refrigerator.

BRANDIED APRICOT TORTE

- 1 pkg. (10¾ oz./298 g) frozen loaf pound cake
- 1 cup (250 mL) apricot preserves
- 2 tablespoons (25 mL) brandy or homemade Apricot Brandy, page 201, divided
- 2 tablespoons (25 mL) butter or margarine
- 1 tablespoon (15 mL) light corn syrup
- 2 squares (1 oz./30 g each) semisweet baking chocolate

6 servings

1 Trim crust, top and sides from the pound cake. Cut lengthwise into thirds. Set aside. Place the preserves in 2-cup (500 mL) measure. Microwave at High 1½ to 2 minutes, or until hot and bubbly. Press through wire strainer into small bowl. Discard pulp. Add 1 tablespoon (15 mL) brandy to strained liquid. Set aside.

2 To assemble cake, place bottom layer on wire rack. Spread with 2 tablespoons (25 mL) strained preserves. Add second layer and spread with 2 tablespoons (25 mL) strained preserves. Add top layer. Spread top and sides with remaining preserves. Refrigerate about 1 hour.

3 To prepare chocolate frosting, place butter, remaining 1 tablespoon (15 mL) brandy and the corn syrup in 2-cup (500 mL) measure. Microwave at High 1½ to 2 minutes, or until butter melts and mixture just comes to a boil. Add chocolate, stirring to melt. Cool until warm. Spread top and sides of cake with frosting. Refrigerate about 30 minutes, or until frosting is firm. Transfer to serving plate.

EASY GERMAN CHOCOLATE CAKE

- ½ cup (125 mL) butter or margarine, divided
- ⅔ cup (150 mL) packed brown sugar, divided
- ⅔ cup (150 mL) flaked coconut, divided
- ⅔ cup (150 mL) finely chopped pecans, divided
- 1½ cups (375 mL) all-purpose flour
- 1⅓ cups (325 mL) granulated sugar
- ¼ cup (50 mL) cocoa
- 1½ teaspoons (7 mL) baking powder
- 1 teaspoon (5 mL) salt
- 1 cup (250 mL) milk
- ⅔ cup (150 mL) shortening
- 3 eggs
- 1 teaspoon (5 mL) vanilla

One 2-layer cake

1 Cut wax paper to fit bottoms of two 9" (2.5 L) round cake dishes. Place ¼ cup (50 mL) butter in each lined dish. Microwave, one dish at a time, at High 45 seconds to 1¼ minutes, or until butter is melted and bubbly. Mix ⅓ cup (75 mL) brown sugar, ⅓ cup (75 mL) coconut and ⅓ cup (75 mL) pecans into butter in each dish. Spread into an even layer. Set dishes aside.

2 Place remaining ingredients in large bowl. Blend at low speed of electric mixer, scraping the bowl constantly. Beat 2 minutes at medium speed, scraping bowl occasionally. Divide and spread the batter into cake dishes.

3 Place one dish on inverted saucer in microwave oven. Reduce power to 50% (Medium). Microwave 6 minutes, rotating ½ turn after half the time. Increase power to High. Microwave 2 to 4 minutes, or until cake is light and springy to the touch, rotating dish once. Sides will just begin to pull away from dish. Let stand directly on counter 5 minutes. Invert onto serving plate. Remove wax paper. Spread any topping from wax paper onto cake top. Repeat with remaining cake. Invert onto wire rack. Cool. Place second layer on top of first layer with frosting side up.

CARAMEL APPLE-TOPPED SPICE CAKE

- 3 tablespoons (50 mL) butter or margarine
- ¼ cup (50 mL) packed dark brown sugar
- 1 medium cooking apple
- 1 cup (250 mL) all-purpose flour
- ⅔ cup (150 mL) granulated sugar
- ¾ teaspoon (4 mL) ground cinnamon
- ½ teaspoon (2 mL) baking soda
- ½ teaspoon (2 mL) salt
- Pinch ground nutmeg
- ⅓ cup (75 mL) shortening
- ⅓ cup (75 mL) buttermilk
- 2 eggs
- ½ teaspoon (2 mL) vanilla

One 9" (23 cm) cake

1 Cut wax paper to fit bottom of 9" (2.5 L) round cake dish. Place butter in 2-cup (500 mL) measure. Microwave at High 30 to 45 seconds, or until melted. Stir in brown sugar. Microwave at High 30 seconds, or until boiling. Stir with fork until smooth. Spread evenly in wax-paper-lined dish.

2 Core and peel apple. Slice thinly. Arrange five slices in center of dish over caramel mixture. Arrange remaining slices around edge of dish, overlapping if necessary. Set aside.

3 Combine remaining ingredients in large bowl. Blend at low speed of electric mixer, scraping bowl constantly. Beat 2 minutes at medium speed, scraping bowl occasionally. Spread batter over apple slices. Place dish on inverted saucer in microwave oven.

4 Reduce power to 50% (Medium). Microwave 6 minutes, rotating ½ turn after half the time. Increase power to High. Microwave 2½ to 5½ minutes, or until cake is light and springy to the touch, rotating dish once. Let stand directly on counter 5 minutes. Invert onto serving plate.

BAKED APPLES

- 4 Rome or other firm red cooking apples
- ½ cup (125 mL) golden raisins
- ¼ cup (50 mL) chopped pecans or walnuts
- ¼ cup (50 mL) light brown sugar
- 2 tablespoons (25 mL) lemon juice

- 1 teaspoon (5 mL) ground cinnamon
- ¼ teaspoon (1 mL) ground ginger
- ¼ teaspoon (1 mL) ground nutmeg
- Plain or vanilla low-fat or nonfat yogurt (optional)

4 servings

1 Preheat oven to 350°F/180°C. With corer or paring knife, remove 1" (2.5 cm) diameter core from each apple without cutting through the bottom. Pare 1½" (4 cm) strip of peel around top of each apple.

2 In small bowl, combine raisins, pecans or walnuts, sugar, lemon juice, cinnamon, ginger and nutmeg. Spoon mixture evenly into apples.

3 Place apples in 8" (2 L) square baking pan. Fill pan halfway with water. Bake apples about 1 hour or until soft. Remove apples from pan with slotted spoon, and cool slightly. Serve with yogurt, if desired.

TIP: *If filling at top of apple begins to burn while baking, cover it loosely with a small piece of foil.*

CHERRY CHEESE ROLL

- 1 cup (250 mL) ricotta cheese
- 1 egg
- 2 tablespoons (25 mL) powdered sugar
- ¼ teaspoon (1 mL) almond extract
- ¼ cup (50 mL) sliced almonds
- 1 round sheet lefse or large crepe (about 12"/30 cm)
- 1 cup (250 mL) cherry pie filling
- Sliced almonds (optional)

4 servings

1 In small mixing bowl, blend ricotta cheese, egg, powdered sugar and almond extract. Stir in almonds. Spread mixture evenly down center of lefse.

2 Fold in opposite sides of lefse to enclose filling. Place roll on 12" (30 cm) platter.

3 Microwave at 50% (Medium) 7 to 11 minutes, or until center of roll is hot, rotating platter once or twice. Top with pie filling. Microwave at High 1 to 2½ minutes, or until pie filling is hot. Top cheese roll with sliced almonds.

GINGERBREAD

- 2¼ cups (550 mL) all-purpose flour
- ¼ cup (50 mL) unsweetened cocoa
- 1 teaspoon (5 mL) baking powder
- 1 teaspoon (5 mL) baking soda
- 1 teaspoon (5 mL) ground cinnamon

- ½ teaspoon (2 mL) ground ginger
- ¼ teaspoon (1 mL) ground nutmeg
- ¼ teaspoon (1 mL) ground cloves
- ¼ teaspoon (1 mL) salt
- 1 cup (250 mL) packed brown sugar
- ¼ cup (50 mL) margarine, softened

- ¼ cup (50 mL) unsweetened applesauce
- 1 cup (250 mL) skim milk
- ½ cup (125 mL) molasses
- ¼ cup (50 mL) frozen cholesterol-free egg product, defrosted, or 1 egg
- Powdered sugar

9 servings

1 Heat oven to 350°F/180°C. Spray 9" (2.5 L) square baking pan with non-stick vegetable cooking spray. Set aside. In medium mixing bowl, combine flour, cocoa, baking powder, baking soda, cinnamon, ginger, nutmeg, cloves and salt. Set aside.

2 Combine brown sugar, margarine and applesauce in large mixing bowl. Beat at medium speed of electric mixer until creamy. Add milk, molasses and egg product. Beat at medium speed until well blended. Gradually beat in flour mixture at low speed until well blended. Beat at medium speed for additional 4 minutes.

3 Pour mixture into prepared pan. Bake for 50 to 55 minutes, or until wooden pick inserted in center comes out clean. Before serving, lightly dust top of gingerbread with powdered sugar.

APPLE BRUNCH MUFFINS

- 6 tablespoons (75 mL) apricot preserves
- 3 plain or sourdough English muffins, split
- 1 medium red cooking apple, cored and thinly sliced (1 cup/250 mL)
- 1 tablespoon (15 mL) frozen orange juice concentrate, defrosted
- 1 tablespoon (15 mL) sugar
- ½ teaspoon (2 mL) apple pie spice

1 Heat oven to 350°F/180°C. Spray baking sheet with nonstick vegetable cooking spray. Set aside.

2 Spread preserves evenly on muffin halves. Top evenly with apple slices. Brush slices with concentrate.

3 Combine sugar and apple pie spice in small bowl. Sprinkle mixture evenly over apples. Arrange muffin halves on prepared baking sheet. Bake for 15 to 18 minutes, or until apples are tender.

6 servings

PUMPKIN PIE BREAD

- 1¼ cups (300 mL) all-purpose flour
- 2 teaspoons (10 mL) pumpkin pie spice
- 1 teaspoon (5 mL) baking powder
- ½ teaspoon (2 mL) baking soda
- ½ teaspoon (2 mL) salt

- 1⅓ cups (325 mL) sugar
- 1 cup (250 mL) canned pumpkin
- ⅓ cup (75 mL) fresh orange juice
- ⅓ cup (75 mL) processed prunes*
- ¼ cup (50 mL) frozen cholesterol-free egg product, defrosted, or 1 egg

- 2 tablespoons (25 mL) vegetable oil
- ½ teaspoon (2 mL) vanilla

16 servings

Process whole pitted prunes in food processor or blender until smooth. Approximately ½ cup (125 mL) whole prunes equals ⅓ cup (75 mL) processed prunes.

1 Heat oven to 350°F/ 180°C. Spray 9" x 5" (2 L) loaf pan with nonstick vegetable cooking spray. Set aside.

2 Combine flour, pumpkin pie spice, baking powder, baking soda and salt in large mixing bowl. Set aside. In medium mixing bowl, combine sugar, pumpkin, juice, prunes, egg product, oil and vanilla. Beat at medium speed of electric mixer until well blended. Add pumpkin mixture to flour mixture. Stir just until dry ingredients are moistened. Pour mixture into prepared pan.

3 Bake for 50 minutes to 1 hour, or until wooden pick inserted in center comes out clean. Let stand 10 minutes. Remove loaf from pan. Cool completely on wire rack before slicing.

↑ CHOCOLATE-COVERED CHERRIES

- ¼ cup (50 mL) butter or margarine
- 2 cups (500 mL) powdered sugar
- ¼ cup (50 mL) sweetened condensed milk
- 36 maraschino cherries
- 1 lb. (500 g) chocolate-flavored candy coating, broken into squares
- 1 tablespoon (15 mL) shortening

3 dozen cherries

1 Place butter in medium mixing bowl. Microwave at 30% (Medium Low) 15 to 45 seconds, or until softened, checking after every 15 seconds. Add powdered sugar. Mix well. Blend in condensed milk. (Mixture will be stiff.)

2 Cover each cherry with about 1 teaspoon (5 mL) sugar mixture. (For easy handling, coat hands with powdered sugar.) Place cherries on wax-paper-lined baking sheet. Chill cherries 30 minutes.

3 Combine chocolate and shortening in 1-quart (1 L) casserole. Microwave at 50% (Medium) 5 to 8 minutes, or until the mixture can be stirred smooth, stirring once or twice.

4 Dip coated cherries in chocolate using two forks. Place on prepared baking sheet and chill until set. (If necessary, microwave chocolate at 50% [Medium] 1 to 3 minutes, or until remelted.)

5 Redip cherries in chocolate. Let cherries cool until chocolate sets. Cover loosely with wax paper. Set aside in cool place 2 to 3 days to allow centers to soften.

↑ CHOCOLATE APRICOT CHEWS

- 1 pkg. (3 oz./85 g) cream cheese
- 1 tablespoon (15 mL) powdered sugar
- ¼ teaspoon (1 mL) vanilla
- 1 pkg. (6 oz./175 g) dried apricot halves
- 1 pkg. (6 oz./175 g) semisweet chocolate chips
- 1 tablespoon (15 mL) shortening

About 15 candies

1 In small bowl, microwave cream cheese at High 15 to 30 seconds, or until softened. Add powdered sugar and vanilla. Mix well. Place small amount of cream cheese mixture between two apricot halves. Press halves together lightly. Repeat with remaining apricot halves and cream cheese mixture. Arrange stuffed apricots on plate. Chill 15 minutes, or until cream cheese filling is firm. Line a baking sheet with wax paper and set aside.

2 In small mixing bowl, combine chocolate chips and shortening. Microwave at 50% (Medium) 3½ to 4½ minutes, or until chocolate is glossy and mixture can be stirred smooth, stirring once or twice. Using two forks, dip stuffed apricots into chocolate mixture, turning to coat completely. Or dip one half only. Arrange apricots on prepared baking sheet. Chill 15 to 20 minutes, or until chocolate is set. Serve chilled.

↑ CARAMEL PECAN CLUSTERS

Remove wrappers from 12 caramels. Set aside. Line a baking sheet with wax paper and set aside. In small mixing bowl, combine ¼ lb. (125 g) chocolate-flavored candy coating and 1 teaspoon (5 mL) shortening. Microwave until mixture melts. Stir in 2 tablespoons (25 mL) finely chopped pecans. With spoon, dip each caramel into chocolate mixture to coat. Drop dipped caramels onto prepared baking sheet. Let clusters cool until set. Store in airtight container or plastic food-storage bag.

12 clusters

CHOCOLATE CHEWS

- 2 squares (1 oz./30 g each) unsweetened chocolate
- 2 tablespoons (25 mL) butter or margarine
- ⅓ cup (75 mL) light corn syrup
- ½ teaspoon (2 mL) vanilla
- 2 cups (500 mL) powdered sugar, divided
- ½ cup (125 mL) nonfat dry milk powder

1¼ lbs./625 g

1 In medium mixing bowl, combine chocolate and butter. Microwave at 50% (Medium) 3 to 4½ minutes, or until chocolate is glossy and mixture can be stirred smooth, stirring once or twice. Blend in corn syrup and vanilla. Microwave at High 1 minute.

2 Mix in 1¾ cups (425 mL) powdered sugar and the dry milk powder. Spread remaining ¼ cup (50 mL) powdered sugar on wooden board. Turn chocolate out onto sugared board and knead until extra sugar is absorbed. Divide dough into 8 equal portions. Roll each portion into ½" (1 cm) diameter rope. Cut each piece into 1½" (4 cm) lengths. Let chocolate chews cool. Wrap each in wax paper.

CANDY PIZZA

- 1 recipe pizza base (below)
- 2 cups (500 mL) stir-ins (opposite)
- ½ to ¾ cup (125 to 175 mL) toppings (opposite)
- 1 recipe frosting (opposite)

1½ lbs. (750 g)

1 Line baking sheet with wax or parchment paper. Set aside. Microwave candy pizza base. Add combined choice of stir-ins. Mix well to coat.

2 Spread the base mixture evenly on the prepared baking sheet to 10" (25 cm) diameter. Sprinkle with combined choice of toppings. Set aside.

Microwave frosting. Drizzle frosting over candy pizza. Chill at least 1½ hours, or until set. Peel off wax paper. Break candy apart, or serve in wedges.

Candy Pizza Base

Light Chocolate:
In medium mixing bowl, combine 1½ cups (375 mL) milk chocolate chips and 3 squares (1 oz./30 g each) semisweet chocolate. Microwave at 50% (Medium) 4 to 6 minutes, or until chocolate can be stirred smooth, stirring twice.

White Chocolate:
In medium mixing bowl, combine ¾ lb. (375 g) white candy coating (broken into squares) and 1 tablespoon (15 mL) shortening. Microwave at 50% (Medium) 2½ to 5½ minutes, or until mixture can be stirred smooth, stirring twice.

Peanut Butter:
In medium mixing bowl, combine 1½ cups (375 mL) peanut butter chips and 3 oz. (90 g) white candy coating. Microwave at 50% (Medium) 4 to 6 minutes, or until mixture can be stirred smooth, stirring twice.

Dark Chocolate:
In medium mixing bowl, combine 1½ cups (375 mL) semisweet chocolate chips and 3 squares (1 oz./30 g each) unsweetened chocolate. Microwave at 50% (Medium) 4 to 6 minutes, or until chocolate can be stirred smooth, stirring twice.

Mint Chocolate:
In medium mixing bowl, combine 1½ cups (375 mL) mint-flavored semisweet chocolate chips and 3 squares (1 oz./30 g each) semisweet chocolate. Microwave at 50% (Medium) 4 to 6 minutes, or until chocolate can be stirred smooth, stirring once or twice.

Butterscotch:
In medium mixing bowl, combine 1½ cups (375 mL) butterscotch chips and 3 oz. (90 g) white candy coating. Microwave at 50% (Medium) 4 to 6 minutes, or until mixture can be stirred smooth, stirring twice.

Candy Pizza Stir-ins

Use one or more of the following, to equal 2 cups (500 mL):

- Crisp rice cereal
- Toasted round oat cereal
- Corn flakes cereal
- Crisp square rice, wheat or corn cereal
- Coarsely crushed pretzel sticks
- Coarsely crushed shoestring potatoes
- Salted mixed nuts
- Chopped nuts
- Salted dry-roasted peanuts
- Whole or slivered almonds
- Miniature marshmallows

Candy Pizza Toppings

Use one or more of the following toppings, to equal ½ to ¾ cup (125 to 175 mL):

- Miniature jelly beans
- Jellied orange slices, cut up
- Candied fruit
- Candied cherries, cut up
- Maraschino cherries, drained
- Red or black licorice pieces
- Shredded coconut
- Candy-coated plain or peanut chocolate pieces
- Candy-coated peanut butter pieces
- Chocolate-covered raisins
- Candy corn

Candy Pizza Frosting

- ¼ lb. (125 g) white or chocolate-flavored candy coating
- 1 teaspoon (5 mL) shortening

  Frosts one candy pizza

In 2-cup (500 mL) measure, combine candy coating and shortening. Microwave until melted. Drizzle frosting over candy pizza.

BASIC TRUFFLES

- 2 bars (4 oz./113 g each) sweet baking chocolate, cut up
- ⅓ cup (75 mL) whipping cream
- 3 tablespoons (50 mL) butter or margarine
- ½ teaspoon (2 mL) vanilla

Coatings:

- Powered sugar
- Cocoa
- Finely chopped nuts
- Shredded coconut

24 truffles

1 Line an 8 x 4" (1.5 L) loaf dish with plastic wrap. Set aside. In 1-quart (1 L) measure, combine chocolate, whipping cream and butter. Microwave at 50% (Medium) 4 to 6 minutes, or until chocolate melts and mixture can be stirred smooth, stirring once. Beat mixture until smooth and shiny. Blend in vanilla. Pour mixture into prepared loaf dish. Refrigerate 4 hours. Lift chocolate mixture from dish and cut into 24 equal portions. Let stand 10 minutes.

2 Coat hands lightly with powdered sugar and roll each portion into ¾" (2 cm) ball. Place desired coating in small bowl and roll each ball to coat. Place each truffle in paper candy cup and chill at least 1 hour before serving. Store truffles in refrigerator no longer than 2 weeks.

Variation: *Follow recipe above, except omit vanilla and substitute another complementary flavored extract (maple, almond, cherry, orange, peppermint, etc.).*

TIP: *Work quickly when rolling mixture into balls. Chocolate mixture is rich, and melts easily.*

- 2 bars (4 oz./113 g each) sweet baking chocolate, cut up
- ⅓ cup (75 mL) whipping cream
- 3 tablespoons (50 mL) butter or margarine
- 1 tablespoon (15 mL) liqueur (almond, cherry, orange, etc.)

Coating:

- ½ lb. (250 g) white or chocolate-flavored candy coating, divided
- ¼ cup (50 mL) shortening, divided

Decoration:

- 1 square (1 oz./30 g) semisweet chocolate
- 1 teaspoon (5 mL) shortening

10 truffles

TIP: *For pastel-colored truffles, or decorative toppings, tint white candy coating with 1 or 2 drops food coloring.*

1 Line an 8" x 4" (1.5 L) loaf dish with plastic wrap. Set aside. In 1-quart (1 L) measure, combine the chocolate, whipping cream and butter. Microwave at 50% (Medium) 4 to 6 minutes, or until chocolate melts and mixture can be stirred smooth, stirring once. Beat until smooth and shiny. Blend in liqueur. Pour into prepared loaf dish. Refrigerate 4 hours.

2 Lift chocolate mixture from dish and cut into 10 equal portions. Let stand 10 minutes. Line a baking sheet with wax paper and set aside. Coat hands slightly with powdered sugar and roll each portion into 1¼" (6 cm) ball. Place on prepared baking sheet. Chill 15 minutes.

3 Combine ¼ lb. (125 g) candy coating and 2 tablespoons (25 mL) shortening in 2-cup (500 mL) measure. Microwave until mixture melts. Using fork, dip each chocolate ball in candy coating. Place on prepared baking sheet. Chill until set.

4 Combine remaining candy coating and shortening in clean 2-cup (500 mL) measure. Microwave until melted. Redip truffles and chill until coating is set.

5 Place semisweet chocolate square and 1 teaspoon (5 mL) shortening in small bowl. Microwave at 50% (Medium) 2½ to 4½ minutes, or until chocolate is glossy and mixture can be stirred smooth, stirring once. Drizzle melted chocolate in decorative design over tops of coated truffles. Chill before serving. Store truffles in refrigerator no longer than 2 weeks.

Use your microwave whenever a recipe calls for melted chocolate. No double boiler is needed because microwave energy penetrates from all sides rather than just the base as in range-top cooking. Microwaving also eliminates the need for constant stirring and reduces the possibility of scorching.

CHOCOLATE-DIPPED SNACKS & FRUIT

Coating:

- ½ lb. (250 g) chocolate-flavored candy coating or white candy coating

Or:

- ½ lb. (250 g) confectioners' candy coating plus 1 tablespoon (15 mL) shortening

Dippers:

- Potato chips, broken into 1" to 1½" (2.5 to 4 cm) pieces
- Pretzels
- Candied Peel (page 279)
- Candied Pineapple (page 278)
- Fresh strawberries

About 6 dozen pieces

1 Place candy coating in 2-cup (500 mL) measure or small deep bowl. Microwave at 50% (Medium) 3 to 4½ minutes, or until coating is glossy and can be stirred smooth, rotating after each minute. Stir to melt any small pieces. If coating begins to set, resoften at 50% (Medium) at 1-minute intervals, or until of proper dipping consistency.

2 Use two forks to dip pieces into coating. Let excess coating fall back into bowl. Cool on wire rack until set. Store pretzels or potato chips in wax-paper-lined container in cool, dry place. Refrigerate chocolate-coated fruit until serving time.

CHOCOLATE-COVERED MARSHMALLOWS

- 1 cup (250 mL) chocolate chips
- ¼ cup (50 mL) shortening
- 2 cups (500 mL) chopped nuts
- 1 pkg. (10 oz./300 g) large marshmallows
- 50 wooden picks

50 marshmallows

1 Place chocolate chips and shortening in 2-cup (500 mL) measure. Microwave at 50% (Medium) 1½ to 3½ minutes, or until chips are shiny and soft. Stir until smooth.

2 Place nuts in shallow dish. Insert pick in top of each marshmallow. Dip in chocolate to cover completely. Roll in nuts, coating about three-fourths of the way up. Set on wax paper. Repeat with remaining marshmallows. Let stand until firm. Stir together leftover nuts and chocolate. Drop by spoonfuls onto wax paper. Wrap marshmallows and candy drops individually in plastic wrap or store in covered container.

BUTTERMILK PRALINES

- 2 cups (500 mL) sugar
- 1 teaspoon (5 mL) baking soda
- 1 cup (250 mL) buttermilk
- ¾ cup (175 mL) butter or margarine
- 1 teaspoon (5 mL) vanilla
- 2 cups (500 mL) pecan halves

4 dozen pralines

1 Butter 3-qt. (3 L) mixing bowl. Stir in sugar, baking soda, buttermilk and butter. Microwave at 50% (Medium) 30 to 40 minutes, or until a soft ball forms in cold water, stirring 2 or 3 times during cooking. Add vanilla. Beat at high speed of electric mixer until soft peaks form. Stir in pecans.

2 Drop by teaspoons (5 mL) onto wax paper. Cool until firm. Store in tightly covered container in freezer no longer than 3 months or in refrigerator no longer than 1½ months.

CHOCOLATE BOURBON BALLS

- 1½ cups (375 mL) fine vanilla wafer crumbs
- ⅓ cup (75 mL) bourbon
- 1 cup (250 mL) semisweet chocolate chips
- 2 tablespoons (25 mL) butter or margarine
- ½ cup (125 mL) finely chopped pecans
- 1¼ to 1½ cups (300 to 375 mL) powdered sugar, divided

4 dozen balls

In small bowl, mix cookie crumbs and bourbon. Set aside. Place chips and butter in large bowl. Microwave at 50% (Medium) 2 to 5 minutes, or until chips are soft. Stir until smooth. Stir in pecans and crumb mixture. Gradually mix in enough sugar until mixture just holds together. Shape by teaspoons (5 mL) into balls; place on wax paper. Roll in remaining sugar to coat. Store in refrigerator, tightly covered, no longer than 2 weeks.

COCONUT DATE BALLS

- 2 cups (500 mL) chopped dates
- ¾ cup (175 mL) sugar
- ½ cup (125 mL) butter or margarine
- 1 egg
- 2 tablespoons (25 mL) milk
- 1 teaspoon (5 mL) vanilla
- ½ teaspoon (2 mL) salt
- 2 cups (500 mL) crushed corn flakes
- ½ cup (125 mL) chopped pecans
- 1 cup (250 mL) flaked coconut

5½ dozen balls

1 In medium bowl, combine dates, sugar and butter. Microwave at High 4 minutes, stirring 2 or 3 times. Stir until all butter is absorbed. In small bowl, mix egg, milk, vanilla and salt. Stir a small amount of hot dates into egg mixture, then return to dates, stirring constantly.

2 Reduce power to 50% (Medium). Microwave 5 to 8 minutes, or until thickened and mixture forms a ball when stirred. Mix in corn flakes and pecans. Shape into 1" (2.5 cm) balls; roll in coconut. Place on wax paper. Chill until set. Store in refrigerator or at room temperature, tightly covered, no longer than 2 weeks.

APRICOT CHEWS

- ½ cup (125 mL) butter or margarine
- 1 cup (250 mL) granulated sugar
- ⅓ cup (75 mL) all-purpose flour
- ½ teaspoon (2 mL) salt
- 2 eggs
- 1 cup (250 mL) chopped dried apricots
- 3 cups (750 mL) wheat flake cereal, coarsely crushed
- 1 cup (250 mL) chopped pecans
- 1 teaspoon (5 mL) vanilla
- ½ to ¾ cup (125 to 175 mL) powdered sugar

4½ dozen chews

1 Place butter in 2-qt. (2 L) bowl or casserole. Microwave at High 45 seconds to 1¼ minutes, or until melted. Blend in granulated sugar, flour, salt and eggs. Stir in apricots. Microwave at High 3½ to 6 minutes, or until very thick, stirring every 2 minutes. Cool 5 minutes.

2 In large bowl, combine cereal and pecans. Stir in apricot mixture and vanilla until all ingredients are well distributed. Shape into 1" (2.5 cm) balls. Place powdered sugar in plastic bag. Shake a few apricot balls at a time in bag until coated. Repeat. Refrigerate 2 to 3 hours, or until chilled.

THIN MINT LAYERS

- 1 pkg. (6 oz./175 g) semisweet chocolate chips
- 3 tablespoons (50 mL) butter or margarine, divided
- 1 cup (250 mL) powdered sugar
- ⅛ teaspoon (0.5 mL) peppermint extract
- 2 to 5 drops green food coloring
- 3 to 4 teaspoons (15 to 20 mL) milk

25 mints

1 In 2-cup (500 mL) measure, combine chocolate chips and 2 tablespoons (25 mL) butter. Microwave at High 45 seconds to 1½ minutes, or until chips are soft. Stir until smooth. Spread in 8" x 8" (2 L) baking dish. Chill about 1 hour, or until set.

2 In medium bowl, combine sugar, remaining butter, the peppermint extract and food coloring. Beat with electric mixer, adding milk as needed, until smooth and stiff frosting consistency. Spread on chilled chocolate layer. Chill 3 to 4 hours, or until firm. Cut into about 1½" (4 cm) squares. Store in refrigerator, tightly covered, no longer than 1 week.

CHOCOLATE DESSERT & LIQUEUR CUPS

Dessert Cups:

- 12 paper cupcake liners
- 4 squares (1 oz./30 g each) semisweet baking chocolate
- 2 teaspoons (10 mL) shortening

Liqueur Cups:

- 20 paper candy cups
- 2 squares (1 oz./30 g each) semisweet baking chocolate
- 1 teaspoon (5 mL) shortening

10 liqueur cups

1 Double paper liners to yield six dessert cup forms or ten liqueur cup forms. Arrange on a flat plate. Set aside. Place desired amount of chocolate and shortening in 2-cup (500 mL) measure.

2 Microwave at 50% (Medium) 3½ to 4 minutes (dessert cups) or 2½ to 3½ minutes (liqueur cups), or until the mixture is glossy and can be stirred smooth, stirring after each minute.

3 Spoon 1 tablespoon (15 mL) melted chocolate into each double thickness dessert cup liner or 1 teaspoon (5 mL) melted chocolate into each liqueur cup form. Tilt cups to coat sides to within ⅛" (3 mm) of top. Continue to tilt to form thick chocolate shell.

4 Return coated liners to flat plate. Refrigerate dessert cups 1 hour before removing paper, and liqueur cups 30 minutes. Return to refrigerator until serving time. Fill dessert cups with sherbet or ice cream; fill liqueur cups with liqueurs.

FRUIT-FLAVORED CRISPY BARS

- ⅓ cup (75 mL) butter or margarine
- ¼ cup (50 mL) fruit-flavored gelatin (half of 3-oz./85 g pkg.)
- 1 pkg. (10 oz./300 g) marshmallows
- 8 cups (2 L) crisp rice cereal

24 bars

1 Grease 12" x 8" (3 L) baking dish. Place butter in large bowl. Microwave at High 45 to 60 seconds, or until melted. Mix in gelatin. Stir in marshmallows, tossing to coat.

2 Microwave at High 1½ to 2 minutes, or until marshmallows melt, stirring after half the time. Immediately stir in cereal until well coated. Press into prepared dish with back of lightly buttered large spoon. Cool. Cut into 2" (5 cm) squares.

Remaining Gelatin: *Microwave ½ cup (125 mL) water at High 1 to 2 minutes, or until boiling. Stir in gelatin until dissolved. Stir in ½ cup (125 mL) cold water. Chill. 2 servings.*

CHOCOLATE-COVERED BANANAS

- 3 large firm bananas
- 6 wooden popsicle sticks
- 1 cup (250 mL) semisweet chocolate chips
- 2 tablespoons (25 mL) shortening
- ½ cup (125 mL) chopped peanuts

6 servings

1 Peel bananas; cut each in half crosswise. Insert wooden sticks. Place on wax-paper-lined plate or baking sheet. Place chocolate chips and shortening in 2-cup (500 mL) measure. Microwave at 50% (Medium) 2½ to 4 minutes, or until chips are glossy and can be stirred smooth.

2 Spoon melted chocolate over each banana to coat. Allow any excess to drip back into bowl. Sprinkle bananas with peanuts. Place on wax-paper-lined plate. Freeze until firm. Wrap in wax paper, label and freeze no longer than 2 weeks.

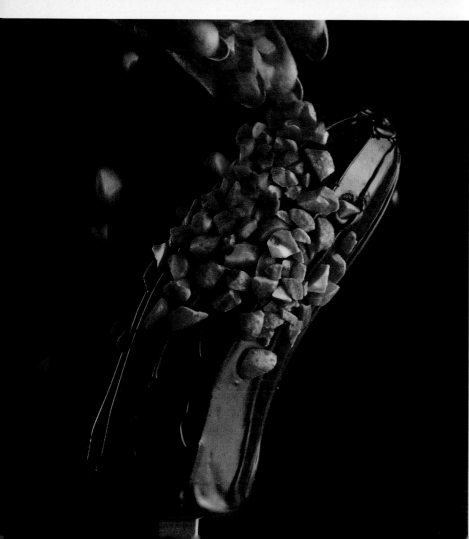

ORANGE-SPICED PECAN BRITTLE

- ½ cup (125 mL) granulated sugar
- ½ cup (125 mL) packed brown sugar
- ¼ cup (50 mL) dark corn syrup
- 2 tablespoons (25 mL) water
- ¼ teaspoon (1 mL) salt
- ¼ teaspoon (1 mL) ground cinnamon
- ¼ teaspoon (1 mL) ground nutmeg

- 1 cup (250 mL) chopped pecans
- 1 tablespoon (15 mL) butter or margarine
- 1 teaspoon (5 mL) baking soda
- ½ teaspoon (2 mL) orange extract or homemade Orange Extract, page 278

¾ lb. (375 g) or
2 cups (500 mL) crushed

1 Line large baking sheet with foil. In large bowl, combine granulated sugar, brown sugar, corn syrup, water, salt, cinnamon and nutmeg. Microwave at High 5 minutes. Stir in pecans. Insert microwave candy thermometer. Microwave at High 1½ to 4½ minutes, or until temperature is 300°F/150°C (hard crack stage*), stirring after each minute.

2 Stir in butter, baking soda and orange extract until light and foamy. With rubber spatula, quickly spread to thin layer on prepared baking sheet. Cool. Break apart. Serve as a snack, or crush for use as a dessert topping. Store in airtight container no longer than 2 months.

Hard Crack Stage: *Syrup separates into hard, brittle threads when dropped into cold water.*

AMARETTO GLAZED ALMONDS

- 3 tablespoons (50 mL) Amaretto
- ½ cup (125 mL) blanched whole almonds

½ cup (125 mL)

Place Amaretto in 9" (23 cm) pie plate. Stir in almonds, tossing to coat. Microwave at High 4 to 5 minutes, or until glazed and light golden brown, stirring after each minute. Almonds will continue to toast after they are removed from oven. Spread on sheet of foil to cool. Store in airtight container. Serve as a snack or dessert garnish.

FRUIT-FLAVORED POPCORN BARS

- 1 bag (10 oz./300 g) large marshmallows
- ¼ cup (50 mL) butter or margarine, cut up
- 3 tablespoons (50 mL) fruit-flavored gelatin powder (any flavor)
- 8 cups (2 L) popped popcorn
- ½ cup (125 mL) dry-roasted peanuts (optional)

16 popcorn bars

1 Grease 9" (2.5 L) square baking dish. Set aside. In large mixing bowl, place marshmallows and butter. Microwave at High 2 to 3 minutes, or until marshmallows puff and mixture can be stirred smooth, stirring 2 or 3 times.

2 Add gelatin. Mix well. Add popcorn and peanuts. Stir to coat. With buttered fingers, press popcorn mixture into prepared baking dish. Let mixture cool, and cut into 16 bars.

Fruit-flavored Popcorn Sculptures:
Follow recipe above, except shape popcorn mixture into any desired shape on greased baking sheet.

RED HOT POPCORN BALLS

- 6 tablespoons (75 mL) butter or margarine
- ½ cup (125 mL) red cinnamon candies
- 10 large marshmallows
- ⅓ cup (75 mL) packed brown sugar
- 2 tablespoons (25 mL) light corn syrup
- 8 cups (2 L) popped popcorn

6 popcorn balls

Popcorn Sculptures: Follow either popcorn recipe, except shape prepared popcorn mixture into any desired shape on greased baking sheet. Decorate with prepared frosting, jelly beans or decorator sprinkles.

1 In large mixing bowl, combine butter and cinnamon candies. Microwave at High 3½ to 4 minutes, or until candies are melted and can be stirred smooth. Add marshmallows, brown sugar and corn syrup. Microwave at High 1 to 1½ minutes, or until marshmallows puff and mixture can be stirred smooth, stirring 2 or 3 times. Add popcorn. Stir to coat.

2 With buttered fingers, shape popcorn mixture into 6 balls. Let popcorn balls cool. Wrap with plastic wrap, and tie with ribbon, if desired.

CARAMEL CORN

- 3 tablespoons (50 mL) butter or margarine
- ¾ cup (175 mL) packed brown sugar
- ⅓ cup (75 mL) shelled raw peanuts
- 3 tablespoons (50 mL) dark corn syrup
- ½ teaspoon (2 mL) vanilla
- ¼ teaspoon (1 mL) baking soda
- Pinch salt
- 5 cups (1.25 L) popped popcorn

5 cups (1.25 L)

Soft Crack Stage: Syrup separates into hard but not brittle threads when dropped into cold water.

1 Place butter in 8-cup (2 L) measure or large bowl. Microwave at High 30 to 45 seconds, or until melted.

2 Stir in brown sugar, peanuts and corn syrup. Insert microwave candy thermometer.

3 Microwave at High 3 to 4 minutes, or until mixture reaches 280°F/135°C (soft crack stage*).

4 Mix in vanilla, baking soda and salt. Place prepared popcorn in large bowl.

5 Pour hot mixture quickly over popcorn, stirring to coat. Microwave popcorn at High 2 minutes, stirring after half the time.

6 Stir again. Cool about 30 minutes, stirring occasionally to break apart.

LOLLIPOPS

- 1 cup (250 mL) sugar
- ½ cup (125 mL) light corn syrup
- ¼ cup (50 mL) water
- ¼ teaspoon (1 mL) orange, lemon (page 278) or peppermint extract
- Food coloring (orange, yellow or red)
- 12 wooden popsicle sticks or lollipop sticks

12 lollipops

Hard Crack Stage: Syrup separates into hard, brittle threads when dropped into cold water.

1 Mix sugar, corn syrup and water in 8-cup (2 L) measure. Use wet pastry brush to wash sugar crystals from sides of measure. Insert microwave candy thermometer.

2 Microwave at High 9 to 12½ minutes, or until mixture reaches 310°F/155°C (hard crack stage*), stirring every 2 minutes. Stir in desired extract and food coloring.

3 Pour over sticks arranged on buttered foil, or pour into lollipop molds, below. Let stand about 1 hour, or until hard. Wrap in plastic wrap. Store in a cool, dry place.

HOW TO MAKE LOLLIPOP MOLDS

1 Cut 1" (2.5 cm) off top of twelve 9-oz./275 mL wax-coated paper drinking cups.

2 Grease inside of top portion of cup. Punch small hole in side of mold; insert stick.

3 Place molds on buttered foil. Fill as directed, above.

GRANOLA

- 3 cups (750 mL) old-fashioned rolled oats
- ½ cup (125 mL) shredded coconut
- ⅓ cup (75 mL) sliced almonds, chopped
- ⅔ cup (150 mL) honey
- ¼ cup (50 mL) packed dark brown sugar
- ¼ cup (50 mL) vegetable oil
- 1 teaspoon (5 mL) ground cinnamon
- 1 teaspoon (5 mL) vanilla
- 1 teaspoon (5 mL) molasses
- ½ cup (125 mL) raisins
- ⅓ cup (75 mL) chopped dried apples

6 cups (1.5 L)

- 6 cups (1.5 L) Granola (opposite)
- ½ cup (125 mL) butter or margarine
- ½ cup (125 mL) packed dark brown sugar
- Pinch salt
- 2 eggs, slightly beaten
- ¼ teaspoon (1 mL) almond extract

12 bars

1 Prepare granola as directed, except omit raisins. Set aside. Place butter in 2-cup (500 mL) measure or medium bowl. Microwave at High 45 seconds to 1½ minutes, or until melted. In medium bowl, combine brown sugar, salt, eggs and almond extract. Beat in butter until combined. Stir in granola until coated. Press into greased 12" x 8" (3 L) baking dish.

2 Microwave at High 6 to 9 minutes, or until firm to the touch, rotating dish ½ turn and pressing mixture with spatula every 2 minutes. Cut into twelve 4" x 2" (10 x 5 cm) bars. Cool completely before removing from dish. Store in refrigerator no longer than 1 week.

HOW TO MICROWAVE GRANOLA

1 Mix rolled oats, shredded coconut and chopped almonds in large bowl. Set aside.

2 Combine remaining ingredients, except raisins and apples, in 8-cup (2 L) measure. Microwave at High 2 to 3 minutes, or until boiling, stirring after each minute.

3 Pour the honey mixture over the oats, tossing to coat. Microwave at High 4½ to 7 minutes, or until the mixture begins to stiffen and appear dry, stirring every 2 minutes. For crisper cereal, microwave 30 to 60 seconds longer, or until the coconut begins to brown lightly.

4 Stir in raisins and apples. Allow mixture to cool about 1 to 1½ hours, stirring to break apart 1 or 2 times during cooling.

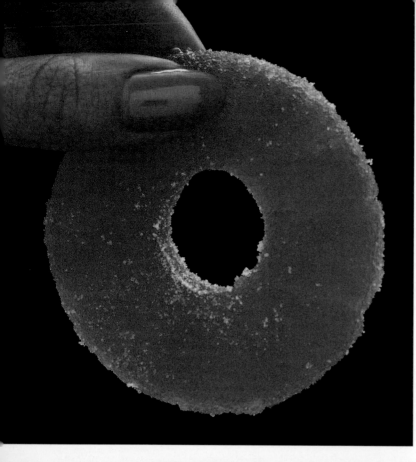

← CANDIED PINEAPPLE

- 1 cup (250 mL) sugar
- 1 can (20 oz./ 570 mL) pineapple slices, packed in own juice, drained and ⅓ cup (75 mL) juice reserved
- 2 tablespoons (25 mL) light corn syrup
- Sugar

10 slices

1 In 3-qt. (3 L) casserole, combine 1 cup (250 mL) sugar, ⅓ cup (75 mL) reserved pineapple juice and the corn syrup. Arrange five pineapple slices in single layer over sugar mixture. Microwave at High 8 to 12 minutes, or until sugar dissolves and slices are glossy and transparent on edges, turning over and rearranging every 4 minutes. Remove slices to wire rack to cool. They will become more transparent as they stand.

2 Add remaining slices to hot syrup. Microwave as directed above. Cool. When slices have cooled completely, coat with sugar. Cover with wax paper and let stand on wire rack at least 24 hours to dry. Re-coat with sugar. Slices will be slightly sticky. Store in airtight container with wax paper between layers no longer than 2 weeks.

← LEMON OR ORANGE EXTRACT

- 1 lemon or orange
- ½ cup (125 mL) vodka

½ cup (125 mL)

Remove peel from lemon with vegetable peeler or zester. Do not include white membrane. Place peel in 4-oz. (125 mL) bottle. Add vodka. Microwave at High 30 to 45 seconds, or until bottle is warm to the touch. Cap bottle. Let stand at room temperature about 2 weeks before using.

STEWED FRUIT

- 1 cup (250 mL) dried fruit (prunes, apricots, apples or mixed dried fruit)
- ½ cup (125 mL) water

1 cup (250 mL)

Place dried fruit in 1½-qt. (1.5 L) casserole; sprinkle with water. Cover. Microwave at High 2 to 4 minutes, or until water boils, stirring after each minute. Let stand, covered, 5 minutes. Stir before serving. Sprinkle with cinnamon, if desired.

CANDIED PEEL

- 3 large oranges
- 1 lemon
- 6⅓ (1.575 L) cups water, divided
- ⅔ cup (150 mL) granulated sugar
- ¼ cup (50 mL) powdered sugar

1 cup (250 mL)

1 Remove peel from oranges and lemon with vegetable peeler or zester. Do not include the white membrane of fruit.

2 Combine 2 cups (500 mL) water and the strips of peel in 4-cup (1 L) measure or medium bowl. Microwave at High 4 to 6 minutes, or until the water boils. Drain.

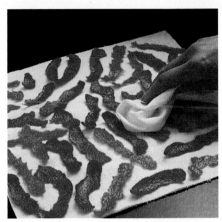

3 Repeat process 2 more times, boiling all the peel in 2 cups (500 mL) of water each time. Rinse peel. Drain on paper towels; pat dry.

4 Combine ⅓ cup (75 mL) water and the granulated sugar in 3-qt. (3 L) casserole. Stir in peel. Microwave at High 6 to 8 minutes, or until sugar dissolves and peel is glossy and transparent, stirring every 2 minutes.

5 Remove peel with slotted spoon to rack. Cool. Sift powdered sugar over peel. Let cool completely. Store in airtight container no longer than 1 month.

6 Serve as a dipper for chocolate fondue, or add one strip of peel to cup of coffee or hot chocolate to flavor the drink.

Gifts from
the Kitchen

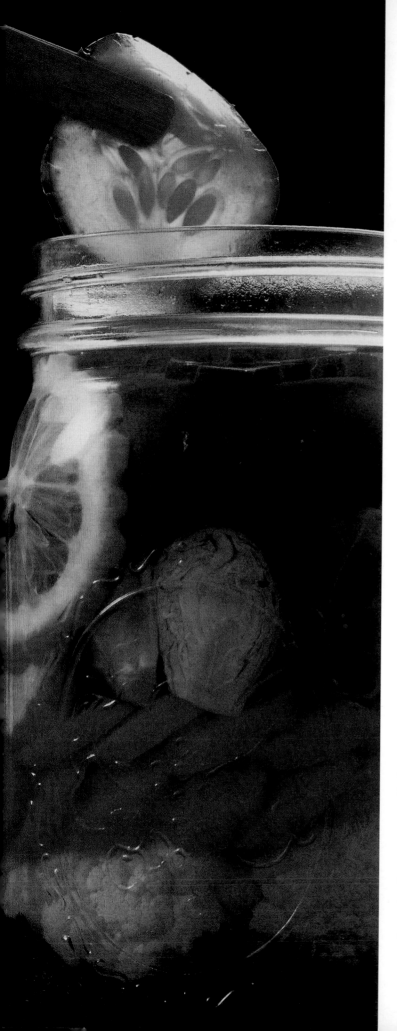

Putting up pickles and relishes once meant hours of effort at harvest time. With most ingredients available year-round, modern cooks can microwave small batches of these items as they are needed. Microwaving is cooler, cleaner, and faster than conventional methods, and small batches can provide more variety. These home-made specialties have true, natural flavor. They make welcome gifts when presented in an attractive bottle.

Experiment with a variety of pickles, your own home-made salsa, or trend-setting specialty mustards, which add spice to meals and cost less than those purchased from gourmet food shops.

The recipes on pages 282-290 are packed into sterilized jars after microwaving. They are not pressure- or water bath-canned, so they do require refrigeration.

ANTIPASTO JAR

Pickling Liquid:

- 1 cup (250 mL) water
- ½ cup (125 mL) Onion-Garlic Vinegar (page 291), or cider vinegar
- 1 tablespoon (15 mL) salt
- 1 tablespoon (15 mL) vegetable oil

Three cups (750 mL) fresh vegetables: Use a combination of the following to equal 3 cups (750 mL):

- Broccoli flowerets and stalks, sliced ¼" (5 mm) thick
- Brussels sprouts (¼ lb./125 g), cut in half lengthwise
- Sliced carrots, ¼" (5 mm) thick
- Cauliflowerets
- ½ cup (125 mL) water

One cup (250 mL) fresh vegetables: Use a combination of the following to equal 1 cup (250 mL):

- Fresh whole mushrooms, 1" (2.5 cm) diameter
- Green or ripe olives
- Green pepper, cut into 1" (2.5 cm) pieces
- Sliced cucumber

Garnish: Add one or more of the following:

- 1 lemon slice
- 1 bay leaf
- 1 sprig fresh dill, basil or oregano

1 quart (1 L)

PICKLED CARROTS

- 12 oz. (375 g) fresh tiny whole carrots
- ¼ cup (50 mL) water

Pickling Liquid:

- ½ cup (125 mL) cider vinegar
- ⅓ cup (75 mL) sugar
- ½ to 1 teaspoon (2 to 5 mL) salt
- Pinch celery seed

- Pinch mustard seed
- Pinch dried crushed red pepper
- 4 whole cloves
- 4 whole peppercorns
- 2 small cloves garlic, peeled
- 1 bay leaf
- 1 stick cinnamon

1 pint (500 mL)

1 Wash and scrub or peel carrots; trim ends. Place in 1½-qt. (1.5 L) casserole. Add water; cover. Microwave at High 3 to 4 minutes, or until tender-crisp, stirring after half the time. Place under cold running water until cool. Drain. Pack into sterilized 1-pint (500 mL) jar or two ½-pint (250 mL) jars. Set aside.

2 In 2-cup (500 mL) measure, combine pickling liquid ingredients. Microwave at High 1 to 2 minutes, or until boiling, stirring after half the time to dissolve the sugar and salt. Pour over carrots in the jar. Cover. Refrigerate 1 week before serving. Store in refrigerator no longer than 1 month.

1 Mix pickling liquid in 4-cup (1 L) measure. Microwave at High 3½ to 5½ minutes, or until boiling, stirring after half the time.

2 Combine desired 3 cups (750 mL) vegetables in 2-qt. (2 L) casserole. Add ½ cup (125 mL) water. Cover.

3 Microwave at High 2 to 4 minutes, or until color of vegetables intensifies, stirring once.

4 Place immediately under cold running water until cool. Drain. Add remaining 1 cup (250 mL) vegetables.

5 Pack vegetables into sterilized 1-qt. (1 L) jar, layering if desired. Include choice of garnish.

6 Pour pickling liquid over the vegetables. Cover. Refrigerate 2 to 3 days before serving. Store in refrigerator no longer than 1 month.

WATERMELON PICKLES

- 1 lb. (500 g) watermelon rind
- ½ cup (125 mL) sugar
- ½ cup (125 mL) cider vinegar
- 1 tablespoon (15 mL) chopped cyrstallized ginger
- 2 teaspoons (10 mL) grated fresh orange peel or 1 teaspoon (5 mL) dried orange peel
- 4 whole cloves
- 1 stick cinnamon

1 pint (500 mL)

1 Trim dark green outer skin from rind. Cut trimmed rind into 1" (2.5 cm) chunks. (Yields 3 cups/750 mL.) Place chunks in 1½-qt. (1.5 L) casserole. Add sugar, tossing to coat. Cover and let stand overnight.

2 Stir in vinegar, ginger, orange peel and cloves. Add cinnamon. Microwave, uncovered, at High 10 to 13 minutes, or until chunks are transparent, stirring every 3 minutes. Remove cinnamon stick. Spoon into hot sterilized 1-pint (500 mL) jar; cover. Refrigerate 1 week before serving. Store in refrigerator no longer than 1 month.

CABBAGE RELISH

- 2½ cups (625 mL) shredded green or red cabbage
- ¾ cup (175 mL) chopped red onion
- ½ cup (125 mL) chopped green pepper
- 1 cup (250 mL) white vinegar
- ⅔ cup (150 mL) sugar
- 2 teaspoons (10 mL) salt
- ½ teaspoon (2 mL) celery seed
- ½ teaspoon (2 mL) mustard seed
- ¼ teaspoon (1 mL) ground turmeric

2 pints (1 L)

1 In medium bowl combine cabbage, red onion and green pepper. Divide mixture equally between two sterilized 1-pint (500 mL) jars. Set aside.

2 In 4-cup (1 L) measure, combine vinegar, sugar, salt, celery seed, mustard seed and turmeric. Microwave at High 2 to 4 minutes, or until boiling, stirring after half the time to dissolve sugar and salt. Divide between two jars; cover. Refrigerate 1 week before serving. Store in refrigerator no longer than 1 month.

APPLE-PEAR CHUTNEY

- 2 medium apples, cored and chopped
- 2 medium pears, peeled, cored and chopped
- 1½ cups (375 mL) packed dark brown sugar
- 1 cup (250 mL) cider vinegar
- ¾ cup (175 mL) chopped onion
- ⅔ cup (150 mL) chopped green pepper
- ½ cup (125 mL) chopped dates
- 1 tablespoon (15 mL) chopped crystallized ginger
- 1 teaspoon (5 mL) salt
- 1 teaspoon (5 mL) dry mustard
- 4 whole cloves
- 4 whole allspice
- 2 bay leaves
- 1 stick cinnamon

2 pints (1 L)

1 Combine apples, pears, brown sugar, vinegar, onion and green pepper. Process in food processor, turning motor on and off 4 to 6 times, or place in blender and process 10 to 15 seconds, or until chopped but not puréed. (Process in two batches, if necessary.) Place the mixture in 2-qt. (2 L) casserole. Stir in remaining ingredients.

2 Microwave at High 18 to 25 minutes, or until very thick, stirring 3 or 4 times. Cool to room temperature. Discard bay leaves and cinnamon stick.

3 Divide equally between two sterilized 1-pint (500 mL) jars; cover. Refrigerate 1 week before serving. Store in refrigerator no longer than 1 month.

NOTE: *Use as a condiment for meat or curry dishes.*

CORN RELISH

- 3 cups (750 mL) frozen whole kernel corn
- ½ cup (125 mL) chopped green pepper
- ¼ cup (50 mL) chopped onion
- 2 tablespoons (25 mL) chopped pimiento, drained
- 1 cup (250 mL) white vinegar
- ⅔ cup (150 mL) sugar
- 1 teaspoon (5 mL) salt
- 1 teaspoon (5 mL) celery seed
- ½ teaspoon (2 mL) mustard seed
- ½ to ¾ teaspoon (2 to 4 mL) red pepper sauce

2 pints (1 L)

1 In medium bowl, combine corn, green pepper, onion and pimiento. Microwave at High 1½ to 2½ minutes, or until corn is defrosted but cool to the touch, stirring after half the time. Divide equally between two sterilized 1-pint (500 mL) jars. Set aside.

2 In 4-cup (1 L) measure, combine remaining ingredients. Microwave at High 2 to 4 minutes, or until boiling, stirring after half the time to dissolve sugar and salt. Divide mixture between the two jars; cover. Refrigerate 1 week before serving. Store in refrigerator no longer than 1 month.

TRANSFORM LEFTOVERS

Save watermelon rind for Watermelon Pickles, opposite. Use leftover cabbage in Cabbage Relish, opposite. When you fix a selection of raw vegetables for a relish or appetizer tray, set some aside to make an Antipasto Jar (page 282) the next day.

MIXED PICKLE RELISH

- 1 cup (250 mL) peeled, seeded and chopped cucumber
- 1 cup (250 mL) chopped onion
- 1 cup (250 mL) chopped red pepper
- 1 cup (250 mL) chopped green pepper
- 1 tablespoon (15 mL) pickling salt
- ⅔ cup (150 mL) sugar
- ½ cup (125 mL) white wine vinegar
- 2 teaspoons (10 mL) dry mustard
- ½ teaspoon (2 mL) grated fresh gingerroot
- ¼ teaspoon (1 mL) ground turmeric
- Pinch ground allspice
- Pinch cayenne
- 1 clove garlic, minced

1-pint (500 mL) jar

1 In colander, place cucumber, onion, red and green peppers. Sprinkle with salt. Toss lightly to mix. Let colander stand over bowl 1½ hours, stirring occasionally.

2 Place salted vegetables in 1½-quart (1.5 L) casserole. Add the remaining ingredients. Mix well. Microwave at High 20 to 30 minutes, or until mixture thickens slightly, stirring twice. Spoon mixture into sterilized 1-pint (500 mL) jar. Cover and refrigerate overnight before serving. Store relish in refrigerator no longer than 1 month.

CHRISTMAS OVERNIGHT PICKLES

- 1 large cucumber (¾ lb./375 g), peeled and cut crosswise into 3 pieces
- 4 whole allspice
- 4 whole cloves
- ½ cup (125 mL) water

- ½ cup (125 mL) cider vinegar
- ½ cup (125 mL) sugar
- ¼ teaspoon (1 mL) salt
- ¼ teaspoon (1 mL) ground nutmeg

- ½ teaspoon (2 mL) red food coloring
- ½ teaspoon (2 mL) green food coloring

4 to 6 servings

1 Scoop out and discard seeds from cucumber; slice hollow pieces into ¼" (5 mm) rings. Divide cucumber rings evenly between two plastic food-storage bags. Add 2 allspice and 2 cloves to each bag. Set aside.

2 Combine remaining ingredients, except food colorings, in 2-cup (500 mL) measure. Microwave at High 2 to 5 minutes, or until mixture boils, stirring once to dissolve sugar and salt. Divide mixture into two portions. Stir red coloring into one portion. Stir green coloring into remaining portion. Cool slightly.

3 Pour red vinegar mixture over cucumbers in one food-storage bag. Pour green vinegar mixture into remaining bag. Tie securely and refrigerate bags overnight. Drain pickles before serving. Store in refrigerator no longer than 3 days.

YELLOW SUMMER SQUASH PICKLES

- 3 cups (750 mL) thinly sliced yellow summer squash
- ½ cup (125 mL) coarsely chopped red pepper
- 1 small onion, thinly sliced and separated into rings
- 8 whole peppercorns
- 1 large clove garlic, cut into quarters (optional)
- 1 cup (250 mL) white wine vinegar
- ⅔ cup (150 mL) sugar
- 2 teaspoons (10 mL) pickling salt
- ¼ teaspoon (1 mL) celery seed
- ¼ teaspoon (1 mL) mustard seed

Two 1-pint (500 mL) jars

1 In medium mixing bowl, mix squash, red pepper and onion. Divide mixture and pack evenly into two sterilized 1-pint (500 mL) jars. Place 4 peppercorns and 2 garlic quarters in each jar. Set aside.

2 Combine remaining ingredients in 2-cup (500 mL) measure. Microwave at High 2 to 5 minutes, or until mixture boils, stirring once to dissolve sugar and salt. Pour mixture evenly into jars. Cover and refrigerate at least 5 days before serving. Store in refrigerator no longer than 1 month.

PICKLED EGGS

- Juice from 1 can (16 oz./454 g) sliced beets
- Water
- ⅔ cup (150 mL) cider vinegar
- 3 tablespoons (50 mL) packed brown sugar
- ¾ teaspoon (4 mL) salt
- 6 whole cloves
- 6 whole allspice
- 6 whole peppercorns
- 1 medium onion, thinly sliced
- 6 hard-cooked eggs, peeled

6 servings

Add enough water to beet juice to measure 1 cup (250 mL). (Reserve beets for future use, if desired.) In medium mixing bowl, combine beet juice mixture, vinegar, sugar, salt, cloves, allspice and peppercorns. Add onion. Cover with plastic wrap. Microwave at High 6 to 8 minutes, or until onion is tender-crisp, stirring once. Add eggs. Cover and refrigerate 1 to 2 days, turning occasionally to ensure even-colored eggs. Drain and slice eggs. Serve on platter or in salads.

PICKLED GREEN BEANS

- 1 pkg. (10 oz./300 g) frozen cut, or French-cut, green beans
- 1 small onion, cut in half lengthwise and thinly sliced
- ½ cup (125 mL) sliced black olives
- 1 cup (250 mL) white vinegar
- ⅔ cup (150 mL) sugar
- 2 teaspoons (10 mL) pickling salt
- ¼ teaspoon (1 mL) dried tarragon leaves or dried dill weed

Three ½-pint (250 mL) jars

1 In medium mixing bowl, microwave beans at High 4 to 6 minutes, or until defrosted, breaking apart once. Drain thoroughly. Add onion and black olives. Mix well. Divide mixture and pack evenly into three sterilized ½-pint (250 mL) jars. Set aside.

2 Combine remaining ingredients in 2-cup (500 mL) measure. Microwave at High 2 to 5 minutes, or until mixture boils, stirring once to dissolve sugar and salt. Pour mixture evenly into jars. Cover and refrigerate at least 5 days before serving. Store in refrigerator no longer than 1 month.

PICKLED GARDEN RELISH

- 3 cups (750 mL) fresh cauliflowerets, 1" (2.5 cm) pieces
- 2 medium carrots, cut into 2" x ¼" (5 cm x 5 mm) strips
- ¼ cup (50 mL) water
- 1 medium red pepper, cut into 2" x ¼" (5 cm x 5 mm) strips
- 2 stalks celery, sliced ½" (1 cm) thick
- ⅔ cup (150 mL) whole green or black olives
- ¾ cup (175 mL) white wine vinegar
- ½ cup (125 mL) olive oil
- 2 tablespoons (25 mL) sugar
- 1 teaspoon (5 mL) salt
- ½ teaspoon (2 mL) dried oregano leaves
- ¼ teaspoon (1 mL) pepper

About 6 cups (1.5 L)

1 In 1½-quart (1.5 L) casserole, combine cauliflower, carrots and water. Cover. Microwave at High 3 to 5 minutes, or until vegetables are hot, but still crisp, stirring once. Stir in red pepper, celery and olives. Set aside.

2 In 2-cup (500 mL) measure, blend vinegar, olive oil, sugar, salt, oregano and pepper. Pour vinegar and oil mixture over vegetables. Mix well. Re-cover. Chill at least 8 hours or overnight. Drain before serving.

FLAVORED VINEGARS

To speed the release of flavors into vinegar, microwave until warm to the touch, not hot. Use any well-washed bottle from catsup or other condiments. Avoid flawed or chipped bottles.

ONION-GARLIC → VINEGAR

- 2 cloves garlic, peeled
- 2 pearl onions, peeled
- Wooden skewer, 6" (15 cm) long
- 1 or 2 cups (250 or 500 mL) white or cider vinegar

1 or 2 cups (250 or 500 mL)

Alternate garlic cloves and pearl onions on a skewer. Drop into bottle. Add vinegar. Microwave, uncovered, at High 30 seconds to 1½ minutes, or until bottle is just warm to the touch; check every 30 seconds. Cap and let stand in a cool, dark place 2 weeks before using. After opening, store in refrigerator no longer than 2 months.

HERB VINEGAR

- 1 sprig fresh mint, fresh tarragon, or fresh oregano
- 1 or 2 cups (250 or 500 mL) white or cider vinegar

1 or 2 cups (250 or 500 mL)

Place one or more sprig desired herb in bottle. Add vinegar. Microwave, uncovered, at High 30 seconds to 1½ minutes, or until bottle is just warm to the touch; check every 30 seconds. Cap and let stand in a cool, dark place 2 weeks before using. After opening, store in refrigerator no longer than 2 months.

← WINE JELLY

- 2¾ cups (675 mL) rosé wine, white wine or pink champagne
- 1 box (1¾ oz./57 g) powdered fruit pectin
- 1 stick cinnamon
- 3 whole cloves
- 3½ cups (875 mL) sugar

2½ pints (625 mL)

1 In 3-qt (3 L) casserole or 8-cup (2 L) measure, combine wine, pectin, cinnamon stick and cloves. Microwave at High 5 to 10 minutes, or until boiling, stirring every 3 minutes. Boil 1 minute. Gradually stir in sugar until blended.

2 Microwave at High 3 to 6½ minutes, or until mixture returns to a boil, stirring carefully every 2 minutes to prevent boilover. Boil 1 minute. Skim any foam from top. Pour into hot sterilized ½-pint (250 mL) jars, or glasses. Cover with hot sterilized lids and screw bands. Invert jar and quickly return to upright position. Or, if desired, seal jars with paraffin wax. Store in a cool, dark place no longer than 6 months.

← FRUIT JELLY

- 1 can (6 oz./170 mL)* frozen apple, grape, pineapple or tangerine juice concentrate
- 2 cups (500 mL) water

- 1 box (1¾ oz./57 g) powdered fruit pectin
- 3½ cups (875 mL) sugar

2½ pints (625 mL)

1 In 3-qt. (3 L) casserole or 8-cup (2 L) measure, combine juice concentrate and water. Stir in pectin until dissolved. Microwave at High 7 to 14 minutes, or until boiling, stirring every 3 minutes. Boil 1 minute. Gradually stir in sugar until blended.

2 Microwave at High 5 to 7 minutes, or until mixture returns to a boil, stirring carefully every 2 minutes to prevent boilover. Boil 1 minute. Skim any foam from top. Pour into hot sterilized ½-pint (250 mL) jars. Cover with hot sterilized lids and screw bands. Invert jar and quickly return to upright position. Or, if desired, seal jars with paraffin wax. Store in a cool, dark place no longer than 6 months.

VARIATIONS:

Zesty Grape Jelly: *Stir 1 teaspoon (5 mL) fresh lemon juice into Grape Jelly after skimming foam.*

Mint Apple Jelly: *Stir 5 to 7 drops green food coloring and 1 teaspoon (5 mL) mint extract into Apple Jelly after skimming foam.*

If 6-oz. (170 mL) can not available, use half of 12-oz. (341 mL) can.

LAYERED JELLIES ↑

Jellies can be layered in wine glasses, coffee mugs or creamers as well as pint jars and jelly glasses. Sterilize the containers before use.

Choose jellies that have attractive color contrast and good flavor combination, such as Apple, Mint Apple and Grape, above.

Try Pineapple and Tangerine with a middle layer of Rosé or White Wine Jelly. For variety, suspend a piece of Candied Pineapple (page 278) or a maraschino cherry in the layer of Wine Jelly. Three batches of jelly yield 7½ pints (1.875 L).

1 Fill each jelly glass or other container one-third full. The first layer must begin to set before the next layer is added.

2 Prepare second layer. When first layer is sufficiently set, carefully spoon second layer into jar. Allow to set slightly.

3 Add final layer, carefully spooning over second layer. Top with paraffin wax.

293

BLUEBERRY-KIWI REFRIGERATOR JAM ↑

- 2 cups (500 mL) peeled, cored and sliced kiwi fruit
- 2 cups (500 mL) frozen blueberries
- 2 cups (500 mL) sugar
- 1 pkg. (3 oz./85 g) lemon gelatin

Three ½-pint (250 mL) jars

In medium mixing bowl, combine kiwi fruit, blueberries and sugar. Mix well. Microwave at High 15 to 25 minutes, or until fruit is very soft, stirring 3 or 4 times. Add gelatin, stirring until dissolved. Divide mixture evenly among three sterilized ½-pint (250 mL) jars. Cover and chill until set, about 2 hours. Store jam in refrigerator no longer than 1 month.

Blueberry-Kiwi Light Jam: Follow recipe above, except substitute 1 pkg. (0.3 oz./11 g) low-calorie lemon gelatin for the 3-oz. (85 g) pkg.

CHERRY-ALMOND REFRIGERATOR JAM

- 4 cups (1 L) frozen pitted dark sweet cherries
- 2 cups (500 mL) sugar
- 1 pkg. (3 oz./85 g) cherry gelatin
- ¼ teaspoon (1 mL) almond extract

Three ½-pint (250 mL) jars

In medium mixing bowl, combine cherries and sugar. Mix well. Microwave at High 15 to 25 minutes, or until cherries are very soft, stirring 3 or 4 times. Add gelatin, stirring until dissolved. Stir in almond extract. Divide mixture evenly among three sterilized ½-pint (250 mL) jars. Cover. Chill until set, about 2 hours. Store jam in refrigerator no longer than 1 month.

Cherry-Almond Light Jam: Follow recipe above, except substitute 1 pkg. (0.3 oz./11 g) low-calorie cherry gelatin for the 3-oz. (85 g) pkg.

STRAWBERRY-RHUBARB REFRIGERATOR JAM

- 4 cups (1 L) frozen cut-up rhubarb
- 2 cups (500 mL) sugar
- 1 pkg. (3 oz./85 g) strawberry gelatin
- 2 teaspoons (10 mL) lemon juice

  Three ½-pint (250 mL) jars

In medium mixing bowl, combine rhubarb and sugar. Mix well. Microwave at High 15 to 25 minutes, or until rhubarb is very soft, stirring 3 or 4 times. Add gelatin, stirring until dissolved. Mix in lemon juice. Divide mixture evenly among three sterilized ½-pint (250 mL) jars. Cover. Chill until set, about 2 hours. Store jam in refrigerator no longer than 1 month.

Strawberry-Rhubarb Light Jam: Follow recipe above, except substitute 1 pkg. (0.3 oz./11 g) low-calorie strawberry gelatin for the 3-oz. (85 g) pkg.

APPLE
← BUTTER

- 3 lbs. (1.5 kg) cooking apples, peeled, cored and cut into quarters
- ¼ cup (50 mL) apple cider
- 1½ cups (375 mL) granulated sugar
- ½ cup (125 mL) packed brown sugar
- 2 tablespoons (25 mL) cider vinegar
- 1½ teaspoons (7 mL) ground cinnamon
- ¼ teaspoon (1 mL) ground allspice
- Pinch ground nutmeg

   Three ½-pint (250 mL) jars

1 Place apples in 3-quart (3 L) casserole. Add apple cider. Cover. Microwave at High 18 to 23 minutes, or until apples are very soft, stirring once or twice. Place mixture in food processor or blender, and process until smooth.

2 Return apple mixture to 3-quart (3 L) casserole. Stir in remaining ingredients. Microwave, uncovered, at High 30 to 45 minutes, or until mixture is very thick, stirring 3 or 4 times. Spoon mixture evenly into three sterilized ½-pint (250 mL) jars. Cover and refrigerate overnight before serving. Store Apple Butter in refrigerator no longer than 1 month.

PEAR HONEY

- 2 lbs. (1 kg) pears (4 medium), peeled and cored
- 2¼ cups (550 mL) sugar
- 1 can (8 oz./227 mL) crushed pineapple
- 1 tablespoon (15 mL) lemon juice
- ½ teaspoon (2 mL) grated lemon peel

   Three ½-pint (250 mL) jars

Cut each pear into 6 pieces. Place in food processor or blender. Process until finely chopped. Place chopped pears in 3-quart (3 L) casserole. Stir in remaining ingredients. Mix well. Microwave at High 30 to 40 minutes, or until pears are translucent and very tender, stirring 2 or 3 times. Divide mixture evenly among three sterilized ½-pint (250 mL) jars. Cover and refrigerate overnight before serving. Store in refrigerator no longer than 1 month.

BRANDIED FRUIT

- ¾ cup (175 mL) water
- ½ cup (125 mL) packed brown sugar
- ⅓ cup (75 mL) granulated sugar
- ½ teaspoon (2 mL) ground cinnamon
- Pinch ground allspice
- Pinch ground nutmeg

- ½ to ¾ cup (125 to 175 mL) brandy
- 1 cup (250 mL) dried apricots
- 1 cup (250 mL) dried apples
- 1 cup (250 mL) pitted prunes
- ½ cup (125 mL) raisins
- ¾ cup (175 mL) drained maraschino cherries (optional)

1 quart (1 L) fruit

1 In medium mixing bowl, combine water, sugars, cinnamon, allspice and nutmeg. Mix well. Microwave at High 4 to 6 minutes, or until mixture boils and sugar dissolves, stirring once.

2 Stir in remaining ingredients. Microwave at High 9 to 14 minutes, or until apricots and apples are tender, stirring once or twice. Cover and refrigerate at least 3 days before serving. Store in refrigerator no longer than 3 weeks. Serve fruit over plain cake or ice cream, if desired.

FRUIT SYRUPS

- 1 bag (16 oz./500 g) frozen raspberries, blackberries or blueberries
- 1 cup (250 mL) sugar
- ¾ cup (175 mL) light corn syrup

1 pint (500 mL)

1 Place frozen fruit in medium bowl or 4-cup (1 L) measure. Cover with plastic wrap. Microwave at High 6½ to 10 minutes, or until boiling, stirring every 3 minutes.

2 Line strainer with cheesecloth; place in 8-cup (2 L) measure or 3-qt. (3 L) casserole. Pour hot fruit into lined strainer.

3 Mash fruit with back of spoon to press the juice through strainer. (Yields about ½ to ¾ cup/125 to 175 mL juice.) Discard pulp.

4 Add sugar and corn syrup to the strained juice. Microwave at High 3 to 6 minutes, or until boiling, stirring every 2 minutes.

5 Boil 1 minute. Skim any foam from top. Pour the syrup into hot sterilized 1-pint (500 mL) jar or catsup bottle; cap.

6 Refrigerate or store in a cool, dark place no longer than 6 months. Serve over pancakes, waffles or desserts.

FRESH STRAWBERRY SYRUP ↑

- 1 pint (500 mL) fresh strawberries, hulled
- 1 cup (250 mL) sugar
- ¾ cup (175 mL) light corn syrup

1 pint (500 mL)

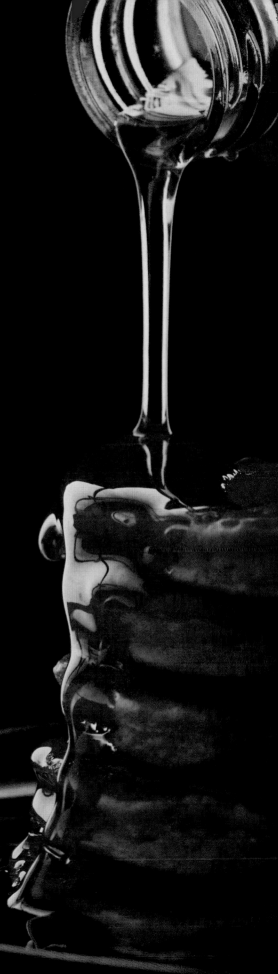

1 Cut strawberries in half. Place in large bowl. Mash with fork. Cover. Microwave at High 4 to 5 minutes, or until boiling, stirring every 2 minutes. Line strainer with cheesecloth; place in 3-qt. (3 L) casserole or 8-cup (2 L) measure. Pour hot fruit into lined strainer. Mash fruit with back of spoon to press the juice through strainer. (Yields ½ to ¾ cup/ 125 to 175 mL juice.) Discard pulp.

2 Add sugar and corn syrup to strained juice. Microwave at High 3 to 6 minutes, or until boiling, stirring every 2 minutes. Boil 1 minute. Skim any foam from top. Pour syrup into hot sterilized 1-pint (500 mL) jar or catsup bottle; cap. Refrigerate or store in a cool, dark place no longer than 6 months. Serve over pancakes, waffles or desserts.

Heat Syrup for Serving: *Remove cap from bottle or jar. Microwave at High 30 to 60 seconds, or until bottle is warm to the touch.*

FRESH PLUM SYRUP →

- 1 lb. (500 g) very ripe purple plums
- 1 cup (250 mL) sugar
- ¾ cup (175 mL) light corn syrup

1 pint (500 mL)

1 Cut plums in half; remove pits. Cut halves into small pieces. Place in large bowl; cover. Microwave at High 5 to 8 minutes, or until plums cook down and mash easily, stirring every 2 minutes.

2 Line strainer with cheesecloth; place in 3-qt. (3 L) casserole or 8-cup (2 L) measure. Pour hot fruit into lined strainer. Mash fruit with the back of spoon to press juice through strainer. (Yields ½ to ¾ cup/125 to 175 mL juice.) Discard pulp.

3 Add sugar and corn syrup to strained juice. Microwave at High 3 to 6 minutes, or until boiling, stirring every 2 minutes. Boil 1 minute. Skim any foam from top.

4 Pour syrup into hot sterilized 1-pint (500 mL) jar or catsup bottle; cap. Refrigerate or store in a cool, dark place no longer than 6 months. Serve over pancakes, waffles or desserts.

SOFTENING CREAM CHEESE

In small mixing bowl, microwave cream cheese as directed in chart (below), or until softened. DO NOT microwave cream cheese in the foil wrapper. For use in dips and spreads, blend softened cream cheese with favorite flavors, as directed in chart (opposite).

Amount	Power Setting	Microwave Time
1 pkg. (3 oz./85 g)	High	15 to 30 seconds
1 pkg. (8 oz./250 g)	50% (Medium)	1½ to 3 minutes

TIP: Cream cheese softens quickly in the microwave and spreads easily. Softened cheese is easier to blend in your favorite appetizer, main dish or dessert recipe.

HOW TO MAKE FLAVORED CREAM CHEESES

1 Microwave 8 oz. (250 g) cream cheese in small mixing bowl as directed in chart (above), stirring once or twice.

2 Blend in additional ingredients for desired flavor (opposite).

3 Serve flavored cream cheeses as directed (opposite); store cream cheese as recommended.

Flavor & yield	To 8 oz. (250 g) cream cheese blend in:	Serving suggestions	Store up to:
Cheddar & Chive Cream Cheese about 1¼ cups (300 mL)	½ cup (125 mL) finely shredded Cheddar cheese, 1 tablespoon (15 mL) sliced green onion, 1 teaspoon (5 mL) freeze-dried chives, pinch garlic powder	Dip for vegetables; topping for hot cooked vegetables; spread for crackers, bread	2 weeks
Cocoa Cream Cheese Frosting about 1¼ cups (300 mL)	½ cup (125 mL) powered sugar, 2 tablespoons (25 mL) cocoa, ½ teaspoon (2 mL) vanilla	Frosting for graham crackers, brownies, bars, cakes	2 weeks
Italian Herb Cream Cheese about 1 cup (250 mL)	2 tablespoons (25 mL) fresh snipped parsley, ½ teaspoon (2 mL) Italian seasoning	Spread for sandwiches or crackers; topping for hot cooked vegetables	2 weeks
Lemon-Basil Cream Cheese about 1¼ cups (300 mL)	2 teaspoons (10 mL) lemon juice, ½ teaspoon (2 mL) dried basil leaves (crushed), ¼ teaspoon (1 mL) garlic powder	Dip for vegetables; spread for bagels, French bread, cheese croissants	2 weeks
Mustard Relish Cream Cheese about 1¼ cups (300 mL)	2 tablespoons (25 mL) sweet relish, 1 tablespoon (15 mL) chopped onion, 2 teaspoons (10 mL) Dijon mustard	Spread for bagels, sandwiches, crackers	2 weeks
Orange Spice Cream Cheese about 1 cup (250 mL)	2 tablespoons (25 mL) sugar, 2 tablespoons (25 mL) orange juice, 1 teaspoon (5 mL) grated orange peel, pinch ground allspice	Spread for fruit muffins, bagels, croissants, quick breads	2 weeks
Red Wine Onion Cream Cheese about 1¼ cups (300 mL)	2 tablespoons (25 mL) chopped onion, 2 tablespoons (25 mL) red wine, pinch salt, pinch pepper	Dip for vegetables and crackers	2 weeks
Strawberry Cream Cheese about 1⅓ cups (325 mL)	½ cup (125 mL) fresh sliced strawberries, 2 tablespoons (25 mL) sugar, 1 teaspoon (5 mL) vanilla	Dip for fruit; spread for pound cakes, quick breads	3 days

CANDY COATING ORNAMENTS

- ¼ lb. (125 g) chocolate or white candy coating
- 1 heat-sealable pouch, 1-qt. (1 L) size
- Coloring book (optional)

About 10 ornaments

Choose the Right Pouch: *Be sure to use a heat-sealable, boilable pouch when melting candy coating. Do not use ordinary food-storage or freezer bags; they are not designed to withstand the high temperature.*

1 Break candy coating into pieces. Place in heat-sealable pouch. Do not seal pouch.

2 Microwave at 50% (Medium) 3 to 4 minutes, or until soft to the touch. (Candy should be warm, not hot.)

3 Sqeeze softened candy coating into one corner of pouch. Snip corner with scissors to form writing tip.

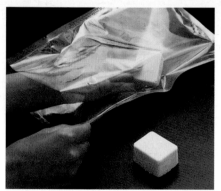

4 Draw designs with candy coating onto wax paper, or trace designs onto wax paper over coloring book for pattern ideas.

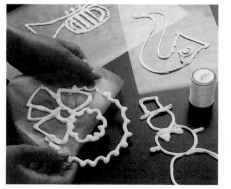

5 Let stand until firm. Peel design off wax paper. Place thread through ornaments for hanging.

6 Decorate ornaments while still soft. Use red hot candies, chocolate shot or miniature marshmallows, if desired.

DOG BISCUITS

- 1 cup (250 mL) whole wheat flour
- ½ cup (125 mL) all-purpose flour
- ¾ cup (175 mL) non-fat dry milk powder
- ½ cup (125 mL) quick-cooking rolled oats
- ¼ cup (50 mL) yellow cornmeal
- 1 teaspoon (5 mL) sugar

- ⅓ cup (75 mL) shortening
- 1 egg, slightly beaten
- 1 tablespoon (15 mL) instant chicken or beef bouillon granules
- ½ cup (125 mL) hot water

1½ dozen cutouts or 5½ dozen nuggets

VARIATION:

Cheese Dog Biscuits: *Omit bouillon granules. Add ¼ cup (50 mL) canned grated American cheese food to dry ingredients. Continue as directed below.*

1 Combine flours, milk powder, rolled oats, cornmeal and sugar in medium bowl. Cut in shortening until mixture resembles coarse crumbs.

2 Stir in egg. Stir instant bouillon granules into hot water until dissolved. Slowly pour into the flour mixture, stirring with a fork to moisten.

3 Form dough into ball and knead on floured board 5 minutes, or until smooth and elastic. Divide dough in half and roll out each ½" (1 cm) thick.

4 Make cutouts with cookie cutter. Or, make nuggets by rolling dough into 1" (2.5 cm) diameter log; cut off ½" (1 cm) pieces.

5 Arrange 6 cutout shapes or 24 nuggets on 10" (25 cm) plate. Microwave at 50% (Medium) 5 to 10 minutes, or until firm and dry to the touch.

6 Rotate plate every 2 minutes and turn shapes over after half the time. Cool on wire rack. Shapes will crisp as they cool.

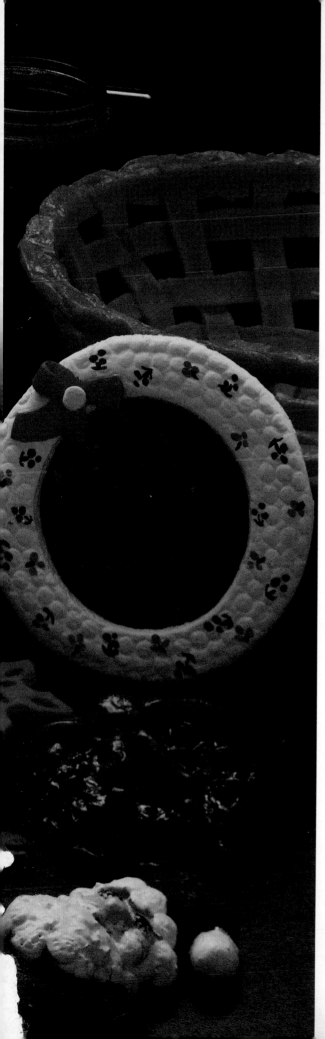

DOUGH ART

The microwave oven dries baker's clay in minutes rather than the hour or two needed conventionally. Use this inedible dough to make baskets, picture frames, ornaments, candle holders, necklace pendants or to sculpt small figures.

The dough can be applied to microwave oven-safe objects, such as clay pots or glass jars. To test dish safety, place in oven. Place ½ to 1 cup (125 to 250 mL) water in glass measure. Set on or next to dish. Microwave at High 1 to 2 minutes. If dish remains cool, it is microwave-safe. Before shaping dough over glass bottles, jars or bowls, check the glass carefully for flaws. Do not use imperfect glass, as heat and steam from the dough could cause it to break.

Always elevate objects on a microwave roasting rack. The dough adheres to glass and clay, so no glue is needed. If you plan to remove the shaped object from the glass after microwaving, first spray the glass with a nonstick vegetable spray. Allow items shaped over glass to cool in the oven; rapid temperature changes can cause the glass to break.

Useful tools for dough art are a rolling pin; a ruler; cookie cutters, pastry cutter, drinking glass with floured rim, or a small knife for cutting out objects; a drinking straw for making holes to hang ornaments; flat wooden sticks for sculpting or engraving designs; wooden picks for interior support of arms, legs or neck of sculptured figures; garlic press to produce textures like hair or fur; and a paintbrush to moisten pieces for joining. After thorough drying, paint your work with acrylic or enamel colors or finish with a sealer to prevent brittleness.

HOW TO MAKE DOUGH ART*

- 3 cups (750 mL) all-purpose flour
- ¾ cup (175 mL) salt
- ¾ teaspoon (4 mL) powdered alum
- Food coloring (optional)
- 1¼ cups (300 mL) water

1 In large bowl, combine flour, salt and alum. If colored dough is desired, add food coloring to water. Mix water into flour. Shape dough into ball. Knead dough on lightly floured surface about 5 minutes, or until dough is smooth. Store in plastic bag.

2 If dough becomes too stiff, sprinkle lightly with water while kneading. If dough is too moist, knead in additional flour to achieve desired consistency. Most dough shapes are microwaved on microwave roasting rack or microwave baking sheet sprayed with nonstick vegetable cooking spray. Microwave at 30% (Medium-Low) at 2-minute intervals.

3 Microwave dough drying is *not* a complete drying process. Small areas of most objects may remain moist but firm to the touch. Allow all microwave-dried pieces to air-dry for at least 24 hours before finishing. All dried objects require finishing to prevent brittleness or breakage. Paint both sides of exposed areas with acrylic sealer, shellac, varnish or lacquer.

***NOTE:** This dough is for decoration only.

HOW TO MAKE DOUGH BASKETS

1 Prepare dough as directed (page 305). Select glass bowl the size and shape desired for basket. Dough is shaped over outside of bowl. Spray outside of the bowl with nonstick vegetable cooking spray. Place bowl upside down.

2 Roll dough on lightly floured surface to ¼" (5 mm) thickness. Using pastry wheel or knife, cut ½" (1 cm) wide strips long enough to go across side, bottom and other side of bowl with 1" (2.5 cm) overhang on each side.

3 Weave bottom by starting in center and laying parallel strips across bottom. Pull back every other strip to center and place another strip at right angles. Lift alternate strips and place another strip at right angles. Continue with additional strips until bottom is woven.

4 Cut ½" (1 cm) wide strips long enough to go around bowl. Weave in and out of strips on bowl until sides are completed. Join ends of strips by moistening with small amount of water. (A paintbrush works well.) Trim strips even with top of bowl.

5 Form rope long enough to go around top of basket by rolling two equal pieces of dough between hands. Lay pieces side by side and twist one over the other, starting at center. Moisten top basket edge with water and press rope onto woven pieces. Moisten ends to join.

6 Microwave one basket at a time at 30% (Medium-Low) 4 minutes, rotating 2 or 3 times. Check; rotate if basket is not dry. Continue to microwave at 2-minute intervals, checking and rotating after each minute. Cool in oven. Remove from bowl and finish as directed (page 305).

HOW TO MAKE DOUGH CUTOUTS

1 Prepare dough as directed (page 305). Spray microwave baking sheet with nonstick vegetable cooking spray.

2 Roll dough on lightly floured surface to ¼" (5 mm) thickness. Dip edges of cutters in vegetable oil. Cut desired shapes.

3 Arrange four pieces at a time on prepared baking sheet. Cutouts can be appliquéd with small designs, if desired.

4 Shape designs for appliqué out of very small pieces of dough. Moisten area on cutout to be decorated. Place appliqué on wet area as directed (page 309).

5 Punch small hole at top of cutout with wooden pick or drinking straw if object is to be hung. Microwave pieces at 30% (Medium-Low) 2 minutes.

6 Check; rotate if pieces are not dry. Continue microwaving at 2-minute intervals, checking and rotating after each minute. Cool and finish as directed (page 305).

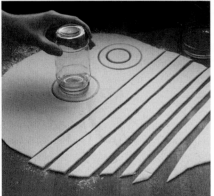

HOW TO MAKE PICTURE FRAMES

1 Prepare dough as directed (page 305). Spray microwave baking sheet with nonstick vegetable cooking spray. Roll dough on lightly floured surface to ¼" (5 mm) thickness.

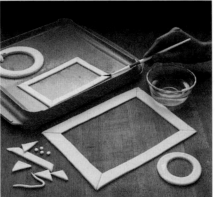

2 Use pastry wheel or knife to cut ½" to 1" (1 to 2.5 cm) wide strips long enough to form 3" x 5" (8 x 13 cm) or 5" x 7" (13 x 18 cm) rectangles. Cut circles with a jar, using a smaller jar to cut out center.

3 Assemble the frame on prepared baking sheet. Wet cut edges with water and press together gently. Appliqué with cutout designs, if desired.

4 Microwave at 30% (Medium-Low) 2 minutes. Check; rotate if pieces are not dry. Microwave at 2-minute intervals, checking and rotating after each minute.

5 Cool and finish as directed (page 305). Cut cardboard to fit back and cover with fabric. Glue cardboard onto three edges of frame back.

6 Leave one edge of frame open to insert picture. Attach picture hanger, paper clip or easel backing.

HOW TO MAKE APPLIQUÉS FOR CLAY POTS

1 Prepare dough as directed (page 305). Cut or shape desired designs. Wet one side of cutout designs and area on pot where designs are to be applied.

2 Press designs onto dampened surface. Place pot directly on microwave oven floor. Microwave at 30% (Medium-Low) 2 minutes; check. Rotate if piece is not dry.

3 Microwave at 1-minute intervals, checking and rotating after each minute. Cool in microwave oven. Finish as directed (page 305).

HOW TO MAKE DECORATED JARS

1 Prepare dough as directed (page 305). Roll dough on lightly floured surface to ¼" (5 mm) thickness. Press dough over jar until it adheres.

2 Appliqué as desired. Place in microwave oven upside down on roasting rack. Microwave at 30% (Medium-Low) 2 minutes; check. Rotate if the piece is not dry.

3 Microwave at 1-minute intervals, checking and rotating after each minute. Cool in microwave oven. Finish as directed (page 305).

PATTERNS

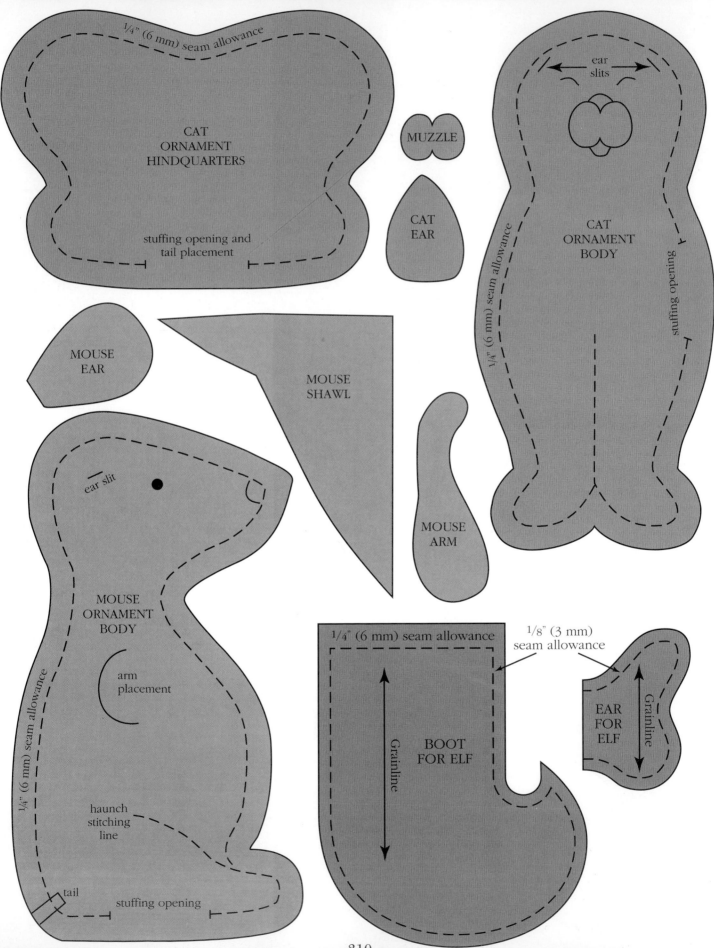

1/4" (6 mm) seam allowance

CAT
ORNAMENT
HINDQUARTERS

stuffing opening and
tail placement

MUZZLE

CAT
EAR

ear
slits

CAT
ORNAMENT
BODY

1/4" (6 mm) seam allowance

stuffing opening

MOUSE
EAR

MOUSE
SHAWL

ear slit

MOUSE
ARM

MOUSE
ORNAMENT
BODY

1/4" (6 mm) seam allowance

arm
placement

haunch
stitching
line

tail

stuffing opening

1/4" (6 mm) seam allowance

1/8" (3 mm)
seam allowance

Grainline

BOOT
FOR ELF

EAR
FOR
ELF

Grainline

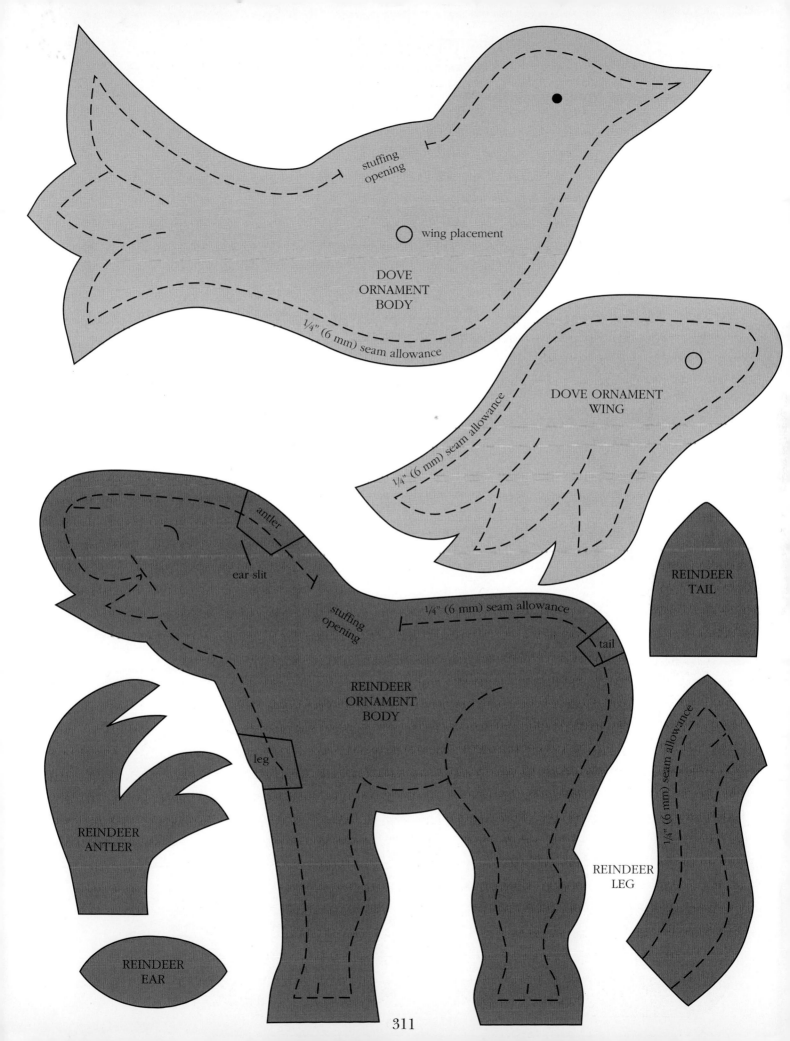

stuffing
opening

○ wing placement

DOVE
ORNAMENT
BODY

¼" (6 mm) seam allowance

DOVE ORNAMENT
WING

¼" (6 mm) seam allowance

antler

ear slit

stuffing
opening

¼" (6 mm) seam allowance

tail

REINDEER
ORNAMENT
BODY

leg

REINDEER
ANTLER

REINDEER
EAR

REINDEER
TAIL

REINDEER
LEG

¼" (6 mm) seam allowance

311

BACKGROUND TREE TEMPLATE
FOR HOLIDAY PLACEMATS

Place on fold

DOVE GARLAND

Place on fold

ROCKING HORSE ORNAMENT
Dimensions 3½" × 4¼" (9 × 10.8 cm)

PACKAGE
ORNAMENT
Dimensions
4⅝" × 3½"
(11.7 × 9 cm)

Place on fold

Place on fold

Place on fold

Dimensions
6⅛" × 6¾"
(15.4 × 17 cm)

PARTRIDGE
ORNAMENT

CANDLE
ORNAMENT
Dimensions
4¼" × 3¼" (10.8 × 8.2 cm)

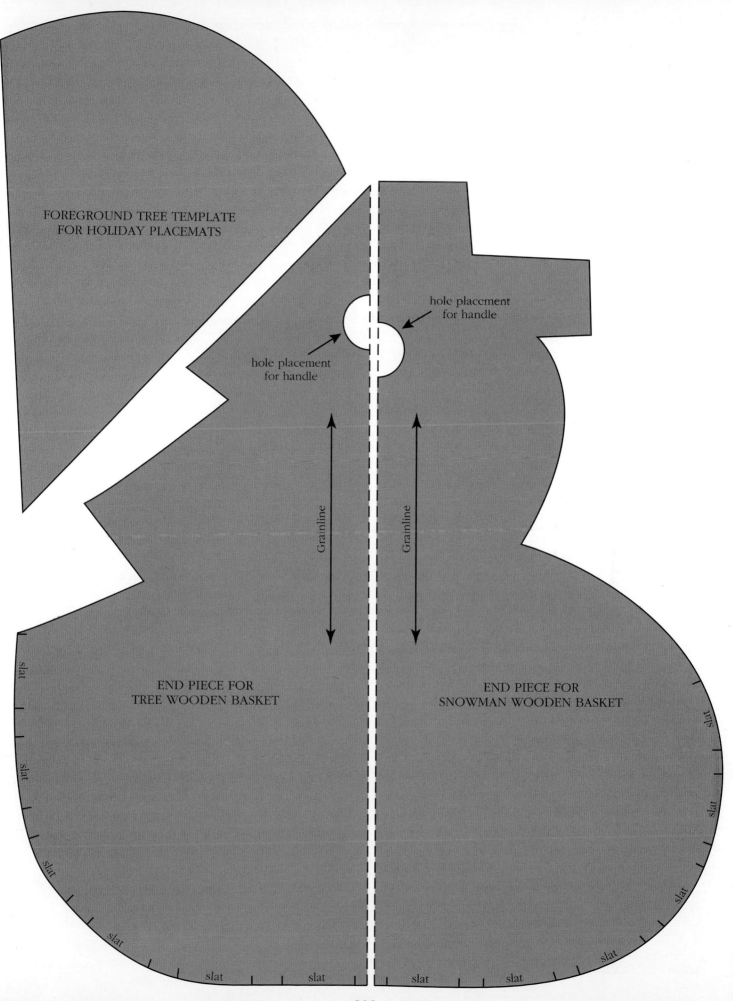

FOREGROUND TREE TEMPLATE
FOR HOLIDAY PLACEMATS

hole placement
for handle

hole placement
for handle

Grainline

Grainline

END PIECE FOR
TREE WOODEN BASKET

END PIECE FOR
SNOWMAN WOODEN BASKET

slat

slat

slat

slat

slat

slat

slat

slat

slat

slat

slat

slat

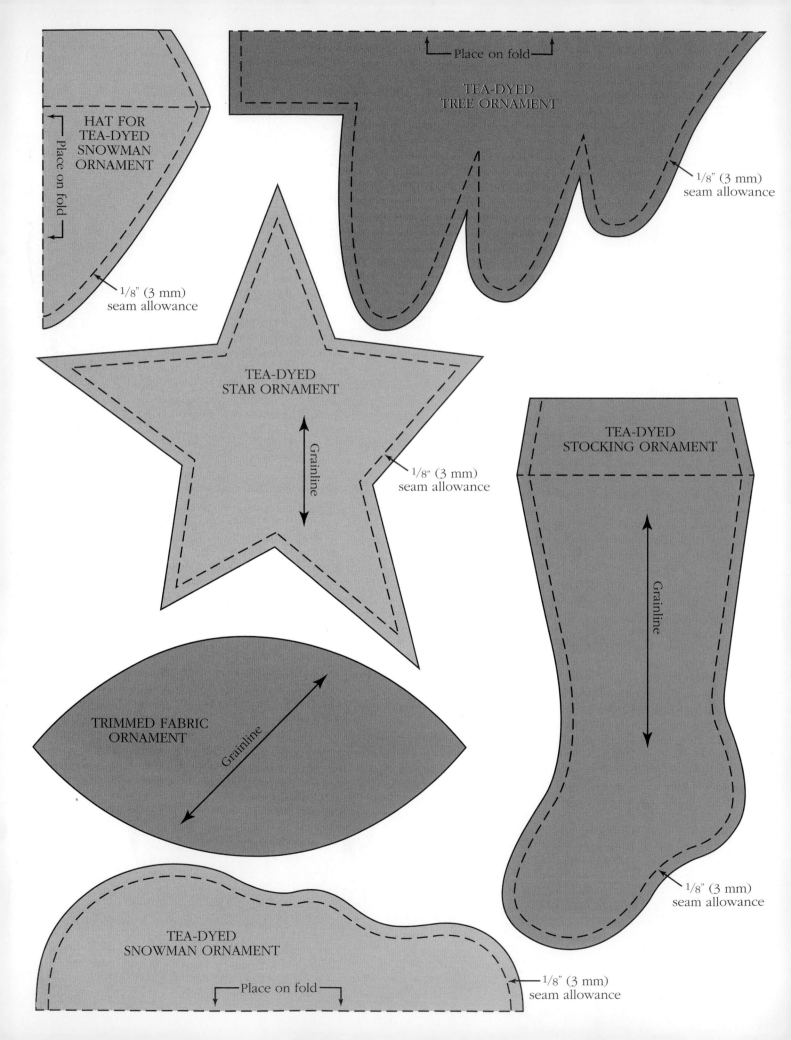

HAT FOR
TEA-DYED
SNOWMAN
ORNAMENT

Place on fold

1/8" (3 mm)
seam allowance

Place on fold

TEA-DYED
TREE ORNAMENT

1/8" (3 mm)
seam allowance

TEA-DYED
STAR ORNAMENT

Grainline

1/8" (3 mm)
seam allowance

TEA-DYED
STOCKING ORNAMENT

Grainline

1/8" (3 mm)
seam allowance

TRIMMED FABRIC
ORNAMENT

Grainline

TEA-DYED
SNOWMAN ORNAMENT

Place on fold

1/8" (3 mm)
seam allowance

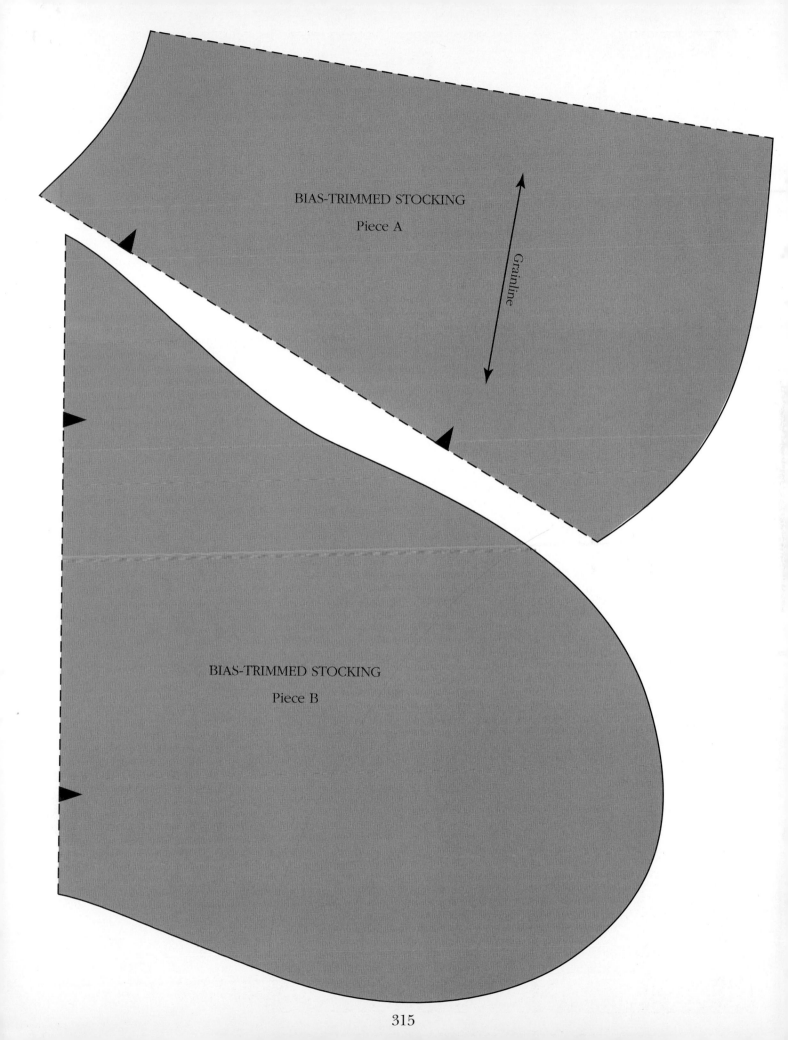

BIAS-TRIMMED STOCKING

Piece A

Grainline

BIAS-TRIMMED STOCKING

Piece B

A

Almonds, amaretto glazed, 271
Angel tree topper, paper-twist, 8-12
Animal crackers, 180
Antipasto jar, 282
Antipasto kabobs, 177
Appetizers, 166-177
Apple butter, 296
Apple-pear chutney, 285
Appliquéd almond cookies, 214
Apricot brandy, 201
Apricot chews, 268
Apricot date balls, 235
Arrangements, floral, 91-98
Artichoke dip, hot, 184

B

Baked apples, 255
Baskets,
    dough, 306
    wooden, 124-127, 313
Beverages, 194-201
Bias-trimmed stockings, 143-145
    patterns, 315
Biscochitas, Mexican, 236
Biscotti, chocolate-dipped, 227
Blueberry-kiwi refrigerator jam, 294
Bow tree topper, wire-mesh, 9, 12-13
Brandied apricot torte, 252
Brandied fruit, 297
Brandied ginger snaps, 213
Bread,
    pumpkin pie, 259
    spinach-filled, 189

C

Cabbage relish, 284
Cakes, 251-254
Canapés, 169-170
Candied peel, 279
Candied pineapple, 278
Candy, 260-268, 271, 275
Candy coating ornaments, 301
Candy-filled chocolate wheels, 224
Cappuccino, 199
Caramel apple-topped spice cake, 254
Caramel pecan clusters, 261

Carolers, 135-141
Cat ornament, felt, 58-59, 310
Cauliflower, whole, 175
Centerpieces, floral, 91-93, 97-98
Cheese ball, 191
Cheese dip in pepper, 193
Cheese loaf, layered, 183
Cheese roll, cherry, 256
Cheese sauce, 183
Cheesy seafood snack dip, 192
Cherry-almond refrigerator jam, 294
Chipped beef dip, 190
Chips, seasoned, with Lone Star
    Caviar, 187
Choco-brandy balls, 222
Chocolate almond rosettes, 219
Chocolate apricot chews, 261
Chocolate bourbon balls, 267
Chocolate chews, 261
Chocolate-covered bananas, 270
Chocolate-covered cherries, 260
Chocolate-covered marshmallows, 267
Chocolate dessert and liqueur
    cups, 269
Chocolate-dipped palmiers, 239
Chocolate-dipped snacks and fruit, 266
Chocolate-ginger rocking horse, 224
Christmas overnight pickles, 287
Chutney, apple-pear, 285
Cinnamon-stick star tree topper,
    9, 13
Coaster sets, holiday, 99-101
Cocoa peppermint pretzels, 210
Cocoa, Mexican hot, 196
Coconut date balls, 268
Coffee, Irish, 199
Coffee liqueur, 201
Cookie-cutter ornaments, 18-19
Cookies, Christmas,
    basics, 204
    decorating, 242-243, 246-247
    recipes, 207-241
    using a pastry bag, 244-245
Copper ornaments, 23-25
Corn relish, 285
Crab canapés, 170
Cream cheese, softening and
    flavoring, 300-301
Curry dip, 191

D

Desserts, 250-259
Dips, 184-194
Dog biscuits, 303
Dough art, 305-309
Dove ornament, felt, 61, 311

E

Eggs, pickled, 289
Elves, Santa's, 130-133
Extracts, lemon or orange, 278

F

Fabric ornaments, trimmed,
    30-31, 314
Fabric tree, fringed, 129
Fattigmands, 216
Felt ornaments, 54-61
    patterns, 310-311
Finger rolls, ham salad, 173
Floral arrangements, 91-98
Florentine canapés, 170
Folded star ornaments, 27-29
French lace cookie cups, 237
Frosting, to decorate cookies,
    242-243
Fruit, 266, 270, 278-279, 292
Fruitcake, holiday, 251
Fruit-flavored crispy bars, 270
Fruit jelly, 293
Fruit syrups, 298-299

G

Garden relish, pickled, 290
Garlands, 70-75
    scherenschnitte, 39, 42, 312
German chocolate cake, easy, 253
Gingerbread, 257
Gold-leaf ornaments, 32
Granola, 276-277
Greek amaretto cookies, 231
Greek holiday cookies, 238
Green beans, pickled, 289

H

Ham salad finger rolls, 173
Hand-cast paper ornaments, 47-50
Hanging pine balls, 163

Holiday horns, 209
Holiday meringue cookies, 208
Holiday thumbprint cookies, 213
Hummus, 185

J

Jalapeño cheese dip, 191
Jellies and syrups, 292-299

K

Kabobs, antipasto, 177
Kolachkes, poppy-raspberry, 228
Krumkake, orange-spiced, 220

L

Lace doily ornaments, 51-53
Lamppost, 141
Layered bean dip, 188
Lemon blossom spritz, 214
Lemon extract, 278
Linens,
  see: table linens
Liqueur, 200-201
  cups, 269
Lollipops, 275

M

Madeleines, 217
Mantels, decorating, 148-149
Marbleized ornaments, 33
Metal ornaments, 23-25
Mexican biscochitas, 236
Mexican hot cocoa, 196
Mexican snack dip, 192
Mint truffle cookies, 211
Mixed fruit warmer, 194
Mixed pickle relish, 286

Mouse ornament, felt, 54-57, 310
Muffins, apple brunch, 258
Mushrooms, sausage-stuffed, 168

N

Napkins, holiday, 111-112
Nuts,
  amaretto glazed almonds, 271
  roasted peanuts, 181
  spiced, 172

O

Orange extract, 278
Ornaments,
  candy coating, 302
  cookie-cutter, 18-19
  felt, 54-61, 310-311
  folded star, 27-29
  gold-leaf, 32
  hand-cast paper, 47-50
  ideas for, 66-67
  lace doily, 51-53
  marbleized, 33
  metal, 23-25
  papier-mâché, 44
  quick and easy, 68-69
  ribbon roses, 63-65
  scherenschnitte, 39-41, 43, 312
  spice, 21
  string-ball, 35-37
  tea-dyed, 15-17, 314
  trimmed fabric, 30-31, 314

P

Paper ornaments,
  folded star, 27-29
  hand-cast, 47-50
  scherenschnitte, 39-41, 43, 312
Paper-twist angel tree topper, 8-12
Papier-mâché ornaments, 44
Pâté, chicken liver, 170
Patterns, 310-315
Peanuts, roasted, 181
Pear honey, 296
Pecan brittle, orange-spiced, 271

Pepper wedges, savory, 193
Pfeffernüsse, German, 241
Pickled carrots, 283
Pickled eggs, 289
Pickled green beans, 289
Pickles and relishes, 282-290
Pineapple, candied, 278
Pine balls, hanging, 163
Pizzas, candy, 262-263
Pizza, pita, 176-177
Pizzelles, 221
Placemats, 103-107, 111, 113-116
  patterns, 312-313
Plum pudding, 250
Polynesian appetizers, 167
Popcorn,
  balls, red hot, 273
  bars, fruit-flavored, 272
  caramel corn, 274
  mix, fruity, 179
Poppy-raspberry kolachkes, 228
Poppy seed pinwheels, 213
Potato skins, baked, 173
Pralines, buttermilk, 267

Q

Quick and easy ornaments, 68-69

R

Raspberry liqueur, 201
Reindeer ornament, felt, 59-60, 311
Relishes and pickles, 282-290
Ribbon roses, ornaments, 63-65
Rolls, ham salad finger, 173
Rosettes, 219
Rum balls, 232
Runners, table, 103-105
Russian tea, 198

S

Salmon-cucumber canapés, 169
Santa's elves, 130-133
Sauce, cheese, 183
Sausage,
  balls, 172
  pickled, 171
  in stuffed mushrooms, 168

Scherenschnitte ornaments and garlands, 39-43, 312
Seafood and avocado dip, 194
Shrimp,
  in beer, 166
  spiced, 166
  wrap-ups, 167
Skirts, tree, 78-87
Snacks, 178-194
Snowballs,
  chocolate, 233
  orange, 222
Snowman ornament, tea-dyed, 15, 17, 314
Sour cream cutouts, 207
Special-occasion sugar cookies, 207
Spice ornaments, 21
Spicy Greek jewels, 235
Spinach balls, 172
Spread, sun-dried tomato and garlic, 182
Stained glass cookies, 227
Star ornaments,
  folded, 27-29
  tea-dyed, 15-16, 314
Star tree topper, cinnamon-stick, 9, 13
Stewed fruit, 278
Stocking ornament, tea-dyed, 15-16, 314
Stockings,
  bias-trimmed, 143-145, 315
  woolen, 147
String-ball ornaments, 35-37
Sweets, 260-279
Syrups and jellies, 292-299

T

Table arrangements, 94-95
Table linens, 103-117
  napkins, 111-112
  placemats, 103-107, 111, 113-116, 312-313
  runners, 103-105
  toppers, 119-121
Tea, Russian, 198
Tea-dyed ornaments, 15-17
  patterns, 314
Texas Mary, 197
Thin mint layers, 268
Three-cornered hats, 240
Tin ornaments, 23-25
Tomatoes, stuffed cherry, 168
Topiary trees, 161-162
Toppers,
  table, 119-121
  tree, 9-13
Torte, brandied apricot, 252
Tree ornament, tea-dyed, 15-16, 314
Tree skirts, 78-87

Tree toppers, 9-13
Tree trimming, 76-77
Trees,
  fringed fabric, 129
  topiary, 161-162
  wall, 157-159
Truffles,
  basic, 264
  deluxe, 265

V

Vegetable platters, 175
Viennese kiss cookies, 229
Vinegars, flavored, 291

W

Wall trees, 157-159
Watermelon pickles, 284
Wine jelly, 292
Wire-mesh bow tree topper, 9, 12-13
Wooden baskets, 124-127
  patterns, 313
Woolen stockings, 147
Wreaths, embellishing, 150-156

Y

Yellow summer squash pickles, 288

Z

Zucchini, crab-stuffed, 171
Zucchini dip, fresh, 190

Creative Publishing international, Inc. offers a variety of how-to books. For information write:
  Creative Publishing international, Inc.
  Subscriber Books
  5900 Green Oak Drive
  Minnetonka, MN 55343